The Construction and Representation of Race and Ethnicity

The Construction and Representation of
Race and Ethnicity
in the Caribbean and the World

Mervyn C. Alleyne

UNIVERSITY OF THE WEST INDIES PRESS
Barbados • Jamaica • Trinidad and Tobago

University of the West Indies Press
1A Aqueduct Flats Mona
Kingston 7 Jamaica
www.uwipress.com

09 08 07   5 4 3

CATALOGUING IN PUBLICATION DATA

The construction and representation of race and ethnicity in the
Caribbean and the World / Mervyn C. Alleyne.

p. cm.
Includes bibliographical references.

ISBN: 976-640-114-4 (casebound)
ISBN: 976-640-179-9 (paperback)

1. Race awareness – West Indies. 2. Ethnicity – West Indies.
3. Ethnic attitudes. 4. Sociolinguistics. 5. Bias-free language.
6. Identity (Psychology) – West Indies. I. Title.

F2169.A55 2002   305.8'009729 -dc21

Cover illustration: Aubrey Williams, *Supernova* (1975).
Collection of the University of the West Indies.

Book and cover design by Robert Harris.
E-mail: roberth@cwjamaica.com

Set in Plantin Light 10/14 x 27

Printed on acid-free paper.
Printed in the United States of America.

Contents

Preface

*T*his book examines different ways in which inter-
acting individuals and groups perceive themselves and see others in relation
to themselves; and how, on the basis of these perceptions, they construct
categories in order to organize the mass of human phenomena surrounding
them. A related area of interest is the way in which these categories are
represented verbally.

It is a natural human instinct to classify; and the ability to classify and then
to represent verbally is an essential aspect of human cognition. Other animal
species have an innate instinct to classify (into male/female, friendly/hostile,
edible/non-edible, and so on). But this does not go beyond instinct into
cognitive, that is, mental, intellectual, processes. Of course, the human species
is not content merely to classify and then to organize its behaviour on the basis
of these classifications. The human being develops a complex structure of
categories and subcategories, contrasting but also overlapping and intersecting. In addition, the human assigns meanings, denotations and connotations,
and values, and develops "attitudes", to these categories. What we may call
race and ethnicity have come to constitute perhaps the most complex and
controversial of such categories. They have emanated from all human societies
and go back as far in human history as we can fathom.

The idea to write this book had a clear and definite moment of conception.
One morning in October 1995, Mr Desmond Green came to my office to ask
my support for the campaign which he was waging to have dictionaries of
English rewritten. He is a passionate defender of the equality of mankind and
of the need to erase negative (including racist) ideas from the minds of men

and women. An urgent necessity, as he saw it, was to rewrite dictionary entries under the headword "black" in order to remove the stigmatic metaphorical and connotative meanings. And there is an amazing number of such; for example, "black-hearted", "black comedy", "black market", "black sheep", "black spot", "black list", "blackguard", "black mark", "blackmail", "black book", "black magic". Interestingly, later, in 1997, it was reported that the National Association for the Advancement of Colored People (NAACP) of the United States wished to start a campaign to sanitize the word "nigger". It called on its members to join a letter-writing campaign to protest Merriam-Webster's definition of "nigger" in its latest dictionary as a "black person" or "a member of any dark-skinned race".

I immediately empathized with Mr Green's concerns. But I realized that dictionaries reflect usage (more than they compel usage) and that therefore his was a noble but totally unrealistic idea. First of all, it would be impractical and undoubtedly futile to try to bring editors of dictionaries around to his way of thinking. These include not only English dictionaries but also dictionaries in other languages (especially those of western Europe). Second, dictionaries are used by a minority of persons. Even if changes were made in a dictionary, popular usage, and most of all popular thinking underlying usage, would not necessarily be affected at all. Even if "black" were cleaned up, were the entries under "white", "whiten" to be analogously corrected? And what about "denigrate", "darken", "obscure", "candid", "fair", "clear", and the like? These, and a host of other words, support a marked contrast between negative black and positive white.

Were we in Jamaica at the point where we could write our own dictionary of (Jamaican) English? This was more a political than a linguistic, philosophical or moral matter, and would require a fuller treatment than I can give it here. However, I do adumbrate the issue in the chapters dealing with the three Caribbean territories of Puerto Rico, Martinique and Jamaica. There, I examine the question of emerging regional standard norms of Spanish, French and English respectively, and the role they may play in the construction of ethnic and national identities.

I did not want to be negative to Mr Green's concerns and therefore pondered how I might assist. It occurred to me then and there that it would be useful to understand the scope of this phenomenon both in time and in space. When and where and how did the semantic expansions of "black" (and "white") take place?

I began with the dictionaries of Modern English, then Middle English, and Old English (Anglo-Saxon). I kept being pushed further and further back in time until I had come to antiquity and the end of the pre-Hellenic era. Immediately, all that I had previously read about the history of racism and had accepted (uncritically, because it was not my "field") appeared very questionable. Racism directed against black people did not start with European adventurers and with slavery in the "Age of Discovery" after all.

The idea that racism as we know it today began in the age of European mercantilist expansion and specifically with New World slavery is firmly entrenched in the scholarship on race in Western societies. The main issue has been the symbiotic links between race and New World slavery. The claim was/is that racism, as we know it today, had in fact been "invented" and it then gained substance in order to justify the special kind of slavery that brought Africans to the New World.

Sanjek is very strong and assertive on the subject:

> Race is the framework of ranked categories segmenting the human population that was developed by Western Europeans following the global expansions beginning in the 1440s. . . . Racism was something new in human history when it arose following European world expansion. . . . [quoting Ralph Linton, an anthropologist of the 1930s] Prior to the sixteenth century, the world was not race conscious and there was no incentive for it to become so. (1994a, 1–3)

There is a strong association in the human mind between the way people look and the way they behave. In fact, assumptions about behaviour and behavioural stereotypes are constructed on the way people look. There is a strong link, therefore, between race (the way people look; see later) and ethnicity (the way people behave), the former being a very salient component of the latter. In the same way that colours which are used to represent the two major "races" have developed pejorative connotations (in the case of "black") and ameliorative connotations (in the case of "white"), so too has the vocabulary representing the ecology and ethnicity/culture of the peoples of the world.

The outstanding cases are the connotations of "jungle" and "tribe". These words in English (and their counterparts in other European languages) now connote (and may even denote) wild, uncontrolled disorder. In Jamaica, as elsewhere, the "law of the jungle" refers to uncontrolled anarchy, with everybody, man and beast, free to roam about hurting one another. This is far from the real state of a jungle in its pristine form, where a very clear natural order exists in which, for example, killing takes place for the purpose of satisfying hunger and in self-defence. Unmotivated, senseless acts of conflict and slaughter between and among men and beasts are not at all typical of the jungle. Such acts are in fact more typical of "civilized" cities and countries.

The word "tribe" and its other western European cognates come from Latin, *tribus*, which originally had a neutral referential application. It referred to divisions of the Roman population (for example, *tribus urbana*, the city group; *tribus rustica*, country folk). There may have been three such divisions, and the root of the word may be related to Latin *tres*, three. In modern languages, the root is to be found in such noble terms as tribute, tribunal, tribune, contribute. But the connection of these words with their parent, tribe, has now been lost. Tribe itself now refers chiefly to African ethnic groups, and also to other ethnic groups seen as still in a pre-civilized, "savage" state. Thus the Yoruba and the Igbo are "tribes", but the Northern Ireland Catholics and Protestants are "ethnic groups", as are the Serbs and Croats, or the Basques and Catalans.

In Jamaica, in a particularly insensitive usage, ultra-partisan politics is referred to as "tribal politics", and the political parties so engaged are called "tribes". Even a racially and ethnically conscious performer (singer) like Jacob Miller wrote an outstanding reggae composition calling for an end to "tribal war" in Jamaican society and politics. This is a particular connotation of "tribe" developed and propagated chiefly by Hollywood films, which portrayed African peoples as constantly shouting, fighting and performing acts of cruelty. Again, like "jungle", "tribe" connotes senseless disorder, but this is certainly not an exclusive property of African ethnic groups.

However, these are not the only cases. European languages are replete with cases of positive denotations/connotations associated with words expressing aspects of European ecology and culture, and negative ones associated with words expressing other ecologies and cultures. For example, "classical", "modern", "civilized", as against "traditional", "folk", "savage", "primitive". "Savage" is ultimately from Latin *silvaticus* (or its colloquial variant, *salvaticus*) meaning "of the forest". In English, its etymological denotative meaning is now subordinate to its connotative expansion "wild", "ruthless", "cruel". Its nearer antecedent is French, *sauvage*, which, in one of its meanings – uncultivated – retains part of the Latin denotation. In French, *un arbre sauvage* is a "tree growing in the wild", one which has not been planted by humans. This meaning has been completely lost in English.

Even "clothed" and "naked" no longer have merely simple denotative meanings but contain connotations of decency and morality, and indecency and immorality, respectively. This particularly hurts the evaluation of some groups living in equatorial climates where it is more natural and sensible for the body not to be covered (either by hair or by clothes), as indeed it may be more natural and sensible there for the skin to contain high proportions of melanin and for noses to be wide and flat. In addition to a racial hierarchy, we now have in today's world what may be referred to as a hierarchy of cultures.

When I was offered a Rockefeller resident fellowship at the University of Puerto Rico, I decided to make the history of the construction and representation of race and ethnicity in the world and in the Caribbean the subject of my research. I wish to thank Professor Lowell Fiet, the Caribe 2000 programme and the University of Puerto Rico for the opportunity to spend the academic year 1996–97 at the Rio Piedras Campus and on the "Finca", where I was made most comfortable. I owe a debt of gratitude also to my own University of the West Indies for granting me leave to take up the Fellowship, and to Mr Reginald Pierce who assisted me with the library research and skilfully edited the manuscript. Professor Jean Bernabé, dean of the Faculty of Arts and Human Sciences of the *Université des Antilles et de la Guyane*, also supported the research by affording me the opportunity of a visiting appointment on the Martinique campus. And lastly, my family relieved me of parenting duties, particularly my daughter Malene, who, at the tender age of fourteen, realized the importance of the research and encouraged me to pursue it. The book is dedicated to her.

CHAPTER ONE

Introduction

*W*hatever may be the theory of human evolution to which one subscribes, the incontrovertible fact is that one of the salient aspects of this evolution is the separation of humans into different modes of organization and classification. Apart from family, and, later in the evolution, clan, tribe, caste, class, nation, there are two such classifications which are fundamental to humans and which are the subject of this book: race and ethnicity. Race and ethnicity are lower-level categories for which the bases were laid from the time humans moved from their original location(s) and lost contact with each other. With successive migrations and splitting up, differences in physical (phenotypical and genotypical) traits and features, and in behavioural, philosophical, aesthetic, symbolic (cultural and ethnic) patterns emerged and increased further as the millennia went by.

Racial differentiation has been slower and less fragmented than ethnic differentiation. It has been impossible to calculate the number of "ethnic" groups in the contemporary world or at any period of human history, just as it has been impossible to calculate the number of languages (language being an important mark of ethnicity). On the other hand, it is significant that there have been attempts to specify the number of "races". It must be noted, however, that there is no universal agreement concerning this number. This uncertainty serves to indicate that there are no clear-cut objective scientific criteria on which to base the category and concept of race. This leads to a widespread view among scientists that race is not a valid, viable scientific concept. Physical anthropologists have more or less abandoned any idea that racial categories can be unambiguously established and counted.

However, the people of the world (at least the educated people of the world to whom such calculations matter) have come to believe that there are three or four major "races": Negroid, Caucasoid, Mongoloid; or, in another terminology, black, white, yellow, red.

Following the lead of social scientists, I am taking both race and ethnicity to be social constructs. However, they are based on objective features that can be specified and that, particularly in the case of race, are transmitted genetically from generation to generation and have remained as well-known and widely accepted criteria for classification. On the other hand, there are cases which suggest that, in the final analysis, their existence in the social order is determined by the perception of people, which may change over time or disappear according to circumstances.

Even colours, which are the prime physical and visible bases for the social construction of race, are themselves socially constructed. To understand this, we merely have to consider that one of the most dramatic examples of the non-translatability or non-commensurability of languages is the lexicon of the colour spectrum. Different cultures demarcate different zones of this commonly occurring natural spectrum for naming purposes. The number of colours existing naturally or observable on a colour spectrum is enormous. The average English speaker codifies only a very small subset of these, about eight. The male English speaker codifies even fewer than the female. Other cultures demarcate and codify differently.

Race, then, is the socialized perception of phenotypical characteristics. These phenotypical characteristics constitute only one of the features recognized and used for human classification. Behaviour and customs (language, clothing, foods, religion) constitute another set of features and, together with race, provide the basis for ethnicity.

It is this perception of similarities and differences that is the basis on which individuals and groups identify themselves as belonging to the same race and ethnic group, and, on the other hand, identify others as belonging to a different race and ethnic group. This perception, and the behaviours that it leads to, are the interest of this book, rather than the scientific assessment and validation of the concepts. This does not mean that the scientific category has no bearing on, or relationship to, the social constructs. The former is based on measurement, the latter on perception and social consensus. However, the perception is based fundamentally on a capacity to observe and measure and is not random and capricious. Whereas it is true, as we shall later see, that there may be disagreement as to assignment of particular individuals to a particular race or racial (phenotypical) category, it is also true that in the vast majority of cases the society or the community are in general agreement as to the assignment.

It has to be re-emphasized that the categories of race and ethnicity that are actually established by any society depend on social, economic, political and ideological factors, historical and contemporary. The category of "negro" or "black" in the United States is established on the basis of "one drop" of black blood; but the category of "Native American" is not similarly and analogously established. One drop of Native American blood will place the person in the dominant blood category. In the Caribbean, the categories are established differently and are arranged in much more complex systems (see later). Chinese immigrants to Cuba in the latter half of the eighteenth century were classified as white. A particularly dramatic example of the politically based construction of race is the case of the category "honorary white" in South Africa, to which some Indians were assigned.

Ethnicity and race are socially constructed, contextual representations that play themselves out at specific historical periods. Racial meanings are contested and transformed as people counterpose their own constructions of identity, community and history. Thus the vocabulary and meanings constantly change: one drop of black blood makes you black in the United States, but white in Latin America.

Race, therefore, is not a genetic attribute – this has been clearly established now – but rather a socialized perception of biological phenotypical characteristics.

Race: The "Scientific" Concept and Its Physical/Objective Features

The scientific concept of race has been the subject of considerable debate and has followed the development of interested sciences such as biology, genetics and physical anthropology. Various criteria to determine race have been used at different periods, including size of skull and other skeletal features. At present, the great interest in genes and DNA has led inevitably to the dominance of gene pools in the study of race. Contemporary studies have taken two directions: first, the difficulty or impossibility or inappropriateness of establishing clear biological racial distinctions, and of dividing human populations into discrete racial categories; and second, the question of the equality or inequality of races, that is, of the inherent, biologically based, superiority or inferiority of races.

There is increasingly wide (but certainly not universal) agreement that gene pools are so randomly distributed across human populations that if two members of the same putative race were chosen at random, they could show fewer common features than would be shown if any one of them were to be compared with someone of another putative race. It is then suggested that races do not exist and that race is not a viable scientific concept. This scientific view of race is reinforced by the recent statement of the International Genome Organization supporting the theory of the single emergence of *homo sapiens* in Africa. A study of chromosome distribution among Europeans and Africans has led to the conclusion that Europeans (and perhaps other inhabitants of the globe) are descended from a few hundred Africans who migrated from the African homeland some twenty-five thousand years ago. This argument is sometimes injected into discussions of social conflict, the suggestion being that there is no rational foundation for such conflict.

It should be emphasized that the scientific case, though in some ways relevant to the social phenomenon of racial conflict, should be clearly distinguished from it. What is important and significant in this latter case is that people perceive themselves as being similar or different from others on the basis of certain salient physical attributes, and that "race" (or its equivalent in other languages or at other stages of the same language) is one of the terms used to express this.

The same perception based on visible salient physical attributes is also applied to other forms of biological species (such as animals and plants) and, in many languages, the same term "race" is used. It is interesting to observe that in this case it is the animals (such as dogs, cats, cows and chickens) that form part of the human social ambiance that are so characterized, thereby lending support to the notion that the construction of race is a social imperative. When this perception of similarities and differences among human individuals and groups takes place in a context of competition, scarce re-sources, and so on, racial conflict may arise and has arisen throughout human history.

As mentioned above, the social construction of race is based upon the perception of certain salient phenotypical (and to a lesser extent, in some cases, genotypical) features. Colour of the skin may be generally the most salient. Shills believes that colour identification is a

> primordial quality, one of the earliest sensibilities of man as a vehicle of self-identification. The awareness of differences in skin color heightens aware-ness of other differences. It does so not just by symbolizing those differences, but by serving as a focus of self-identification as a member of a species with a distinctive biological origin and separateness. (1968, 14)

Franklin seems to agree:

> If Freud was correct in his theory that the overriding pleasure instinct first becomes gratified within one's own body, then it may be argued that even within a society a person will be attracted to those who most resemble himself [*sic*]. If, in addition to this, people of the same or similar color share common experiences . . . it merely serves to intensify color affinity. (1968, ix)

Indeed, it can be argued that the world is organized on the basis of physical differences, and that humans learn to react differently to these differences. This applies both ontogenetically, in the evolution and development of humans and their senses, and phylogenetically, in the maturation of children. Differences such as edible/non-edible, hard/soft, hot/cold, pain/pleasure be-long here. Many of the abstract expressions of English and other languages are based on original physical concepts. States are seen as physical locations: "in love", "under stress", "beyond contempt". Ideas and thoughts are still seen as physical objects: "hard problem", "weighty issue", and so on. In Romance languages, the main form expressing the abstraction "to be" is derived from a verb of location, *stare*. Similarly, in the Jamaican language, the verb of location, *de* (to be in a place), comes to mean also "to exist". Colours may belong here, being primordial physical perceptions which become abstrac-tions; and, like the other physical concepts, their precise values are learned through associative learning.

Colour may be a primordial perception but it is not always a sufficient criterion for human classification. There may be other features needed in the totality required to distinguish one "racial" group from another. Thus skin colour may have to be supplemented or complemented by other features to make the differentiation.

Texture of the hair also has a high degree of salience. The significance of hair texture as a socioracial marker is indicated by the fact that it is the object of constant tending and modification, unlike skin colour which is relatively immutable. However, skin colour does also come in for some tending as some persons in the zone of the skin colour continuum near the black pole shun the rays of the sun which are thought to cause darkening of the skin; conversely, persons near the white pole now seek the sun in order to remove the whiteness (though at an earlier period such persons avoided the sun and employed other devices to enhance whiteness). There is also the practice observed in some young women of using products reputed to bleach the complexion of the skin in order to mitigate its blackness. And it is not uncommon, in the Caribbean as well as in many other parts of the world, for a person to choose a mate (or have a mate chosen for him or her) of lighter complexion, one of the goals of which is to have offspring closer to the white-skin pole of the continuum. Although these practices do not (all) alter the racial classification of an individual, they place the individual in a socially more advantageous phenotypical category, built on both racial and aesthetic/erotic (sexual) considerations.

For the Caribbean, shape and size of the bottom are additional features which sometimes, but not always, run parallel to skin colour and hair texture. For example, a well-formed bottom generally coincides with dark skin colour. When it is found exceptionally on a white or near white woman this is seen as a sign that the person has "black blood" in her ancestry.

In different places and in different times, shape of the nose, mouth, eyes, face, legs and torso has also come into play. There have been less diagnostic features such as colour of the hair and of the eyes and shape of the fingers that have been used for racial (or subracial) classification. And, finally, size of the penis (again real or imagined) has emerged as a criterion of racial classification. It has also become a very significant and complex factor in the psychology of interracial relations.

The importance of physical features/shape in human classification emerges also in the way in which they also relate to class. Texture and complexion of the skin may indicate peasant class as against urban class. In earlier times, pallor indicated aristocratic status. A number of other defining features have been constructed for class: an upright stance indicates aristocracy; squatness identifies the peasantry.

As we have said, the social case does not require the rigour of a scientific classification. One event that has considerably weakened the scientific case but has also complicated the social case is racial mixture. There have presumably always been mixtures of races throughout human history. But such mixtures have accelerated in the contemporary period in such a way as to considerably blur the external physical distinctions among peoples. This is particularly so in the Caribbean, where different "races", placed in very small geographical space, and involved in intimate social relations based on asymmetrical distributions of power, have been engaged in miscegenation to a degree that makes perceptions difficult or ambiguous, and leads to a gradation of colour and other physical attributes.

In the Caribbean, as in other parts of the contemporary world, skin colour belongs to a continuum of shades which is the result of racial mixing and which is perceived as ranging from one pole, black, to another pole, white. A continuum of hair texture parallels the skin colour continuum and ranges from "straight" to "woolly". Hair texture differences are particularly salient, and are focused on in the contemporary Caribbean with as much (and perhaps more) attention and concern as skin colour. As we said above, hair texture may supplement or complement skin colour in the racial classification of an individual, but it may also contradict and confuse, and sometimes even supersede, the classification based on skin colour. Hair texture differences have also attracted a special terminology that is not only descriptive but also expresses a social value ("good", "bad", "kinky", "pepper grain", and others).

However, miscegenation has obviously not affected all individuals. This has had three results for the Caribbean and elsewhere. First, race remains a clear perception and is applied to still well-constituted groups, although the outer limits of the groups may not be at all precise. Second, mixed persons may come to constitute other groups that may not be classified as "races", but that are given their own designations. Populations use these designations and, in relation to them, there is wide agreement about the physical attributes that provide the meaning of these terms (*mulatto, mestizo, dougla, coolie rayal, black chinee, échappé coulie,* and others) in different parts of the Caribbean.

The same applies to the particular criterion of skin colour. There remain two well-constituted groups that are categorized on this basis as "black" and "white". But miscegenation has produced a gradation of colour (reinforced by other physiognomic features which coincide), which leads to a breakdown or disruption of clear-cut racial classification. It creates a new subracial categorization with its own terminology ("red", "brown", "light brown", "dark brown", as well as black and white). In the case of the Caribbean, the two poles of the colour gradation correspond to two racial categories that are still unambiguously recognized (black and white). But increasingly, as more mixing takes place between races and between colours, shade, rather than precise colour, has become (or is becoming) the dominant factor in the social organization.

Third, an ideological factor and a wealth factor may intervene to distort the colour and racial picture by becoming dominant indices of classification. In the same way that "money can whiten", ideology can also both whiten and blacken. The Black Power militants in Trinidad in the 1970s attempted to incorporate (East) Indians in the category "black", thus giving to "black" a new class and ideological dimension. According to Rodney, a leading ide-ologue of Black Power:

> Black Power in the West Indies . . . refers primarily to people who are recognizably African or Indian. . . . Black Power is not racially intolerant. It is the hope of the Black man that he should have power over his own destinies. This is not incompatible with a multiracial society. . . . Black Power must proclaim that Jamaica is a black society. (1969, 28)

And Millette declared: "When I speak about black people in Trinidad and Tobago, I speak of people who are drawn from Indian stock as well as people who are drawn from African stock" (1974, 47).

This leads some scholars to suggest that at this point, class, rather than race, is the dominant principle of social ordering (see, for example, Lewis 1972; Braithwaite 1976). Black and white may move from purely racial categories to redefinition through the incorporation of ideological, class and cultural elements. But note that in the case of Black Power in Trinidad and Jamaica, it is the similarity in colour between African and Indian, as well as their membership in the oppressed class, that allowed such thought of incor-poration. It is safe to assume, hypothetically, that if it were Chinese rather than Indians who shared membership of the oppressed classes with Africans, there would be no thought, even among the most ardent Marxists, of incorporating them into the category "black".

Ethnicity

Physical features are the bases for the construction of racial (and colour) classifications. There are other features that are less visible and tangible and that have come to be associated with races. These are the beliefs, behaviours and artefacts that separate (or are perceived as separating) one group from another. These beliefs and behaviours and artefacts are what are called culture.

A distinction is being made here between culture and ethnicity. Culture and racial identity are the foundation of ethnicity. Culture includes such things as religion (beliefs and ritual), language, music, dress, foods, customs, names and naming. Since these are the most tangible and salient, they, together with race, are therefore the main focus of ethnic identity. Culture also includes less tangible things such as world view, kinship systems, values and morality.

One of the main requirements of ethnicity is recognition not only of similarities and differences in these areas of culture, but also of the need to act in the interest of the perceived group. Humans organize themselves on different bases and exploit these modes of organization to promote their interests. Such modes are family, clan, gender, class, caste, nation, race, ethnicity. Ethnicity entails popular definitions: "Who am I? What am I?" We also see ourselves as a category through analogic representation of "others". In some special circumstances, notably in the Caribbean, self/other definitions become specified in a large measure by the colonial classifiers. These definitions may then be contested, challenged and transformed as people counterpose their own constructions of identity, and represent these constructions with their own vocabulary. The psychological dimension is of the utmost importance, and one is a member of an ethnic group only when one "self-identifies as a member of that group and is willing to be perceived and treated as a member of that group" (Buriel 1987, 135).

Whereas culture is transmitted and ascribed, ethnicity is engendered through recognition of sameness and of common interests which, particularly in situations of competitiveness for scarce resources, leads to common actions to further common interests. Thus, different ethnic groups may belong to the same culture; or at least there may be very minor cultural differences between severely opposed ethnic groups. The Protestants and Roman Catholics of Northern Ireland constitute two ethnic groups, although their cultural differences are, objectively, relatively minor. They would have to be classified as

belonging to the same culture and certainly to the same race. The same applies
to the French Creoles and Anglo-Saxons of Trinidad.

In other words, although race may be a very important factor in the
constitution of ethnicity, the two categories do not necessarily coincide. Jews
constitute perhaps the most assertive ethnic group in today's world. And
although we may speak loosely of the Jewish race, the fact is that there are
many "races" within Jewish ethnicity. The importance of race and particularly
skin colour is dramatically highlighted by the problems of prejudice and
discrimination that the dark-skinned Falasha Jews have encountered in Israel.
In the Caribbean, there were cases of many different ethnicities being con-
flated and collapsed under one "race". Different African ethnic groups
underwent this process. So did different British ethnic groups (Scots, Irish,
Welsh, English).

Socially speaking, it is clear that African Americans are a race, with
remarkably well-defined (though arbitrarily so) genotypical boundaries (one
drop of blood). It is not so clear that they are a separate ethnicity. At least they
are often accused of not acting in concert, like Jews, Chinese, Italians and
others are seen to do. African American ethnicity is rather unstable as it
intersects with class. Socioeconomic advancement for African Americans
often leads to a weakening and dilution of ethnicity and to the creation of
"oreos" (black on the outside, white on the inside).

The most salient expressive indices of African American ethnicity may be
shunned and rejected by upwardly mobile African Americans. Certainly this
is the case with language. The debate on "Ebonics" in education revealed the
extent to which African Americans are divided on the issue. The divisions
here are not along class, but rather ideological lines. However, in terms of
actual language usage and affective association with the language, there is a
class division. The same applies to the "high five" and other ways of expressing
African American ethnicity. They are not the property of middle-class African
Americans.

In the case of African Americans (but also observable in other situations,
for example, among blacks in the Caribbean), the degree of maintenance and
assertion of ethnicity seems to depend to a large measure on preserving a
lower-class status. This is related to a sense of marginalization, of being the
victims of social, economic and cultural oppression. It also has to do with
networks of social interaction. Socioeconomic mobility implies and involves
new networks, requiring interaction with the mainstream, leading to new,

diluted expressions of ethnicity. Lower socioeconomic status implies a high density of in-group interaction, favouring ethnic retention.

However, it should be noted that the Hispanic/Latino ethnic group in the United States preserves its ethnicity to a large extent, regardless of socioeconomic mobility and, as a matter of fact, regardless of race. Black, brown and white Hispanics equally populate the ethnic group. Their ethnicity so dominates their race that, in questionnaires which call for *racial* self-identification, "Hispanic" is given as a category side by side with "black", "white", "Native American", and others. This is similar to the Indians in Trinidad, for example, who as an ethnic group incorporate both the fair Aryan racial type and the dark Dravidian "Madras" type, and retain Indian ethnicity even when they move into the upper classes. North American blacks may not (although this may be a question of degree), and in this sense social class intervenes considerably in the construction of their identity. It is even less clear that they are a separate culture. If they are the latter, the boundaries are certainly blurred, both by objective measurement and by social perception.

It is also quite significant that, although the Greeks and Romans of antiquity held the ethnically different Nordic groups in contempt and considered them to be barbarians, and although the Greeks and Romans of the time did not consider the fair hair, whiter skin and blue eyes of these peoples to be aesthetically or erotically more appealing, there were no problems in the integration of these two types when Greece and Italy were subsequently invaded and occupied by these Nordic barbarians. However, in the case of the Egyptians (and Aethopians), although culturally the Greeks were closer to them than they were to the Nordic tribes, integration with Egypt (and Aethopia) was never achieved. There may have been a host of other factors involved in preventing this integration, but racial/colour differences seem to have played an important part.

While race is often a vital factor in the construction of ethnicity, we have seen that race and ethnicity do not always coincide. Ethnicity is a finer categorization or subcategorization; that is, it is more likely that different ethnic groups belong to the same race and, in spite of this belonging, develop negative attitudes towards, and evaluations of, one another (Serbs and Croats, for example), than that different races belong to the same ethnic group (as in the case of Jews). However, as a result of culture contact, individuals of different races or cultures may come together to constitute a larger ethnic group. When this happens, we are approaching the concept of "nation".

At the present time, a number of countries are grappling with the problem of nationhood and national identity; they are torn between the recognition, acceptance and even celebration of ethnic, racial and cultural diversity on the one hand, and on the other the need to unify the nation beyond the mere participation in public domains such as voting, law, and so on. Jamaica's motto, "Out of Many, One People", and its Latin precursor, *E Pluribus, Unum,* express this desire in a very explicit way. If we ignore recent ethnic minorities recently migrated to France, France would be one nation comprised of one ethnic group, the result of the creation of a larger national ethnicity out of what were in the past a number of different ethnic (and racial) groupings. The United Kingdom is not yet there; neither are the United States, Jamaica or Trinidad and Tobago. Nigeria is very far away.

Racism and Ethnocentrism

Racism intersects with ethnocentrism. Racism is the belief that phenotypical or alleged genotypical characteristics are inherently indicative of certain behaviours and abilities, and it leads to invidious distinctions based on a hierarchical order. Ethnocentrism is the belief in the superiority of one's own culture. It can be basic and harmless when it is simply the belief in the merits of one's own way of life and the equating of "foreign" with "not so good as ours". This is normal and common to all peoples. The Bakari indigenous people of Brazil make a distinction between *kura,* meaning "we" and "good", and *kurapa,* meaning "they", "foreign" and "bad". But ethnocentrism may lead to a hierarchical ordering, especially in the context of culture contact. When a people come to believe that their assumed superiority is based on a superior genetic pool, it is a pathological case of racism and ethnocentrism combined.

There is a macrocosmic stratification among the world's cultures and races. Cultures and races are identified with nations and regions of the world. In the modern history of the world (that is, starting from Graeco-Roman antiquity), these nations and regions have developed in different ways and to different degrees, technologically, militarily and economically. These differentials in development have spilled over into the areas of culture and race. The result is that the race and culture of the most powerful in those areas of military and industrial technology have gained in prestige. The result of this is the current racial and ethnic/cultural hierarchy in the world.

In the macrocosmic picture, it is now both the cultural and phenotypical racial attributes and the military, technological and economic superiority that determine the ethnocentrism of those at the top, as well as the hierarchical ordering. There can be both ethnic and racial segmentation without hierarchy, but hierarchy has been the dominant pattern. Although, as we shall see, colour (and even hair texture, but to a lesser extent) is ascribed intrinsic value in the construction of the hierarchy, it is rather the way of life that is evaluated and its value ascribed to the corresponding colour (and other phenotypical features). This hierarchy is reflected microcosmically within any one territory where different races and ethnicities co-exist.

Beyond what may be called natural, basic ethnocentrism, the scientific and technological advances of European "white" nations, which have led and still lead to military and colonial/imperial domination of other continents and races, are the most important factors that determine the hierarchical ordering. However, from the period of Graeco-Roman antiquity through the Age of Enlightenment to the present time, claims have been made of an innate intellectual superiority of the white race. Jensen (1969), one of the leading proponents of this claim, reported that blacks scored significantly lower on intelligence quotient tests than whites and he attributes this to genetic heritage, and not to discrimination, poor diet, bad living conditions, inferior schooling and other contextual factors. Another proponent, Nobel Prize physicist William Shockely, says that "there is difference in the wiring patterns of white and black brains". It should be noted that both Jensen and Shockely base their claims on inferential knowledge, not on direct knowledge of the brain. So far, no "smart" gene has been identified that is present in white people and absent in black people.

However, it then becomes important for blacks and other races to show that this scientific and technological superiority is a feature of the present cycle of human history, and that indeed Europe is greatly indebted to these other races for this scientific and technological advancement. At earlier cycles, the white peoples of Europe were behind in these areas of endeavour.

A related claim is that certain performance characteristics, which have become the building blocks of racial stereotyping, are really part of the genetic make-up of the race. Blacks are sprinters and have rhythm; whites are long distance runners (that was before the triumphs of the Kenyans and Ethiopians) and have no rhythm. Jews are brainy and have a flair for business. A leading African intellectual, Leopold Senghor, himself claimed that "emotion is black, reason is white" (Senghor 1964, 24). He later tried to wriggle out of the embarrassment by granting blacks the gift of reason, but explaining that European reasoning is analytical and discursive by utilization; Negro-African reasoning is intuitive by participation.

As we suggested above, one of the main factors in the growth of inordinate ethnic arrogance is military might (cf. Britain in the nineteenth century and the United States at the present time). When great inequalities in the distribution of power manifest themselves between two groups, notions of superiority and inferiority find a very nurturing environment. Another factor in the development of these attitudes is the distance, the degree of difference, between two cultures or ethnic groups. Given the natural tendency to consider one's own culture as the norm against which all others are to be evaluated, those behaviours that are most distant are the most "strange", and are likely to become "odd", "weird", "monstrous", "deviant", and the like.

Note the development of the meaning of "strange" itself. The English word comes from Old French *estrange*, which, with the Spanish *extraneo*, is derived from a Latin word, *extraneus*. The root of the Latin word originally meant simply "outside". But already in Latin, the meaning of *extraneus* was expanded from "foreign" to include "strange". These two meanings still exist in French and Spanish. In English, the word *strange* has lost its original denotative meaning "foreign", and has preserved only the metaphorical expansion "strange". (Note, however, that the derivative noun *stranger* combines the etymological meaning and the metaphorical expansion.) Spanish has carried the expansion even further: it has created a derivative verb, *extrañar*, which means "to surprise".

There is likely to be more tolerance for those cultural forms that are different from one's own but not too distant from the accepted norm. This applies to behaviour including customs, beliefs, foods, religion and language. But it may also apply to appearance: physiognomic features, clothing, decorations. According to Wagatsuma, "the type of Negro the Japanese think attractive or handsome or the least objectionable is a light-skinned individual with Caucasian features. For this reason, they all find Hindu Indians generally more acceptable, even though the Hindus' black skin still groups them with African and American Negroes" (1968, 154).

But distance is not always an objective measurement. African scarification may appear weird to a European who finds (at the present time) nothing too odd in tattooing. And a white woman who has lavishly painted herself with cosmetics may similarly seem frightening to an Amerindian who has lavishly painted himself with "war paint". However, the claim of this book is that the physiognomic distance between white and black peoples was, and probably still is, a significant factor reinforcing the power factor and leading to the particular historical attitudes of whites to blacks.

Class, Caste

The other important categories for the taxonomy of human societies are what are usually called class or caste. These have to do with the socioeconomic status assigned to, or held by, different groups of individuals. In ethnically and racially complex societies, ethnic and racial groups as a whole may occupy certain socioeconomic positions *vis-à-vis* other ethnic and racial groups. Class stratification (vertical status relationships) will then coincide with ethnic/racial divisions (horizontal relationships); and it will become a moot point whether the society is organized on the basis of class or on the basis of race/ethnicity. This issue concerning racially, ethnically and socially complex Caribbean societies has been keenly debated in the sociological literature. This book will not be concerned with debating this issue. It seems to us that it is not a question of two mutually exclusive models (one based on race and the other on class), but of one model being more powerful than the other in particular Caribbean societies, at particular periods of Caribbean history. There may be a general movement over time from a racially and culturally plural-type structure towards one of class stratification, with a weakening of plural ethnicities. But the process is far from complete. (East) Indians in Trinidad and Guyana maintain a high level of ethnicity regardless of their social status; and there are still (remnants of) two different types of social stratification, one within the Indian ethnic group and another within the African Creole group. In South Africa, race is overwhelming and all-encompassing, followed by ethnicity, and then by class. In Trinidad, race is less overwhelming than in South Africa, but still more significant in the social order than race is in Jamaica. In Jamaica, although class may be at present the dominant feature, there is still a large part of social relations and social behaviour that is determined by race and ethnicity, however nebulous these concepts may be at the contemporary period, in the opinion of some scholars.

Race in Jamaica is difficult to define, and is constantly being redefined in the context of changing class and ideological relationships; and ethnicity is in the process of being reconstructed. At first, Africans constituted a relatively well-defined racial group striving to construct a new ethnicity in the difficult circumstances of slavery. There was the beginning of a social differentiation based on criteria such as place of birth (bozal versus creole), civil status (free or freed versus enslaved) and occupation (domestic, artisan, driver, field worker). In the course of time, social mobility involved some distancing from the developing black/African ethnic group. But with the development of nationhood and the need to define "Jamaican-ness", ethnicity is expanding from class and race levels to national levels.

Thus the Caribbean shows different processes of racial and ethnic construction and representation, albeit within a very common framework. Three modalities will be examined in some detail: Jamaica, Martinique and Puerto Rico. These were not chosen at random. They represent the three major colonial powers that competed for hegemony in the Caribbean; they represent different models of plantation society; and they represent different contemporary political circumstances. Together they are not, however, totally representative of the Caribbean. Societies such as Trinidad, Guyana, Suriname and Cayenne, which have become extremely complex in the post-emancipation period, are for the most part beyond the scope of this work, and will have to be dealt with in a separate, later work.

CHAPTER TWO

The Origins of Racial and Ethnic Awareness and Evaluation

Nature or Nurture?

*I*n trying to understand when, in the history of human social evolution, race and ethnicity became part of the perception of human populations, and when prejudice and stigmatic evaluations emerged, we may find it useful to examine the development of ethnic and racial awareness and evaluation in children. In other areas of human development (language and posture, for example), phylogenetic mapping, if it does not recapitulate ontogenetic mapping, at least provides some significant insights. Social groups are a universal necessity in human society. Out of the many options available to classify and organize individuals, those which were selected (family, gender, kinship, clan) show similarity across cultures. These are universals of human classification and organization. The question as to whether race and ethnicity are similar universals may be fruitfully examined by examining how the perception and evaluation of these develop in children.

How biologically determined is this awareness and evaluation of race and ethnicity; and how much is it a learned phenomenon in the socialization process? Studies are not at all conclusive on this question. But it is probable that, like language or religion or music, it is already an innate endowment which then waits for specific environmental stimuli to develop its precise configurations, meanings and values.

Certainly this is the case for the perception of colour. Colour discrimination is an innate human attribute that emerges very early in physical and cognitive development. It then requires precise inputs from the physical and cultural environment to determine the precise dissection of the spectrum and the meanings to be assigned to the divisions. This ability would then also apply to race insofar as the most salient index of race is skin colour. The perception of race would belong to a general predisposition to categorize and classify in order to organize and simplify the overwhelming stimulus information coming from the perceptual and tactile world. Again, the physical, social and cultural environment would determine the exact meanings and values to be assigned to perceived categories (that is, in cases where the phenomenon itself does not carry its own meaning and value; for example, fire already in itself suggests as one of its meanings "something to be prevented from touching the skin").

It is reasonable to suppose that colour, rather than other physical attributes such as size of torso, or shape of nose, would be a (or the) most important physical index of classification, ranking very closely with gender and age. Even where differences in colour do not imply differences in race, we could expect these differences to be perceived very early. Thus within the same racial group, for example, the white race, differences between "fair" and "dark" would be perceived early, and their precise meanings (for example, "living indoors" as against "working in the fields") would be learned later. It would be reasonable to suppose that the meanings and values to be assigned to these human classifications would come from precise environmental conditioning later in the socialization process.

Studies of the development of racial perception and classification in children suggest that this ability is part of a general cognitive maturation. Children are able to identify people as white or black at the same age, three to four years old, so that they "can create meaningful categories (for example, cats are distinguished from toys, and cats and dogs from trains). . . . This ability increases in the pre-operational years (3 to 6)" (Ramsey 1987, 58).

Ramsey further reports that when children aged three to five years were presented with a series of three photographs in which there were different arrays of gender and race and were asked to select two out of the three that "go together", they formed groups "along visible traits such as skin colour, gender, hair, clothing. The subjects used race most frequently, gender the next most frequently, and clothing least often. . . . When children were asked to say who was different from them, they often explicitly used race as a defining factor" (p. 59). Katz reports that "a sizeable proportion of 3 year old and most 4 year old children do exhibit awareness of racial cues, as well as preferential patterns" (1983, 51). She suggests that the underlying developmental processes must have taken place during the earlier period.

These studies of race perception have been carried out with white and black children in the United States. The relations between black and white people are so salient and conflictual that one might expect that adult patterns would be picked up very early by children. But one should be cautious about drawing such a conclusion, since a similarly salient and conflictual relationship between Protestants and Roman Catholics in Northern Ireland does not apparently lead to child awareness of the ethnic differences between the two groups before age eleven (Katz 1983, 51). On the other hand, all that this may be demonstrating is something that we have suggested above: that is, that race may be usefully separated from ethnicity, and that racial awareness may be partly innate (that is, to the extent that it is linked to colour), while ethnic awareness has to be learned, and that the learning process takes time.

If the case for early child awareness of colour and race and for the innate nature of this awareness is compelling, the case for the early emergence of colour and race preference is more controversial. Since, as we have said, the studies reported have been conducted in the United States with black and white children, it may be safe to assume that the political and cultural history of that country, including the possible ethnocentrism of the authors, is responsible for the results of the studies. These results show that nursery school children already show a pro-white bias in their evaluative responses to different colours (represented usually by dolls), and that, significantly, this was the case for both black and white children.

There have been attempts to suggest that pro-white colour preferences are a universal-like attribute in humans, and to seek to explain it in other ways than by political cultural conditions of the environment.

The Affective Meanings of Colours

It is obvious that colour has a universal presence in nature. It is also clear that individuals have preferences for certain colours over others and that colours either affect mental states or are used to express these states. Colours do seem to have the capacity to elicit certain types of feelings and emotions. Artists make this assumption, and so do poets, interior decorators, advertisers and fashion designers.

Also, it seems that, initially, some colours were associated with parts of the body, and then from there they came to express emotions and abstract states/virtues. Western European languages are full of metaphorical expressions showing this semantic development of colour terms. In at least some cases, the affective associations and the metaphorical usage are clear and consistent. Yellow, for example, has a rather consistent association with cowardice and other kinds of pejoration in English (cf. yellow-bellied, yellow streak, the yellow press). According to Ferguson (1954, 268), in the Renaissance, yellow was used to suggest jealousy, treason, deceit. The traitor Judas was frequently painted in a garment of dingy yellow. In the Middle Ages, heretics were obliged to wear yellow. In periods of plague, yellow crosses were used to identify contagious areas. In spite of this, however, recently in the United States of America, a yellow ribbon tied to a tree has come to symbolize, perhaps as an exceptional case, faithfulness and confidence in the safe return of lost loved ones.

Other colours are not so consistent in their associations. Blue, for example, may have become associated with distinction (cf. blue blood, blue-eyed boy, blue chip, blue ribbon, blue stocking, Oxford/Cambridge Blue); but on the other hand, it may also be used metaphorically to express melancholy and sadness (cf. the blues, blue devils), or even indecency and profanity (cf. blue movies). Red can express both bravery (from the colour of the blood) and anger, greed, envy (from the colour of the pupils). Black and white as "colours" are, of course, very pertinent to the theme of this book, and we shall elaborate on them below.

All of the above observations apply to western European language and cognition, and particularly to English. The cross-cultural application is very doubtful. The Chinese, for example, are unlikely to accept all of Western colour symbolism. Isaacs cites "a Chinese scholar" who stated that "of the five colors, yellow is the color of the soil and the soil is the core of the universe.

. . . This implies that when Heaven and Earth were created, the Chinese were given the central place" (1968, 77).

In spite of this, there have been studies, particularly in the 1970s, that have sought to discover universals in the affective evaluations of colours. Gergen accepts uncritically that "people of highly dissimilar cultural backgrounds react similarly to a given color . . . [and] that blackness elicits, on the whole, unfavourable responses while whiteness evokes favorable responses" (1968, 114). He further cites a number of "direct and well-controlled tests within Western culture which demonstrate not only that white is rated more positively than black but that both Negroes as well as whites feel similarly in this regard" (p. 119). He then suggests that this holds across cultural boundaries, by citing a number of sub-Saharan cases (pp. 119–20).

Adams and Osgood (1973) selected twenty-three groups of thirty-five to forty teenage male high school students in cities in twenty countries in Europe, Asia and America. The sample had no representative from Africa or Melanesia, and the only possible dark-skinned subjects were those from Mysore in Kannada, India. These students were tested for "affect attribution" on eight colour concepts: colour, white, grey, black, red, yellow, green, blue. The results show that "brightness is more highly evaluated than darkness; white is more highly evaluated than black; black is bad, strong, passive; gray is bad, weak, passive; white is good, weak; red is strong, active; yellow is weak; blue and green are good" (p. 138).

Adams and Osgood, in discussing the possible sources of these evaluations, make the claim that there is a common relationship of human beings to the world they live in:

> In every locale, blue skies and green plants are good things, red blood is vital, clean light-colored things are better than dark, dirty things, and (for a diurnal animal) lightness is more benevolent than darkness. . . . Another common source is common cultural beliefs either stemming from ancient common origins or from more recent cultural influences. (1973, 138)

The authors mention the possibility of another source in the physiology of vision, that is, "some element in the wave lengths in the red region of the spectrum which particularly stimulates color receptors, leading to the association of red with strong emotions" (p. 139).

Williams and Morland cite other studies that claim that "a similar pro-white bias has been documented among pre-school-aged children in a number of other countries including England, Scotland, France, Germany, Italy, and Japan". They conclude that "these findings appear to parallel the findings from studies with young adults, which point to a pan-cultural tendency to evaluate white more positively than black" (1976, 31).

Snowden accepts this conclusion quite uncritically. He notes that "recent studies point out that there seems to be a widespread commonality in feelings about black and white, that among both Negroes and whites the color white tends to evoke a positive and black a negative reaction" (1983, 82–83). And Russell had the audacity to assert that "negative perceptions of blackness are more causes of, than caused by racism" (1977, 65).

Katz sums up the positions as follows:

> A study conducted with 3-day-old infants found not only that facial-like configurations of varying hues were discriminated but that infants preferred high-contrast stimuli. . . . Newborns seem to be sensitive to color cues, figure-ground contrast, border illumination discrepancies. . . . That children by age 3 should employ skin color cues as a basis for person classification, therefore, should not be surprising. . . .What may be more surprising, however, is that nursery school children exhibit differential evaluative responses to different skin colors. White children clearly prefer the color white in both human and nonhuman pictures, and until relatively recently, young black children also exhibited a prowhite bias. . . . Considerable cross-cultural research has demonstrated that the color white is associated with positive attributes in most cultures and the color black with negative ones. . . . Williams and Morland go on to suggest that such affective connotations generalize to skin color cues. . . . These investigators speculate that pro-white bias originates from a basic tendency to prefer light over darkness. . . . Preference for lightness over darkness may be the developmental forerunner of the preference for white skin. The cultural factors (i.e. language connotations, lower status associated with dark skin, and so on) merely serve to reinforce these initial tendencies . . . . (1983, 52–54)

Needless to say, not all scholars have uncritically accepted the above studies and their conclusions about colour symbolism and colour preferences. Banks, questioning the conceptual and methodological rigour of Williams and Morland (1976), concludes that

> scant evidence exists of the tendency of blacks to express preferential evaluative orientations towards white characteristics. Furthermore, the validity of such a phenomenon as a measurement of content or predictive significance for white preference within the real world of social choices, self-esteem, or racial pride seems equally unsupported by empirical evidence. (Banks 1976, 35)

Hraba (1970), responding to the first study of colour preferences based on reactions to dolls (Clark and Clark 1939), had earlier found that when the Clark and Clark doll study was duplicated in Lincoln, Nebraska, with children aged four to eight, it was found that the majority of blacks preferred the black dolls. Like the blacks, the white children preferred the doll of their own race. His conclusion was that black children, even in interracial settings in a white-dominant context, are not necessarily white-oriented.

Fox and Jordan (1973) conducted a study of 360 black, 360 Chinese and 654 white children, ranging in age from five to seven, in integrated and segregated schools in New York City, and reported that a majority of black children preferred and identified with their own racial group. Indeed, all the children showed generally a preference for their own group.

Katz, while not questioning the validity of the Clark and Clark study and other supportive studies, noted that "more recent studies suggest that this pattern may be changing and that [in the United States of America] children may now be exhibiting same-race preferences for both symbolic stimuli and friendship choices" (1983, 61). She observed "a growing shift toward minority self-esteem and positive racial identification. Black pre-school children now show either no bias or a same-race preference in choice tasks" (p. 61). She further made the very significant observation that "although the responses of black children have changed, the responses of young white children have not . . . [they] almost never express a preference to be a member of any racial group but their own" (p. 62). This is paralleled by male children almost never wishing to be female. We are obviously seeing here the effect of a changing political and cultural situation where there is still a strong residue of white male dominance, but where also, under the impetus of Black Power and "Black Is Beautiful" movements, the preferences of black children are becoming more pro-black.

Similarly, Vaughan reports that

> research in New Zealand among Maori and Paheka children has mapped change in intergroup preferences as a function of urbanism and time. Changes within the inter-ethnic community at large, highlighted by the rise of a Brown power movement, seem to have percolated down to young children. Young Maoris who once showed a preference for white figures now tend to choose brown. (1983, 91)

Katz finally agrees completely with Vaughan that

> a strictly cognitive, non-social learning model cannot account for the apparent discrepancies in majority and minority group children's development. Given

the very strong tendency to prefer one's own group . . . it becomes necessary to postulate some intervening variables to account for the breakdown of this tendency in the case of ethnic groups that are associated with lower-class status within a particular society. It should be noted that an analogous situation exists with regard to sex-role socialization as well. Girls at certain ages value their own gender group less than boys do. Thus we cannot explain children's social development fully without taking into cognizance the high prevalence of racist and sexist attitudes in the adults around them. (1987, 94)

In fact, there has also been some questioning as to whether race is really as salient in the perception of young children as the studies suggest. Katz hints at assessment techniques (that is, forced-choice questions) as being responsible for exaggerating the importance of race to children: "In open-ended interviews, race does not seem to be spontaneously mentioned very often by children. Moreover racial cues seem to be less important to children than gender, cleanliness, physical attractiveness and age" (1983, 67).

However, it seems that, for Katz, race is essentially colour, and it is not clear what "physical attractiveness" refers to, other than to constitutive "racial" features. Note that Katz is not claiming that there is no racial perception by children, but that there is no particular significance attached to this perception.

In this survey of the literature, Semaj will be given the last word. His findings suggest three stages in the development of racial awareness:

By age 4 or 5, children understand that people are categorized into various ethno-racial groups, but they do not yet understand the bases for these groupings. . . . They also have problems differentiating between black and white as colors and the concepts "Black" and "White". Nonetheless, they are beginning to learn the evaluation of and the connotations associated with these colors and concepts in the form of stereotypes. . . . Between the ages 6 and 9, racial classification skills are being improved, especially racial classificati on for self. . . . Self-evaluation and group evaluations become related, and so, irrespective of what the dominant culture says, his/her group is better than the out-group. . . . Between the ages of 8 and 11, the [black] child still believes that "Black" is good, but is now either forced to or is more willing to accept that "White" is also good. Perhaps as the result of an increasing number of experiences with prejudice, the child begins to lose some of the naturally positive identification with Blackness achieved at an early age. However, if forced to make a choice between Black and White, the child will often show an increasing uneasiness or a refusal to respond in such a manner. . . . As one 11-year old acknowledged, "you can't say that one is better than the other because both races have good people and bad people". (1980a, 76–77)

Semaj further states:

> The problem with this theory [of the universal preference for white over black)
> is that there is no known data of innate aversion to darkness, and that it overlooks
> the power and extent of European cultural imperialism, slavery, and assorted
> exploitation of people of color, especially Africans. From this theory we would
> expect that all children should prefer white over black, and that when they do
> so it is primarily because of the "natural order of things" and not because of a
> value system developed and dispersed by Europeans. The data reviewed here
> show that young Black children may sometimes show outgroup racial identifi-
> cation and preference, but for reasons best explained by the white bias in the
> culture and not for any innate reasons. (1981, 44)

What is extraordinary about these studies is the way in which they arrive
at conclusions about universality on the basis of very limited sampling. It
will be observed that the Indian subcontinent has only one representative
in the Adams and Osgood tests, and the sample was quite disproportion-
ately weighted in favour of European groups. Conspicuously, Africa and
Melanesia are completely unrepresented and, therefore, the investigation
did not have the benefit of dark-skinned peoples (with the possible partial
exception of the group from Mysore, Kannada, South India) reacting to
black and white (and other colours). Even so, it has to be admitted that it
would probably not have made a significant difference, since the significant
factor in the evaluation of the colours black and white is probably the
Eurocentrism of Europe and the imposition of European values on the
colonized world.

These colonies had different experiences of European colonialism. Where
this colonial presence has been strongest, for example on the slave plantations
of the New World, Europe was able to have virtually complete control over
the significant symbols and their values. In other areas, like India, this was
only partially so, and some native pre-colonial symbolization has persisted. In
Thailand, it seems that the pre-colonial colour of mourning was white. This
has changed to black in more recent times, apparently under the influence of
Western symbolism. It is also interesting to consider the cases of India, China
and Japan. There, before the advent of European colonization and imperialism, lighter-skinned people from the north and west dominated darker-
skinned people of the south and installed a colour prejudice in favour of light
skin colour. This prejudice became reinforced under European colonialism
and imperialism.

The preference for white or light skin colour seems to be intimately linked to the general domination by people of northern regions over people of southern regions, whether it be in Europe, Asia, or Africa. The only undisputed reverse cases that have impacted on recorded world history are the domination by the Moors over the lighter-skinned Iberians (tenth to fourteenth/fifteenth centuries) and that of the very dark Cushites (Aethiopians) over the less dark Egyptians (circa the fifth century BC). As we know, Moorish domination in south-western Europe was itself relatively quickly reversed. The Iberians in fact immediately thereafter began their colonial and enslavement adventures in Africa. We shall see later that these two events may constitute an important factor that could help to account for some slight differences in black/white and Amerindian/white relations among the Iberians (Spanish and Portuguese) when compared with the English, Dutch and French.

As far as the second case is concerned, there seemed to be quite amicable relations, at least of mutual respect and tolerance, between the Cushites and the Egyptians. We may consider that one factor operating here is that this was not a case of polar differences in skin colour.

These considerations lead us to ponder on what would have been the picture of colour symbolism today had the south conquered and colonized the North. Why this has never been the case in any lasting way is of course an intriguing question which may even lead us right back to questions of genetic racial diffferences or of climatological differences. But it is not useful to pursue these hypothetical questions here.

Colour in the Natural World

It is permissible to assume that to some extent the presence of colours in nature has some influence on the way in which the symbolizations are constructed, and on the way in which we use colour terms metaphorically and react affectively to them. But nature is indeed different in different parts of the globe. Even where the colours of nature are the same, the significance of these colours may be different or impact differently upon people's lives. The first colour to be considered is the colour of the people themselves. It is obvious that, under normal circumstances, people would consider their own colour to be the natural one, the norm against which all the other colours are judged. Indeed, until they see another human skin colour they would not even conceive of the possibility of other skin colours. When they do see people of a different colour, they would initially find them quite strange, even abnormal, and depending on how the relationship evolved, they would develop particular attitudes towards the new people and by extension to the new colour. The more the cultural and social behaviour of the "strange" people becomes modified and assimilated in contact, the more this colour and other racial physiognomic features become unnoticed or irrelevant and meaningless (cf. the nose of the Jew in the United States, or the blond hair of some Italians in southern Italy). The more they retain "strange" behaviours, the more the hostility remains and their physiognomic features come under pejoration.

In other words, the tests done by people like Adams and Osgood would have had to be done, ideally, before a population came into contact with another, before differentials in power between the populations emerged, and before one group succeeded in imposing symbols and meanings on the other. Unfortunately, at this point in the history of contact among peoples, we would have to go to the Amazon rain forest or the interior of New Guinea to find a context in which such test results would be untainted. This is obviously a logistical non-starter. We are therefore obliged to use other techniques and evidence to discover innate affective evaluations of colour that may qualify as universals.

There is considerable ambiguity in the way in which colours behave in the natural world; their meanings to humans would therefore be similarly ambiguous. The earth is for the most part dark coloured, with the notable exception of red bauxitic soils, yellow soils, and the sands of deserts. Indeed, there is some folk belief, at least in the Caribbean, probably tested and verified by actual experience, that the darker the soil, the richer it is. "Black" soil is therefore particularly fertile or believed to be so, and red bauxitic soils comparatively quite poor. Given the importance of agriculture in the evolution of human societies, human populations would very early have had a positive affect regarding the colour black. According to Russell,

> Egypt is one of the few cultures [of course of those known to Russell] in which black is not the color of evil, but the color of the fertile life-giving alluvial plains of the Delta. Red was the evil color, the hostile hue of the scorching desert sands. Plutarch and Herodotus comment that the [ancient] Egyptians sacrificed red-headed people. (1977, 78)

The Spiritual Baptists of Trinidad, like other religious groups, have a well-established and highly functional system of colour symbolization. White, black and yellow appear in the head ties of the faithful. While yellow signifies the light and glory of the ascension and white the resurrection, black signifies "the earth that keeps us alive". There are other cases of the positive associations of black with Mother Earth. Some of these will be pointed out later. Of course, once human populations became urbanized, the "blackness" of the earth would have hardly impressed urban dwellers.

For light-skinned populations, the dark earth becomes "dirt" or "filth" when it touches and "soils" the human body and its clothing. For black-skinned people who are scantily dressed for the weather, this effect is not the same. The contrast between England and Jamaica is dramatic in this respect. In English, *dirt* is derived from Norse *drit*, "excrement"; it then underwent semantic change to mean secondarily "soil", "earth". The adjective *dirty* has absolutely no positive connotations arising from the meaning "earth"; it derives its meanings exclusively from the Norse etymon. On the other hand, in Jamaican, *doti* means first of all "earth", "soil" with no negative connotations and is derived from Twi, *doti*, of the same meaning, while there is another word, *dirty* (also pronounced *doti* in Jamaican) borrowed from English with the English meaning.

English *soil* may also be compared. The noun with the meaning "upper layer of earth" is derived from French and ultimately from Latin *solum*, "ground"; the related verb "to soil" has only a pejorative meaning: "to make dirty", "to defile". The Jamaican language has not borrowed either of these terms.

The darkness of clouds portending "bad", "inclement" weather has been a signficant factor leading to the connotations of "gloom", "ill-omen" for the colours grey and black. Like many other abstract concepts in European languages, "sadness" and "gloom" were very early represented by physical concepts using colours. But note that blue associated with a clear sky, and grey associated with a clouded sky, both have the connotation of "sadness" in English (but not, as far as blue is concerned, for French and Spanish).

When a British newspaper reporter covering the arrival of thousands of West Indians who were "beating the ban" (that is, trying to enter the United Kingdom before the anti-immigration laws came into effect) saw them pouring out of the train at Victoria Station and reported that "this is indeed a black day for Britain", it was a case of the physical and abstract concepts being fused. Similarly, one Puerto Rican anti-abolitionist, Don Manuel Zeno

Correa, in an impassioned declaration in 1866, said: "the day that a law frees the Blacks, black must be the consequence!"

It is obvious that this semantic expansion from the physical to the abstract is more likely to happen in those geographical areas which have darkness pervading where you would expect (or prefer) light. By contrast, we would not normally expect such semantic expansions in the languages of peoples living in the Sahara Desert or in tropical climates, generally speaking. In these places, blue skies have no particular attractiveness.

The physical occurrence of whiteness in nature is to a large measure in snow, clouds, old age, and in "white" skin. It is snow which has contributed most to the connotations and metaphorical expansions of white. Whereas snow has posed and does still pose some problems for human mobility and outdoor activity (like tilling the fields), for most people such activity ceased in any event in winter even if there was no snow. When people went indoors during winter in Europe and worked at the spinning wheel, other light craft and manufacture, snow must have been seen primarily as a relief from the darkness of the winter days and as the most beautiful and exquisite expression of nature. The sunshine making the snow glisten was particularly impressive and helped to develop the transition from physical meanings to abstract meanings of such terms as brilliant, bright, gleam. Untainted snow also helped to develop the connotation of purity for the term white, and the contrast of the earth on the snow (slush), together with the contrast of white clouds with the portentous dark clouds, contributed to the development of the antithesis of physical white and black, and of the antithesis of abstract pure and blemished. Here again, these semantic shifts could not and did not find a facilitating physical environment in tropical lands, and would have to await the advent of European colonialism and imperialism to take root there.

In temperate lands, particularly in the most northern (for example, Europe north of the Alps and the Pyrenees), the language usage and the folklore record these developments: "pure as the driven snow", Snow White, Goldilocks. White became associated with virgins and angels. Most dramatically, pallor, which is the state of the human skin most realistically white, came to be the hallmark of beauty in the Middle Ages and Renaissance, although it was known that it signified some unhealthy internal state. And if by chance pallor did not occur naturally, it was achieved cosmetically by dusting liberally with white powder. As we shall see, the use of white powder on the face is still practised by some Caribbean women, of all skin colours.

Conclusion

There has been some shift in the canon of beauty from north of the Alps and the Pyrenees to south, in the Mediterranean and the New World. Now, tan is more highly valued than pallor, and blondes have even become associated with intellectual dumbness. According to Bastide, "[In Brazil], the ideal woman is not a blond or a fair-skinned woman, but a brunette or dark-skinned woman and especially a 'rosy-tinted mulatto woman'. . . . In films, the dark-skinned woman is loving and faithful, while the blond is the vamp who leads a man to ruin" (1968, 34).

In earlier agricultural societies, a white skin denoted a life of luxury indoors (enjoyed chiefly by the nobility) and a tanned skin denoted an outdoor life, working as a peasant in the fields. Today, on the other hand, a white skin denotes an indoor occupation that does not allow the luxury of holidays in the sun, while a tanned skin denotes the highly prized ability to afford such luxuries.

There is other evidence of the way in which colour evaluations are socially and contextually constructed, and of the shift that constantly occurs in the associations. Mention was made earlier of the shift from white to black as the colour of mourning in Thailand. Black is no longer, in Western culture, the exclusive colour of funeral attire but is now equally linked to a high degree of ceremonial formality and elegance. According to Cohen,

> In Western theatre, the color white usually means purity or goodness, while black stands for death, sorrow or villainy. In the Eastern theatre, on the other hand, an actor with a white patch in the center of his face is either a clown or a liar, and black stands for honesty and integrity. (1968, 3)

It is permissible to conclude that physical differences are important in the attempts by human beings to classify themselves and others. This is of course especially so in close multiracial societies, and indeed the world has become such a society. Some cues are more discernible than others. Among the most discernible are gender and racial physiognomic features (skin colour being perhaps at the top of the list). Gender and race are learned early, perhaps already from age three or four. The social significance of these characteristics is learned sometime later; they persist into adulthood and increase in importance in accordance with social relational factors.

These physical cues are so important in some political situations that, when they are absent, governments may attempt to add them; and when they are felt to be too conspicuous, people may try to remove them or hide them. Hitler ordered Jews to wear Stars of David so they could be more easily identified. Francois Truffaut in his film *The Last Metro* – situated in Nazi-occupied Paris in 1942 – has a Nazi radio announcer decrying the fact that it was so difficult to identify Jews because not all of them showed the stereotypical Jewish "racial" features. The announcer asked wistfully: "Wouldn't it be great if the Jews just all had blue skins?" (One may wonder why Truffaut chose blue. It seems to relate to what was noted earlier as the ambiguity of colour symbolism, particularly in the case of blue.)

New World blacks still suffering from the psychological legacy of slavery attempt to remove or hide a whole range of racial features, including the texture of hair (by straightening it), the size of the lips (by frequently tucking them in), and the size of the bottom (women frequently place their hands behind, as it were to cover the area, especially when walking in front of men). In Jamaica and other areas of the Caribbean and North America, some black-skinned young women "bleach" their skins to become less black. In this case, white is not the goal, but rather brown, which is becoming, aesthetically and erotically, the desired colour the world over.

In the final analysis, it is the socioeconomic, political and cultural environ-ment which sets the precise pattern. There is no more dramatic an illustration of this than the fact that congenitally blind white South African children were found to hold negative attitudes towards blacks. As Bastide stated: "color is neutral; it is the mind that gives it meaning. . . . Colors are not important in themselves as optical phenomena, but rather as bearers of a meaning" (1968, 34). Isaacs supports this: "Racial mythologies built around differences in skin color and physical features were among the prime tools of power used in the era of Western Empires" (1968, 80).

Safa is quite trenchant on this issue: "The biological foundations of race have been largely discredited, but the meanings attached to racial construc-tions linger in the popular imagination, linking racial characteristics to behav-ior in a hierarchical order to justify white superiority" (1998, 5).

CHAPTER THREE

History of Race and Ethnicity: Europe

*T*o understand the historical foundations of the race and ethnicity situation in the world today, and in the Caribbean in particular, we shall restrict ourselves to looking at the historical development of racial and ethnic perception, awareness, representation and attitudes in three major cultural zones or "civilizations": Europe, Africa and Asia. As it turns out, these are also the major contributors to the emergence and development of modern Caribbean societies and cultures.

We begin with Greek and Roman antiquity, the foundation of so much of Western culture and thought. This period is a convenient place to begin, because it is here that we find the best preserved documentation of the earliest writings and artistic expressions on race and ethnicity in European civilization. However, it is quite likely that racial/ethnic attitudes that we identify in the era of Greek and Roman (classical) antiquity had been forged much earlier, going back to a period of limited contact between Greece and the other peoples of the then "known" world.

We shall see that some of the connotations and metaphorical expansions of the terms "black" and "white" had already become entrenched in the Greek and Latin languages of antiquity. If we can judge by the way in which we now know neologisms and new meanings to take considerable time to become part of the standard usage of writers, we may assume that classical Greek and classical Latin have standardized and recorded a usage that had existed for some time in popular usage (that is, in the spoken language).

Graeco-Roman Antiquity

The world of the Greeks was rather small in the period up to the fifth century BC. Within this limited diversity, if the major source of our knowledge, the epics of Homer, is to be believed, there is recognition of differences in language among the peoples of the "known" world, but there is no evidence of any marked prejudice. According to Baldry, "difference of speech does not form the great dividing line which it later became" (1965, 10). The adjective *barbaros* does not occur in the epics, and it is only later that it came to be used to refer pejoratively to non-Greek speech and by extension to non-Greek speakers. Baldry further states that

> no consideration of race or colour causes any antagonism to the Egyptians. Some antipathy to the Phoenicians is expressed, but this may be attributed to trade rivalry. Concerning the Ethiopians, they are "blameless people", burnt-faced men whose colour [according to Homer] does not prevent them from being favourites of the Gods. (1965, 10)

This last statement concerning the Ethiopians is a kind of back-handed compliment, and hints already that colour is a sensitive issue.

From the fifth century BC, the world of the Greeks expanded considerably. Already in the latter half of the sixth century BC, Xenophanes, the philosopher/poet, had remarked that "each race has its own conception of God, modelled on its own appearance: The Ethiopians think their Gods have snub noses and black hair" (Baldry 1965, 11).

We suggested earlier that ethnocentrism, the belief in the merits of one's own way of life and the equating of "foreign" with "not so good as ours", is normal and common to all free peoples. However, it has to be admitted that cultural arrogance reached quite remarkable heights (or depths) in ancient Greece and Rome. The Greeks and Romans imagined themselves to be at the centre of the civilized world and believed that their way of life constituted a standard by which all things removed from that centre should be judged. (It may be argued that this arrogance has continued unabated among the inheritors of Greek and Roman civilization up to today.) It is easier to explain Roman arrogance than Greek arrogance. The Romans were ruthless conquerors and had an unshakeable belief in their military invincibility. We have seen that one of the main factors in the growth of inordinate ethnic arrogance is military might.

The ancient Greeks and Romans and their inheritors possessed a natural tendency towards ethnocentrism and carried it to extremes not recorded for other peoples. The Chinese too are excessively ethnocentric. For them, all non-Chinese (including Europeans) were almost less than human – uncivilized, beasts, devils. However, unlike the Romans and western Europeans, they have never developed the military might that would have enabled them to lord it over other peoples. They certainly seem not to have developed the passion for extending not only political hegemony but also cultural hegemony over the rest of the world. They never passionately sought to impose their religion, their values, their institutions on other peoples in a "civilizing mission".

The belief of the Greeks and Romans in their own superiority is well documented. The Romans with their military might sought to spread *Pax Romana* wherever their conquering armies went. They granted Roman citizenship to those who attended their schools and became assimilated to the Roman way of life. In the development of Europe, the same Latin root *civis* was used to form both the concept "citizen" and the concept "civilized".

But the attitudes of the Greeks and Romans to the peoples in their immediate vicinity were ambivalent. For people who were furthest removed in geography, appearance and custom, the attitudes were more severe and unambivalent. The Egyptians and the Phoenicians, their neighbours across the Mediterranean, were perhaps the greatest puzzle for the Greeks. According to Bernal, these North African peoples (Egyptians) "were despised and feared, but at the same time deeply respected for their antiquity and well-preserved ancient religion and philosophy" (1987, 23).

The actual relations between the Greeks and Egyptians are a source of much controversy. This has implications for our understanding of the history of racial and ethnic attitudes in Europe and in Western civilization in general. As we said earlier, racial attitudes are dependent on the interplay of a number of factors: difference in appearance and culture, conquest/subordination, competitiveness for scarce resources. For example, the different combinations of the above factors explain Western racial attitudes towards Japan at different periods. They also explain the differences in attitudes of the Greeks towards the Egyptians and towards other peoples.

Bernal (1987) identifies two models of the interpretation of the origins of the Greeks which have implications for racial and ethnic attitudes of the Greeks and Europeans in general at different periods of history: the "Ancient Model" and the "Aryan Model", to which he adds the "Revised Ancient Model". The Ancient Model was the conventional view among Greeks in the classical and Hellenistic ages. According to it, Greek culture had arisen as the result of colonization, around 1500 BC, by Egyptians and Phoenicians who had "civilized" the native inhabitants of Greece. Furthermore, the Greeks had continued to borrow heavily from north-eastern African cultures. Greek writers of the classical and Hellenistic periods, interested in their distant past, had, with few exceptions, accepted that Greece had originally been inhabited by "primitive" tribes, Pelasgians and others, and later had been invaded and settled by Phoenicians and Egyptians who introduced "civilization" in the forms of writing, engineering and religion.

The Aryan Model was developed only during the first half of the nineteenth century AD. According to it, there had been an invasion from the north of Europe, unreported in ancient tradition, which had overwhelmed the local "Aegean" or "pre-Hellenistic" culture. Greek civilization is seen as the result of the mixture of the Indo-European speaking Hellenes and their indigenous subjects. For eighteenth- and nineteenth-century Romantics and racists, it was simply intolerable for Greece, which was seen not merely as the epitome of Europe but also as its pure childhood, to have been the result of the mixture of native Europeans and colonizing Africans and Semites. Therefore, the Ancient Model had to be overthrown and replaced by something more acceptable.

Ancient Egypt

A comparison with ancient Egypt may be instructive. Another question of great controversy is whether the ancient Egyptians were black. A host of writers have discussed this at length, and at the end of it all the picture is not at all consistent. The ancient Greek historian, Herodotus, the father of Western historiography, saw the Egyptians as having black skins and woolly hair. But other contemporary witnesses do not present a consistent picture. Ancient Egypt was a focal point for scholars, scientists, merchants and military adventurers. It was visited and invaded by people from the north (Greeks and Romans), from the south (Kushites), from the east (Assyrians), and to a lesser extent from the west (Carthaginians and others).

The Napatan kingdom of Kush (*c.*750 BC–300 BC) conquered Egypt, which it ruled as the twenty-fifth dynasty, and laid the foundation of a state that, with its later capital at Meroe (*c.*300 BC–AD 350), survived for a thousand years, a span longer than any single period of Egyptian unification (Snowden 1983, 26). Egyptian and Kushite forces then fought side by side in Asia to control Assyrian expansionism. All the evidence presented by Snowden suggests some hostility and contempt by the Egyptians for the Kush, their neighbours and enemies from lower down the Nile Valley in East Africa, but no ascribed stigma. Snowden sums up the position as follows:

> The 25th Dynasty was a new experience for Egyptians. . . . They [the Napatan Kushites] appeared to Egyptians in many respects as native rulers rather than as foreign invaders. . . . No strangers to Egyptian culture, numbers of Kushites had been absorbed into the Egyptian army, some occupying high rank in provincial administration. . . . Apparently regarding themselves as defenders and perpetuators of Egyptian culture, the victorious southern rulers initiated a new era of building by renovating and enlarging existing temples and by new construction in various parts of Egypt. . . . It was not surprising, therefore, that some Delta [Egyptian] chieftains looked to Kushite leadership in efforts to cast off the yoke of Assyrian domination of Egypt, which they found more oppressive than Napatan [Kushite] rule. (1983, 41)

It is quite evident that Ancient Egypt was populated by people of different "races", ranging in colour from white to black and with a variety of physiognomic characteristics. The original racial type, situated geographically on the mid-zone of the race/colour continuum from north to south, was most likely brown to dark brown, but especially during the reign of Kushites over Egypt, there was a strong black presence. Racial perception, awareness and attitudes among the Egyptians and Kushites seem to have been relatively mild and personal, but certainly not non-existent. The political and military-based hostility between the (dark) brown Egyptians and the black peoples to the south (Kushites/Nubians) was real, but does not seem to have sunk into marked racial prejudice and animosity. There seems rather to have been racial integration.

The Racial Attitudes of Ancient Greeks

With the Greeks, the picture is different. There are two basic camps concerning the racial attitudes of Greeks (and Romans) towards the dark-skinned people across the Mediterranean in Africa. The evidence for these attitudes comes generally from the works of scholars (historians, philosophers), creative writers and artists (sculptors). Although these categories represent an important and very influential segment of Greek and Roman populations, they omit one very important group – the ordinary citizen, men in the street of the Greek city states and Rome, and the country folk of both regions. It is the attitudes of these persons (constituting the vast majority) which would have been handed down from generation to generation to the modern day in western Europe. The language of this segment of the population is really our only source of knowledge about their attitudes.

The attitudes of historians should be regulated and affected by their relatively higher scientific objectivity and rationalism, which would/should have ruled out race and colour as a criterion for assessing the worth of an individual or of a people. When we see brilliant thinkers like Aristotle expressing racist opinions, we are tempted to conclude that there must have been even coarser views held by the less intelligent and less rational members of Greek society. However, when it comes to racist beliefs, it is remarkable how many otherwise sensible intellectuals are afflicted with this particular pathology, from the great thinkers of the Age of Enlightment (see later) to some twentieth-century thinkers.

The attitudes of creative writers and other artists towards other peoples are gleaned from their artistic representations of those peoples. These representations may be inspired by particular creative sensibilities or by an artistic penchant for satire and caricature, and they may not necessarily be faithful pictures. When we attempt to interpret these artistic creations, there is a division between those who consider some pieces to be "ugly", "grotesque", "caricature", "comic", and those who claim that the pieces are finely executed. It then is very difficult to figure out what is the precise attitude of the artist towards the person he is portraying.

Of the two camps of scholars who have studied racial and ethnic attitudes among the Greeks and Romans of antiquity, one camp claims that the evidence does not show prejudice and the other that it does. Frank Snowden Jr is an African American art historian and his work purports to show that

> when we set about, through a study of the iconographical and written sources,
> to trace the image of blacks as seen by whites from Egyptian to Roman times,
> and to explore the rationale for the attitude towards blacks during this period
> . . . the very striking similarities in the total picture that emerge from an
> examination of the basic sources – Egyptian, Greek, Roman, and early Christian
> – point to a highly favorable image of blacks and to white-black relationships
> differing markedly from those that have developed in more color-conscious
> societies. (Snowden 1983, vii)

This extreme claim of the preface is not borne out by the text of the ensuing
chapters, which in fact provide support for both positions in such a way that
no clear and consistent picture emerges. This is undoubtedly because no clear
and consistent picture existed. There certainly was no state-sponsored racism,
and no institutional racism. All races could be enslaved and black persons could
achieve high social status as Roman senators, writers, teachers, and so on.

As we noted above, the Greeks considered themselves to be superior to all
others, including the fairer Nordic tribes from north Europe. However, there
is no evidence, even among the evidence produced by Snowden, that this
attitude towards the fair-haired, blue-eyed people of the north was the same
as that held towards the black-skinned, woolly haired people of the lower Nile
valley and north-west Africa. Davis was inspired to state (concerning sixteenth-century Europe): "For reasons that can perhaps never be fully explained, it was the African's color of skin that became his defining characteristic and aroused the deepest response in Europeans" (1988, 447). This
obsession with skin colour seems to go as far back as antiquity itself.

The Greeks (and Romans) were quite colour conscious and were the first
on record to use colour terms to designate people and countries. The word
Aethiops, constructed by the Greeks to name the peoples south of the first Nile
cataract, meant literally "burnt-faced person", and the geographical area
where the burnt-faced people lived was called *Aethiopia.* The people were
routinely identified and referred to by other epithets meaning black, while the
Greeks and Romans identified and referred to themselves by adjectives
meaning white, bright, and so on. The names "Moor" and "Mauretania" are
based on Greek *mauron,* black; and other ethnic groups from north-west Africa
were called *Nigritae* (a derivative of *niger,* black) and *Erebidae* (children of
darkness).

The people of Aethiopia and north-west Africa, and indeed of most of
sub-Saharan Africa, did not and do not faithfully represent the colour black;

nor did Greeks faithfully represent the colour white (cream perhaps, or olive, but not white). This use of colour terms by the Greeks and Romans to designate peoples was a clever act of seizing the prerogative of naming and of controlling the significant symbols. The effects are still with us today. Here already we see a remarkable difference between the Greeks and Romans on the one hand and the Egyptians on the other. The latter have left no record of a race and colour consciousness which would have prompted a colour designation of peoples similar and analogous to that practised by the Greeks and Romans.

Greeks and Romans further observed with great care the colour gradations that existed not only in the Mediterranean area but also further afield. They used a variety of adjectives to refer to the differences between peoples that they perceived. Snowden cites Manilius, a first-century AD poet/astrologer who "mentioned groups who were to be included most frequently in a familiar classical color scheme: Ethiopians, the blackest; Indians, less sun-burned; Egyptians, mildly dark; and the Mauri (Moors), whose name was derived from the color of their skin" (1983, 7). From Manilius (*Astronomica*), Herodotus, Aristotle (*Problemata*), Lucretius, Ovid (*Metamorphoses*), Pliny (*Naturalis Historia*), Ptolemy (*Tetrabiblos*), Snowden has collected the following sample of adjectives used to represent human beings on the basis of their colour: *fuscus* (dark), *niger* (black), *nigerrimus* (very black), *furvus* (swarthy), *adustus* (scorched), *perustus* (sun-burned).

This colour consciousness entered into the proverbial sayings of the time: for instance, "can the Aethiopian change his skin or the leopard his spots?"; "to wash an Ethiopian white". These sayings were used to describe futile activity or to illustrate the unchangeability of nature (Snowden 1983, 7). But there is the implication that the unchangeable status quo is somewhat undesirable and that a change would have been an improvement.

Greek and Roman scholars (anthropologists in our modern sense) not only developed elaborate theories of the origins of skin colour based on climatic conditions, but also developed stereotypical character descriptions of the peoples around them. No less a person than Aristotle left this account:

> The people of cold countries generally, and particularly those of Europe, are full of spirit, but deficient in skill and intelligence; and this is why they continue to remain relatively free, but attain no political development and show no capacity for governing others. The peoples of Asia are endowed with skill and intelligence, but are deficient in spirit and this is why they continue to be peoples

of subjects and slaves. The Greek stock, intermediate in geographical position, unites the qualities of both sets of peoples. (Aristotle 1946, book 7: 296)

Of slaves in particular, Aristotle had this to say:

> Tame animals have a better nature than wild, and it is better for all such animals that they should be ruled by man because they then get the benefit of preservation. . . . This general principle must similarly hold good of all human beings generally and therefore of the relation of masters and slaves. . . . The use which is made of the slave diverges but little from the use made of tame animals. . . . It is nature's intention also to erect a physical difference between the body of the freeman and that of the slave, giving the latter strength for the menial duties of life. . . . It is thus clear that, just as some are by nature free, so others are by nature slaves and for these latter the condition of slavery is both beneficial and just. . . . There is, as we have seen, a kind of slavery which exists by nature; but there is also a kind of slave, and of slavery, which exists by law. (Aristotle 1946, book 1: 13–14)

As we have noted, Snowden emerges as the great apologist for the Greeks (and Romans). He forcefully and repeatedly rejects any thesis that these peoples of antiquity were racists and that in this sense they were the forerunners of later Europeans, who, it is true, took racial prejudice and discrimination to even greater heights (or depths), far surpassing the Greeks and Romans. In his attempt to exculpate the Greeks, Snowden notes that "in classical thought the blackness of the Ethiopian was only skin deep. Blacks could have a soul as pure as the whitest of the whites" [sic] (1983, 103). Snowden apparently is oblivious to how patronizing that statement is and how reminiscent it is of the modern day concept of "roast breadfruits" (in Jamaica) and "oreos" (in the United States), that is, persons held in contempt by black militants for being black on the outside but white on the inside. The "roast breadfruit" and the "oreo" seem to have existed at all times. One of the most famous early Ethiopian Christian Fathers, Abba Moses, dressed in white vestments for his ordination at the beginning of the fifth century AD, is said to have wondered whether he was as white inwardly as he was (his clothing, that is) outwardly. Snowden talks about "this tradition of outer blackness and inner whiteness" (1983, 103).

According to Snowden, the most we can impute to the Greeks and Romans is a "somatic norm image. . . . They had, like other people before and after them, narcissistic canons of physical beauty" (1983, 103). It may be true that the Greeks and Romans treated all aliens with a certain degree of disdain, but it is equally obvious that blacks came in for especial treatment. The evidence for this is in the very data presented by Snowden to support his major thesis, and it is difficult to understand how these contradictions were overlooked by his reviewers and publisher.

Snowden's data come from iconographical and written sources, much of it from comments, statements and creative writings of individuals. Where these individuals express favourable attitudes to blacks, it is clear that they are expressing personal attitudes and are going, as it were, against the grain. For example, Snowden cites a Greek poet, Asclepiades, praising the beauty of one Didyme: "Gazing at her beauty, I melt like wax before the fire. And if she is black, what difference to me? So are coals, but when we light them, they shine like rose-buds" (1983, 77). This is of course reminiscent of the formula used today: "She is black, but beautiful." Interestingly, it appears also in the Song of Songs (1:5), where it is not clear whether the Hebrew *kai* is to be translated as "and" or as "but", a choice crucial to an interpretation of the racial attitude underlying the formula. The earliest scriptures in Latin read *et*, "and" (*nigra sum et formosa*, "I am black and beautiful"); but the Vulgate, produced in an age of rising racism in Europe, reads *sed*, "but" (see later).

Snowden did not realize that Theocritus too was really defending himself from accusations of wrongdoing when he cites the Greek writer as "reminding those who call his Bombyca sun-burned that to him she is honey-brown and charming". Poor Theocritus is apparently lightening Bombyca's complexion to make her more acceptable to his compatriots. Snowden also does not realize that Ovid's Sepho has to defend her colour to Pheon by reminding him that the black Andromeda captivated Perseus by her beauty (cf. the need still felt by some blacks on the defensive to cite famous historical figures who were black). Lastly, Snowden notes that "Martial writes that, though he was sought by a girl whiter than a washed swan, than silver, snow, lily, or privet, he pursued a girl blacker than an ant, pitch, jawdaw, or cicada" (1978, 77). Snowden seems not to be aware that Martial is subject to severe psychological conflict because he (Martial) still associates white with beauty and cleanliness and black with ugliness and dirtiness.

Friedman (1981) presents a different picture. He shows how the Greeks developed notions of "monstrous races" living on the periphery of the "known world". He speaks of the "marked ethnocentrism [of the Greeks and Romans] which made the observer's culture, language, and physical appearance the norm by which to evaluate all other peoples". Affergan (1983, 231) notes that some believe that racism was born between the end of the seventeenth century and the Age of Enlightenment because the first great naturalist classifications appeared then (Linne and Buffon). But, he continues,

> la pensée grecque porte en germe toutes les prémisses du raisonnement et de la dénomination racistes. . . le sol grec en était fertile dans la mesure où c'est par la métaphore de la différence et de l'Autre que la question du racisme peut se poser . . . le dispositif se met lentement en place dans l'économie du langage même (barbaroi, ceux qui bafouillent, qui ne parlent donc grec).

> Greek thought embodies embryonically all the premises of racist construction and representation . . . Greek soil nurtured them to the extent that it is through the metaphor of difference and of the Other that the question of racism is posed . . . the whole apparatus is slowly set up in the economy of the language itself (barbaroi, those who stammer, who in other words do not speak Greek).

Diller does not deal at all with the attitude of Greeks towards Ethiopians and only very briefly with their attitude towards Egyptians. As far as other foreign ethnic groups are concerned, for the period under consideration, he states that

> in the field of biology, the doctrine of the equality of man was vigorously asserted by the sophists and denied by Aristotle. . . . The Greeks disapproved of the mingling of peoples because it fostered discord and uncertainty in the state. They regarded Greek culture as far superior to all others. . . . While the Greeks held a national prejudice against barbarians, there is no evidence of sentimental repugnance. (1971, 160)

The Periclean law of the mid-fifth century BC that prohibited intermarriage between citizens and foreigners suggests that there may have been some incidence of concubinage with foreigners among the people but that the rulers wished to prevent it. However, Diller concludes that "for the historical period before Alexander, we must conclude that there was not much race mixture in Greece" (1971, 160).

The Ancient Romans

As far as the Romans are concerned, they were culturally and intellectually very dependent on the Greeks. The main additional source that will be used for knowledge of the attitudes of Romans towards race is the Latin language. Latin records a clear connotative antithesis between black and white that is fundamentally no different from that which occurs in modern western European languages. In fact, there have been no major semantic extensions or restrictions of these terms from classical Latin to modern European languages. And there is nothing to suggest that there is any difference in this respect between classical Latin (the standard written educated form) and vulgar Latin (the spoken form used in informal contexts). Vulgar Latin was taken to other parts of western Europe with the spread of the Roman Empire and evolved into the Romance languages: French, Spanish, Portuguese, Italian and others. The fundamental semantic structures surrounding black and white in western Europe were therefore already laid in the languages of antiquity.

Latin had basically two words each for black and white. There is some suggestion of a difference in meaning between the doublets in each case; but by and large there is so much overlap between the meanings of the members of the doublet in each case as to justify considering them as (near) synonyms. However, the etymologies suggest that, particularly in the case of the doublet for white, the semantic distinction was more evident in the earlier period of the formation of these terms.

For white, there is in Latin on the one hand *albus*, which, in the classical period, tended to refer to the physical phenomenon of whiteness, and on the other hand *candidus*, which had a wider range of denotative meanings and of affective meanings. According to Marouzeau (1949, 68), "albus *ne désigne que la couleur*, candidus *rend l'impression agréable qu'elle fait sur nous*" (*albus* refers only to the colour, candidus to the pleasant effect it has on us). Marouzeau was an outstanding classical and Romance philologist. In this instance, he was categorical in his assignment of meanings, and rather biased (but honest, I suppose) in his attribution of pleasurable connotations to whiteness.

In fact, *albus* did tend to refer to whiteness as a colour, and when used in reference to people was associated with pallor and even ill health (Ernout 1951, 36), whereas *candidus* was associated with light and brightness. Tucker states, in reference to *albus*, that "the Latin use indicates the notion 'pale' rather than 'shining' [expressed by *candidus*] and the whiteness implied is probably that of emptiness, exhaustion (of illness, death)" (1931, 10). Since, in the age of the formation of Latin, pallor was not appreciated, *candidus* was taken over to express the meaning "white"; and it was *candidus* rather than *albus* which the Romans preferred to use affectively with positive connotations to express that colour. (We may note here again that in the Middle Ages and the Renaissance, pallor came to be appreciated after the Germanic invasions had shifted the centre of power in western Europe from Rome to the peoples further north who were of paler skin, hair and eyes.)

However, the meaning of *albus* came to be extended into areas overlapping somewhat with the meanings of *candidus*. *Albus* could also mean "clear", "transparent", "propitious", "favourable", and in this sense and in association with soft light it came to refer to the morning light. Hence French *aube*, Spanish, and Italian, *alba*, "dawn".

Albus began by referring to the physical colour white. It could also be used as a race/colour term applied to people, and it seems that it could have a neutral meaning free from prejudicial, ameliorative connotations. Cicero used the expression *is qui albus aterne fuerit ignoras* ("you can't tell white from black"), which is based on the Latin epigram *albus aterne sit nescire*, not to know a person from Adam (literally, "not to know a white man from a black man"). The meaning of *albus* then moved to incorporate the notion of light, and so on.

Candidus, on the other hand, began by referring to light. It is related etymologically to *candere*, "to burn", "to be ablaze", and its earliest basic meaning was "bright", "radiant". Its incorporation of the meaning white was no doubt influenced by the glistening, shining nature of snow. This would explain why there was a collapse of meanings between bright and white rather than between bright and green, the dominant colour in nature, which also shines and glistens under the sun. The noun *candor* was used to express the whiteness of snow.

Candidus ultimately came to express the neutral colour white, as is suggested by Vitruvius's description of the Nordic peoples: *sub septentrionibus nutriuntur gentes, immanibus corporibus, candidis coloribus* ("there are people living in the northern regions who have huge bodies and are white in colour"). He contrasts these with the southern peoples across the Mediterranean: *meridianae gentes colore fusco* ("southern peoples of dark colour").

Candidus developed a wide range of positive connotative meanings: (1) lucky, prosperous, favourable; (2) happy, kind, morally pure, innocent; (3) (of writers) clear, lucid. The derivative *candidatus* meant "wearing a white toga". This was the ceremonial attire of important people, and it developed the meaning "person aspiring to high office" (cf. English, candidate).

It is no surprise, therefore, that the Romans then applied the term *candidus* to themselves to distinguish themselves racially from the darker peoples across the Mediterranean. This measure represented the continuing co-opting of positive symbols and meaning to characterize Caucasian peoples.

The incorporation of whiteness into the meaning of *candidus*, and the incorporation of brightness into the meaning of *albus*, represented the valorization of the skin colour, white, in a southern European world whose people had a skin colour that was not exactly white, but who were being more and more exposed to peoples of other colours. When Virgil used *candida* to describe Dido, the darling of his hero Aeneas, he meant both fair (white) and beautiful. *Candidus* was even used by Roman writers to describe the gods.

It was only later, after the Germanic invasions of Italy from the north (beginning circa the third century AD), that *candidus* and *albus* disappeared from spoken usage in favour of the Germanic word *blancus* (French *blanc*, Spanish *blanco*, Portuguese *branco*, Italian *bianco*). This neutral colour term then came to be used in reference to Caucasian peoples. *Blancus* assumed the meanings of *albus* and *candidus*, including an association with pallor as well as some of the positive connotative meanings of *candidus*.

Paralleling the pair of words meaning white, Latin also had a pair in the meaning black. Several Latin scholars propose that the relationship between the members was analogous to that between *albus* and *candidus*. However, there is no agreement as to which of the terms for black is opposed to which term for white.

According to Ernout (1951, 36), *ater*, "black", was the physical colour term opposed to *albus*, while *niger* was opposed to *candidus*. For Marouzeau (1949, 67–68), on the other hand,

> *le concept de "noir" s'accompagne assez naturellement* [sic] *d'une impression défavorable. . . . A cette acception répond le Latin* ater, *tandis que* niger *est réservé à l'emploi physique et désigne, sans plus, la couleur noire. La distinction n'est pas ancienne, mais à l'époque classique elle s'affirme. Cicéron emploie* niger *quand il oppose le noir au blanc. . . . Il y a un rapport analogue entre* albus *et* candidus; albus *ne désigne que la couleur,* candidus *rend l'impression agréable qu'elle fait sur nous.*

the concept "black" conveys, virtually by its very nature, an unfavourable impression; this is the meaning rendered by Latin *ater*, while *niger* has a physical meaning and expresses simply the colour black. The distinction is not an old one, but it became clearer in the classical period. Cicero used *niger* when he contrasted white with black. . . . There is an analogous relationship between *albus* and *candidus*; *albus* refers only to the colour, *candidus* expresses the pleasant effect it has on us.

Again, it seems that a distinction between these two terms for "black" may have existed at the early period of their formation, but by the classical period considerable semantic overlap had taken place. Etymologically, *ater* is based on a root meaning "burnt"; its etymological meaning would be "blackened by fire" (Ernout 1951, 95). As we saw, the same notion of "burnt" recurs in the naming of ancient Aethiopians and other African peoples by the Greeks. The origin of *niger* is obscure (no pun intended). But it has been related to a root (unattested) *nei*, meaning "to smear", "to rub over". Note also the irony that the same root *nei* may have also produced English "neat", French *net*, "clean", German *snee*, English "snow".

However, by the classical period, *ater* and *niger* were interchangeable; they both could be used to express the physical colour black, and they both had pejorative semantic extensions. *Ater* and *niger* could mean "terrible", "savage", "wicked", "evil", and they could both be used to express an ill omen or misfortune. When Horace wrote *hic niger est*, he meant that the person was both black and wicked.

But the most dramatic illustration of the early pejoration of black as a human skin colour is to be found in *atrox*, the pre-classical Latin derivative of *ater*. *Atrox*, which became French *atroce*, Spanish *atroz*, Italian *atroce*, English "atrocious", is a compound of *ater* and *oc*, "face" (cf. also Latin *oculus* "eye"), and meant literally "with a black (that is, terrible) face".

Christianity

Following the self-characterization of western Europeans as "radiant", "shining", "white", and the characterization of the peoples to the south as "burnt" (in the case of *ater*) and probably as "smeared over" (in the case of *niger*), and following the co-opting of the positive connotations of white, it was perhaps inevitable that the next great event in western Europe, that is, Christianization, would also co-opt whiteness, creating one of the greatest hoaxes and deceptions in human history.

When Christianity was adopted (and adapted) by Rome and then spread throughout the empire, it came to be grafted onto a social religious system that had already developed a racial and ethnic hierarchy and a colour symbolization which exalted whiteness and downgraded blackness. Classical antiquity had already moved from a symbolic use of black to represent evil to a transposition of this value to people of black pigmentation. In classical antiquity, demons were at times represented as Ethiopians and the devil was depicted as an Egyptian (Snowden 1983, 100). In Greek and Roman drama, scenes of the "lower world" (Hades) were enacted by dark-skinned Egyptians and Ethiopians.

On the other hand, the world in which Christianity emerged (Palestine, now called the Middle East or the Near East) did not have the value polarization of black and white which had begun in Europe and persisted during the Christian era on that continent. Russell has noted that

> the color black is not a symbol of evil in the Old Testament or in the Apocalyptic period. Rather, the symbolization of color of the ancient near east, red, black and white, is ambiguous. Even where color symbolism is striking, as in the Book of Enoch, neither red nor black becomes significantly fixed as evil as both would do in Christian iconography. (1977, 217)

However, it is useful to note that at the specific time when Jesus Christ was born, heralding the age of Christianity, Palestine had already become a part of the Roman Empire and therefore greatly exposed to Graeco-Roman cultural and intellectual influences. As Kristeller states:

> at the time when the new religion began to spread through the Mediterranean area, its sacred writings which were to form the canon of the New Testament were composed in Greek, that is, in a language which showed the marks of a long literary and philosophical tradition, and in part by authors such as Paul, Luke, and John, who had enjoyed a literary and perhaps a philosophical education. (1955, 75)

Ethnicity, the category related to race and which is the other interest of this book, is very marked in Old Testament history. Ethnic and sub-ethnic categories and identities are routinely mentioned, and a great deal of interest is expressed in language, religion and customs. However, only in very few cases is the skin pigmentaton of the groups and individuals noted. There is very little in the Old Testament of what may even remotely be interpreted as clear unambiguous racial prejudices and hierarchies, or value polarizations in colour symbolism.

The Jews and the Egyptians were antagonistic to each other, and their skin colours may have been slightly different. Given their places of origin and their ethnic provenance, Moses was probably light brown and the Pharaoh dark brown. But if Moses was brought up in the house of the Pharaoh, he presumably was able to pass for an Egyptian on the basis of his appearance, especially his skin colour. This is suggesting that either skin colour did not matter and was not a prime factor in identifying people, or that the differences in shades of brown were rather insignificant in the region.

Moses then married a Kushite (Ethiopian) woman. Although he was rebuked for this by Aaron and Miriam, there is no indication that their objection was based in any way on the skin colour of Moses' intended. In fact, God seemed to be on the side of Moses and the Kushite, because His anger was roused against Aaron and Miriam. It is also significant that when Miriam's skin becomes diseased she is depicted as being "white as snow" (Numbers 12:1–15). In other words, this simile, which in ancient China, Japan and Europe was one of the most widely used to flatter and complement beautiful women, is in the context of ancient Palestine and the Near East paradoxically and ambiguously a depiction of degradation and ill health as well as of beauty. We may conclude that the influence of the Romans, the political and military rulers, imposed the simile "white as snow" on the Palestinians, for whom snow was, at most, a rare occurrence, but that the people of the region reinterpreted the expression in terms of their own experience, in which whiteness of skin was associated with the dreaded disease, leprosy.

However, in His endorsement of the Jews by sending His Son amongst them, God was inevitably rather hostile, though not categorically so, to the Egyptians and Ethiopians. On the one hand, He preserved Ebed-Melech, a Kushite eunuch, from the destruction of Jerusalem, but He also proclaimed to Ezekiel that on the day of reckoning "a sword will come upon Egypt and there will be anguish in Kush". The Jews themselves may have had more than a normal affliction with ethnic arrogance, brought on in large measure by their having been "the Chosen People". But they seemed not to have any excessive difficulty with marrying outside their ethnic group (in spite of the record of Aaron's and Miriam's objection to Moses' marriage).

Colour symbolism in the Bible is inconsistent and imprecise. There is no indication that blackness had any particularly negative connotation, except insofar as it is semantically linked with darkness (that is, the absence or antithesis of light). The colour was not particularly associated with death, evil, and so on, as it came to be in the Roman and European era of Christianity. For example, sin in the Bible was likely to be depicted as red or scarlet (see below).

However, black (or dark – there is some uncertainty about the translations from Hebrew) is used figuratively to express suffering and anguish: "My skin is become black/dark upon me [from mourning]" (Job 30:30); "Earth shall mourn and the heavens above be black/dark" (Jeremiah 4:28). In Apocalypse (6:3), a white horse seems to symbolize the victory of Christ, a red one symbolizes war and a black one symbolizes famine, while a pale green horse symbolizes death.

On the other hand, whiteness had clear connotations of moral and spiritual purity and innocence. It is not clear whether this meaning was indigenous to the region or whether it was brought or reinforced by Greek and later Roman influence. The fact that the simile "white as snow" is so widely used when the region had no consistent experience of snow, and the fact that the simile is used both flatteringly (of feminine beauty) and pejoratively (of the ravages of leprosy) suggest that it may have been an importation from Europe.

There are a number of Biblical allusions attesting to the positive connotations of whiteness. The strongest allusions are based on the notion of washing, used metaphorically to refer to the washing away of sins. The basis seems to be the practice of washing cloth with a detergent, bleaching it in sulphur fumes and leaving it in the sun to dry. The cloth became a shining white after this process. White robes were a sign of prestige and of worthiness. One of the injunctions in Ecclesiastes (9:8) is: "At all times, let thy garments be white." The process of washing is then used as an analogy for the purification of sinful man: "Cleanse me of my sin with hyssop, that I may be purified. Wash me and I shall be whiter than snow" (Psalms 51:7).

Later, in the time of the New Testament, this image strengthens as white was worn by the transfigured Jesus Christ for his resurrection (Matthew 17:2). The angels too were dressed in white (John 20:12), and still are up to this day. White became and still is the dress code for brides, baptisms and the clergy.

There, is however, no indication of an anthesis of white and black. Rather, as we have said, the colour symbolical of sin is scarlet or red: "Though thy sins be like scarlet, they shall be white as snow; if they be red as crimson, they shall be white as wool" (Isaiah 1:18).

Interestingly, as we have said, the simile "white as snow" is also widely used in the Bible to indicate a major symptom of leprosy: "Behold his hand was leprous, as white as snow" (Exodus 4:6); "Miriam was leprous, as white as snow" (Numbers 12:10). In Leviticus (13:4), it is the "shining whiteness in the skin" which is the sign of leprosy. And in Kings 5:27, Gehazi, the leper, is also described as "white as snow". It seems then that there was a double value of whiteness: on the one hand, whiteness in skin pigmentation clashed with the "normal" (that is, regionally typical) colour of healthy skin (that is, various degrees of "brownness"), and was viewed as unhealthy and even despicable; on the other hand, whiteness was the result of the washing (that is, cleansing) and bleaching of cloth and could then be used analogically and metaphorically in a moral, religious context for the cleansing of the soul of its sins. It was desirable that the inner self, the soul, be washed clean and whitened; but there was no desire that the outer self, the skin, be similarly "white", as has happened in the case of New World cultures (cf. the bleaching of the skin by some African descendants in the New World).

The best known Biblical reference to black is in the Song of Songs, where, as we said earlier, black is juxtaposed to beauty. But there is some uncertainty as to whether the relationship between the two attributes (blackness and beauty) is one of contrast or complementarity. Snowden says:

> The Song of Songs 1:5 reads, "I am black and (*kai*) beautiful", in the Septuagint; Origen (*Commentarium in Canticum Canticorum* 2:360) writes, " '*fusca sum et formosa* . . .' *In aliis exemplaribus legimus: 'nigra sum et formosa'* ('I am dark and beautiful' . . . In other copies we read: 'I am black and beautiful'); and most of the early commentators read "and" (see Snowden, *Blacks in Antiquity,* p. 331, n. 17). But Courtes, "The Theme of 'Ethiopia' ", in his discussion of the Origen commentary (p. 14), apparently cites the *sed* ("but") reading of the Vulgate 1:4 ("*nigra sum, sed formosa*") [I am black but beautiful]. (1983, 148, n. 212)

We may note that the Septuagint (which reads "black and beautiful") is the Greek version of the Old Testament, considered to have been made about 270 BC. On the other hand, The Vulgate, which begins to spread the reading "black but beautiful", is the Latin version of the Bible prepared mainly by St Jerome in the late fourth century AD. We may be witnessing here an evolution over time in the racial attitudes of Christianity, culminating in the extremely pro-white bias of European Christianity of the Middle Ages (for which there is other evidence; see below). In any event, the Song of Songs reference is a very isolated case, and there are no other examples on which to build an assessment of the nature of the relationship between black and beautiful in the Bible.

Christianity in Europe

The change during the Roman/European era of Christianity was dramatic. Let us begin with Satan. According to Russell (1977, 247), "nowhere does the New Testament describe Satan as actually black. Satan is a spirit not a body . . . He can even transform himself into an angel of light (2 Corinthians 11:14)" (cf. one of his early names, *Lucifer*, meaning literally "bearer of light"). Only in the later Apocryphal literature is blackness specifically assigned to the devil. About AD 120, the Epistle of Barnabas designated Satan as *ho melos*, the black one, and by the time of the Apostolic History of Abdias and the Acts of Phillip, he is completely limned as black, winged and reeking of smoke. In this Apocryphal and Patristic literature, black became the dominant colour of the devil, with red, another colour for the devil in European folklore, remaining in some descriptions.

As the doctrine of Christianity developed, it showed a great deal of ambivalence about race. On the one hand, there are the origins in tribal Judaism which believed that God was on the side of the Israelites. Then Jews were held responsible for the death of Jesus; and this seems to have played a role in the reinforcement and nurturing of anti-Semitism in Europe.

With the coming of Jesus Christ, the religion had become universal and proclaimed that all men were equal before God and that Christ came to the world to save all sinners (regardless of race and ethnicity). When Christianity left the cultural context of Palestine and went to Rome and Europe, it became recontextualized and adopted the colour symbolism of that continent.

European Christianity Europeanized the phenotype of Jesus, Mary and the angels, and God himself. Jesus and his family, belonging to the sub-ethnic group of Canaanites, were more than likely dark brown. When Joseph and Mary fled to Egypt with Jesus to escape the wrath of Herod, they presumably believed that they would or could blend with the Egyptian population (which, as we have said, was most probably brown but with minorities of other shades tending towards both white and black).

Western religious iconography deliberately and methodically proceeded to a progressive whitening and restructuring, by which Jesus took on the phenotypic characteristics first of a European Mediterranean man, then of a Nordic man with blond hair and blue eyes. In the Caribbean today, there are many homes which still hang pictures of this Nordic, Aryan Jesus.

It is true, however, that there have been various representations of Jesus through the ages, even within European Christianity, where different schools of art imposed their own artistic models. He was at different times short, plain-looking, tall, handsome, bearded, clean-faced, long-haired, short-haired. But almost never was he brown or black with non-European phenotypical traits.

Differences also arose in the context of the different geographical cultural zones where Christianity took root. The face of Christ is differently portrayed in Roman, Greek, Nordic, Indian and Ethiopian iconography. In early Christian art in Egypt, the iconography of the Christian subjects in the frescos of a monastery in Bawit is very local for the most part. Christ is almost always a short-haired beardless youth (Morey 1942, 88). And the typical Coptic saint has hair close-cropped on a flat cranium, descending in a narrow border along the face into a beard that widens slightly at the level of the mouth and then contracts to a point (Morey 1942, 84).

The major achievement of European Christianity, and European culture in general, was to transpose a negative, pejorative connotation of darkness (absence of light) and blackness on to the peoples of the world whose skin pigmentation was perceived as belonging to the colour black, or was dark, and were therefore to be reviled by God and man. At the same time, European Christianity, and European culture in general, took a symbolical and allegorical reference to whiteness as the result of a purifying and cleansing process and tacked it on to the people of Europe, having already made the psychological leap to the perception of the skin pigmentation of these people as belonging to the colour white. Christianity was seen as justifying and reinforcing, or was made to justify and reinforce, a social, psychological condition that, as we have seen, existed and was developing from the pre-classical period.

A firm foundation for the pejoration of black people was found in the Biblical story of the curse of Ham. Ham, a son of Noah, violated an important sexual taboo of his tribe by seeing his (drunken) father naked in his tent. For this, he was cursed by God and condemned to be servant to his own brother. Although the Bible itself does not make an issue of the skin colour of Ham and his descendants, this curse was interpreted by many Europeans as signifying God's rejection of black people and his approval of white people. Interest in this curse has far-reaching effects, since it also provided the biblical and transcendental underpinnings for the enslavement of Africans in the Caribbean and the New World in general. As we shall see later, this biblical allusion was also used to justify the particularly abominable form that slavery took in that region.

Early Christian writers and exegetists were quite severe on Ethiopians, who at the time represented sub-Saharan Africa in general. The devil frequently appeared to monks in the guise of an "Ethiopian". "The black Ethiopian was associated with sin and with the diabolical by homiletic writers such as

Paulinus of Nola who explained that they [Ethiopians] were burned black not by the sun but by vices and sin" (Friedman 1981, 65). Fulgentius of Ruspe spoke of baptizing an Ethiopian whom he saw as "one not yet whitened by the grace of Christ shining on him".

Many other examples of the degrading of blacks by early European Christians exist. Gregory of Nyssa wrote in his *Commentarium in Canticum Canticorum* that "Christ came into the world to make blacks white . . . for in the city of God . . . Babylonians become Jerusalemites, the prostitute a virgin, Ethiopians radiantly white". Ethiopians, in the interpretation of Cyril of Alexandria, are "those whose dark minds are not yet illuminated by divine light . . . those whose uncleanness is hard to wash out and who remaining in their blackness will feast upon the heads of the dragons and will be exposed to the sword" (Snowden 1983, 104). The story is told of Saint Benedict of Palermo who, afraid of temptations by women, prayed to God that he might be made ugly. God obliged and turned him black, thus transforming him into Saint Benedict the Moor.

In the medieval Saint Nicolas celebration, which is still held annually in some parts of western Europe, the benevolent saint is represented by a white bishop riding on a white horse and kindly distributing gifts, while his servant is a black youth on foot carrying a dark sack and a birch. This servant is the purveyor of fear and punishment and carries off naughty children, presumably to practise his cannibalism on them. Just when he is about to seize a child, the saint intervenes and saves the day, to the delight of the spectators.

Finally, by way of examples, the famous medieval French epic, *La Chanson de Roland,* while championing the cause of Christianity against the Saracen invaders (Moors), has its hero inveigh against Ethiopia as well: "a cursed land where the black men had great noses and winnowing ears . . . a cursed people, blacker than ink, their only whiteness is their teeth".

However, as we have said, Christianity had to reconcile this racist hostility with its philosophy and doctrine which proclaimed the equality of all men before God. In its approach to Ethiopians, it moved confusingly and confusedly back and forth from a blackness of skin to a blackness of soul; from a categorical rejection to an obsession with Ethiopia as the most dramatic example of sin and therefore as the crowning ecumenical mission of the church, the illustration of the meaning of the Scriptures for all men. Augustine had made it clear that the mission of the Christian church was not to be limited to any one region; rather, it should and would reach even the Ethiopians, the remotest and blackest of men. In fact, in explicating a verse from the Psalms, Augustine states that under the name "Ethiopia" all nations were signified (Snowden 1983, 104).

Several Black Madonnas appeared in the Middle Ages, attesting to the deep-seated ambivalence of Christianity toward blackness. In the opinion of Bastide, "[the black Madonna] represents a sorceress, a worker of miracles . . . a mysterious goddess endowed with extraordinary powers" (1968, 38–39).

The Three Kings were depicted as white men at first. They later came to represent the three great continents: Europe, Asia and Africa. Bastide observes that Balthazar was depicted behind the other two, sometimes kneeling closest to the Babe, but never between the other two – "that would have been equivalent to ignoring his color" (1968, 39). (See, however, chapter 4, Puerto Rico, for a more detailed analysis of the significance of the Three Kings for racial/ethnic representation.)

The Roman Catholic Church was deeply involved in slavery, both in Europe and in the early colonization of the Americas. By the Middle Ages, slavery had disappeared from much of north-western Europe, but was continuing in the countries bordering on the Mediterranean. After the capture of Málaga by the Catholic kings in 1492, the entire population was enslaved and one hundred of them sent to the Pope as a gift (Ladera Quesada 1967, 71). In sixteenth-century Seville, the Christian church was one of the main owners of slaves, including Moors, Africans and "Indians" sent from the New World. In the Americas, the priest Nicolas de Ovando was the first governor of Hispaniola, and he initiated the conquest of Boriquen (Puerto Rico) and Cuba. And he was not the only high official chosen from the ranks of the clergy.

But the ambivalence of the church continued to manifest itself. While it opposed the enslavement of the indigenous peoples of the Americas, it encouraged the enslavement of Africans. While it allowed its members to be involved in mining and to possess slaves, it opposed the harsh treatment meted out to slaves by brutal owners and even offered refuge to persecuted slaves.

The Renaissance

The Renaissance is credited with signalling the re-emergence of Europe, after the decline of the Roman Empire, as the leading world power. In the fifteenth century, in spite of some decline in Africa, there were still several flourishing

African states: the Hafsid kingdom of Tunis, Songhai, Ethiopia, and the kingdoms of Monomotapa in East Africa and the Congo (Delumeau 1973). At the time of the Crusades, the technology and culture of the Arabs and Chinese equalled and surpassed that of Europe. In 1600, that was no longer the case. In January 1492, Granada was recaptured by the Christians from the Moors and this removed any African Moslem hope of further European expansion. In October of the same year, Columbus arrived in the Americas, completing the decline of Africa and the empowerment of Europe.

All the countries of western Europe, and in particular all of those involved in the colonization of the Caribbean, inherited the Graeco-Roman and Christian perceptions of Africa and the rest of the world. The Renaissance rediscovered the ancient sources and largely accepted the myths about monstrous sub-Saharan Africa that had been constructed and recorded by historians such as Herodotus and Pliny (see *The Natural History,* edited and translated by J. Bostock and H.T. Riley, London, 1893, t. V, ch. 8). Solinus, the geographer of the third century BC (see Caius Julius Solinus, *The Excellent and Pleasant Worke,* translated by A. Golding, London, 1587, ch. 42), was also instrumental in passing them on to the Middle Ages. Rabelais was influenced by this vision of Africa, and his famous character Pantagruel is made to declare that "Africa always produces new and monstrous things" (see *Oeuvres Complètes,* Paris 1873, t. 3). A sixteenth-century French geographer, Alphonse de Saintonge, in a work entitled *Cosmographie,* repeated the monstrous myths imagined by Pliny and Solinus: "In the interior, far away, there are people without heads or with heads in their chests . . . There are others with one eye in the forehead . . . North of the Zuna mountains, there are others with feet like those of the goat and others with faces of dogs" (1904, 94).

The Arabs, who helped to preserve and pass on, more than Europeans of the Middle Ages, the works of Graeco-Roman antiquity, also helped to propagate pejorative evaluations of Africa and Africans. Although the Koran preaches equality, in actual practice the enslavement of conquered African populations gave to Arabs a feeling of superiority over Africans even while they converted them to Islam. Lewis cites an Arab author, Mutahar Ibn Tahir al Magdisi of the tenth century, as declaring that "marriage does not exist among them [Africans]; the child does not know who is his father, and they feed on human flesh. . . . As for the Zanj, they have black skin, flat noses, woolly hair. They are not intelligent and understand very little" (1970, 35).

In some countries (France, Spain, Portugal and Italy), there would also have been a strong popular tradition handed down by the Roman soldiers and colonists who arrived there at the beginning of the Christian era, in addition to the knowledge transmitted by the learned tradition when the works of antiquity were revived. In others (England, Holland, Denmark), which had relatively little or no significant Roman colonization, the learned tradition was the major source of Graeco-Roman inheritance. But there is no doubt that the popular tradition was developing along lines similar to that in the Latin countries.

Since the Nordic physiognomy and phenotype was even further removed from the African's than was that of the Graeco-Roman Mediterranean, it is to be assumed that Nordic attitudes may have been harsher. They certainly are perceived to be so in many interpretations of comparative slavery in the New World. As we shall see later, differences in slave regimes and differences in modalities of race and ethnicity in the Caribbean may be partially explained by sociopsychological and religio-philosophical differences between the Nordics and the Mediterraneans.

The area now known as Spain and Portugal was of course occupied for many centuries by dark-skinned Moors from north Africa, and this would have had some effect on the racial knowledge and attitudes of later Spaniards and Portuguese. From about the mid-fifteenth century, Spain and Portugal began to have direct contact with sub-Saharan west Africa, and many Africans began to be brought back to the peninsula. Other western European nations then followed Spain and Portugal in their direct contacts with Africa as an immediate prelude to the exploration, conquest and colonization of the Caribbean and the Americas.

However, for all these European countries, the picture of Africa that the Middle Ages and Renaissance received from the Graeco-Roman legacy, from both learned and popular sources, was the same: Africa was a "dark" land inhabited by monsters and beastly people.

From the fifteenth century, as Europe begins to know the rest of the world, it is interesting to observe the difference in the reactions to the different peoples encountered. These differences in reaction may have to be accounted for by a complex set of factors, but the colour factor remains quite salient. The three major continents – Africa, Asia, America – had different races of different skin colours, and from the first encounter to this day, the most severe racial stigmas were reserved for Africans from south of the Sahara. Cohen puts it this way:

A sixteenth-century painting of the Church of Saint-Jacques in Dieppe depicts Indians from Asia and North America and blacks from Africa. The first two peoples are shown fully dressed, the Africans are represented as naked. In the background behind the Africans appears a snake curled around a tree. Africans were thus perceived as closer to a life of lust and to Satan. Although Asians, Indians and black Africans showed a non-white skin, the French preferred certain races over others. American Indians had bronze skin that appealed to French aesthetic tastes. . . . Often the colouring of the Indian was not even noted, and the same was true of the Chinese . . . But the blacks' physiognomy struck the French immediately. In 1684, when Francois Bernier published the earliest racial classification, he included the American Indian in the same group as whites, but he classified blacks as clearly distinct. (1980, 8)

Davis reports that

early in the 17th century, a French traveller remarked: "it might be properly said, that these men [black Africans] came out of Hell, they were burnt and dreadful to look upon". A century later John Atkins agreed that "the Black colour and Woolly Tegument of these Guineans is what first obtrudes itself on our observation, and distinguishes them from the rest of mankind". (1988, 447)

The question of race became fully engaged in the post–Middle Ages' philosophical debates in Europe, in which there was a marked increase in non-religious intellectual interest that centred on man. Renaissance and Enlightenment thinkers, proclaiming the ascendancy of reason over faith and questioning the premises, beliefs and doctrines of Christianity, sought to emphasize racial differences in order to defeat Christian assumptions about the equality of mankind and the common origin from Adam and Eve. It might be said that Africa ranked relatively low in Renaissance interest in the exotic. According to Atkinson (1935), for the period 1480–1609, of geographical works on "exotic" countries, only five were on Africa, compared with eighty on the Turks, fifty on the East Indies and forty on the Americas.

The Age of Enlightenment

This relative indifference to Africa changed somewhat in the following centuries. With the increasing importance of philosophical materialism, the eighteenth century developed ideas about biology as the source of differences seen at the level of structures and social customs among different peoples.

Thus was born biological racism, more pronounced in France than elsewhere (Cohen 1981, 15).

The eighteenth century is known as the Age of Enlightenment, when reason finally triumphed over superstition and religion. And we tend to identify that century by the works of the great philosophers and intellectuals: Voltaire, Rousseau, Locke, and others. However, what is less known is that these great thinkers and other lesser lights produced some rather strange views about the human species. How widely these strange views were propagated among the general public is difficult to assess, but there is no reason to believe that they were less widely held within the general population.

One such eighteenth-century view was physiognomics. Inherited from Aristotle, physiognomics saw the colours of human races as a revelation of their levels of civilization. As far as this was applied to Africans, according to Bernal, "it is certain that Locke and most eighteenth-century English-speaking thinkers like David Hume and Benjamin Franklin were racist: they openly expressed popular opinions that dark skin color was linked to moral and mental inferiority" (1987, 203).

Eighteenth-century thinkers, in their zeal to debunk religion, claimed to see in physiognomy proof of an affinity between Africans and the primates. The more the African departed from the Negroid prototype, the more noble he appeared. According to Cohen (1980, 92), French officials serving in Senegal in the late eighteenth century depicted lighter-coloured peoples, like the Fulani, as more able and virtuous than their darker neighbours.

With the fading of the Age of Enlightenment towards the end of the century, Eurocentrism continued unabated. The latter half of the eighteenth century saw the birth of a new dimension of Eurocentrism, in which any non-European role in the development of Graeco-Roman civilization and of its progeny, western European culture, was rejected. We saw that Bernal (1987) identified two models of the origin of Greek culture, the Ancient Model and the Aryan Model. He states elsewhere that

> this Ancient Model was discredited in the last quarter of the eighteenth century, through a process that cannot be linked to any new evidence or source of information. It must therefore be associated with other intellectual shifts. I maintain that these were the new predominance of romanticism, racism and the concept of progress. Romanticism was important because in its attack on the universality of the Enlightenment, it emphasized peculiarity and the importance of place and kinship in the formation of cultures. This was accompanied by the

belief that demanding or stimulating environments, particularly the cold ones of mountains or the north, produced the most virtuous peoples. Thus such a virtuous race as the Greeks could not have derived their culture from the south and east. (Bernal 1985, 67)

Slavery

The general concept of "human being not free to negotiate his/her own labour" had several modalities in Medieval and Renaissance Europe. English had several terms for persons in these different conditions: villein, serf, servant, bondsman, slave. Some conditions were already near to what we have come to accept as the meaning of "slave", the only one of these terms to have survived in active usage today. For example, according to Davis (1988, 34), the *villein* was a chattel who could be sold apart from the manor and whose labour was unregulated by law. Evidently, the ruling classes created a pejorative stereotype of this person which has come down to the contemporary period in the meaning of its modern form, "villain". The word originally meant "belonging to the *villa* (the country estate)".

For a limited period in the tenth and eleventh centuries, the documents, which at the time were written in Latin, show that the Germans sought to distinguish the *servi* of their own nations/tribes from the captives who arrived from the East and who were already apparently given a far lower status. These foreigners were called *sclavi*. This term died out with the end of trade in humans from the East. But in the thirteenth century, when the Genovese and Venetians began to bring human cargoes from the Black Sea, the word *sclavus* (singular form of *sclavi)* suddenly came into common usage in Italy and later spread to Northern Europe as a means of distinguishing unfree foreigners from native serfs. In Iberia, *sarracenus* and *captivus* were the terms that gradually replaced *servus,* and were still common in the thirteenth century. *Sarracenus,* of course, was one of the names given to the Moors. In the fourteenth century, with the Reconquest in full swing, *sarracenus* gave way to *(e)sclavus* (cf. Spanish *esclavo*, Portuguese *escravo*, French *esclave*, English *slave*).

European thought and social psychology were progressing in this way through the Middle Ages into the Renaissance when a new world was opened up to Europeans. The transfer to this new world of an economic production system based on serf and slave labour was an event of enormous significance in the history of race and ethnicity. At first, Europeans transferred their system of serfdom, to which they had subjected their own people of the disadvantaged, unprivileged classes. At the same time they enslaved the indigenous peoples of this new world (the Americas, as it came to be known), regardless of social rank. Later, it was sub-Saharan African peoples who were brought as slaves to meet new production targets that could not be met with the serf labour of Europeans and the slave labour of the indigenous peoples.

These complex moves by several European powers, involving different non-white groups in different socioeconomic and ecological settings, have given rise to a number of interpretations concerning race and ethnicity. They range from statements that racism really began with plantation slavery in the New World, to the claims of this book that racism was firmly embedded and entrenched in European cultural and psychological history and that it long pre-dated the establishment of slave-based societies in the Americas.

There is the epochal work of Eric Williams (1966) and his follow-up article (1971) in which he claims that "slavery in the Caribbean is too narrowly defined with the Negro. A racial twist has thereby been given to what is basically an economic phenomenon. Slavery was not born of racism; rather racism was the consequence of slavery" (1966, 6). This statement ignores the complexity of world history in general and the complexity of New World history in particular. There have been different forms of slavery and various forms and degrees of racism throughout world history. It is true of course that racism is not the only form of hostile prejudice perpetrated by man on his fellow man. Williams shows how white servants were treated with the same brutality as was meted out to blacks: "Eddis found the Negroes 'almost in every instance under more comfortable circumstances than the miserable European, over whom the rigid planter exercises an inflexible severity'. The servants were regarded by the planters as 'white trash', and were bracketed with the Negroes as laborers" (1971, 13). In other words, class prejudice in certain socioeconomic contexts can be as punishing as race prejudice.

However, Williams himself later implied that race became a factor in the special condition reserved for Africans: "Racial differences made it easier to justify and rationalize Negro slavery, to exact the mechanical obedience of a plough-ox or a cart-horse, to demand that resignation and that complete moral and intellectual subjection which alone make slave labor possible" (1971, 14).

It is also true, as we have said, that Europeans had enslaved their own people, and that, therefore, the decision to enslave Africans was not in itself a racist act directed exclusively against these peoples. The entire world was accustomed to slavery without exception of race. It is, however, significant that whereas white people were also slaves, Christian repugnance had led to an avoidance of Christians as slaves in Europe. According to Davidson (1971), at first Europe felt no particular guilt about slavery except when they sold white Christians into slavery. Gradually white slavery diminished, and by 1650 it was virtually a thing of the past. By the second half of the fifteenth century, sub-Saharan Africans had become the dominant group in the western Mediterranean slave labour force. We cannot therefore ignore the history of racial attitudes, which had already existed in classical antiquity, and which strengthened through the Middle Ages into the Renaissance.

A comparison of European attitudes towards Africans and the indigenous peoples of the Americas can be quite instructive. The indigenous peoples of the Americas also became the butt of European ethnocentrism. They were seen as primitive savages, cannibalistic, fit to be enslaved and to be brutalized. Their lands were seen as a brutal wilderness to be exploited. Columbus immediately sent three hundred of these indigenous people to the slave markets in Seville. Two hundred died en route and were thrown overboard.

Yet, in an apparent ambivalence of European thought, the indigenous peoples became noble savages, romanticized and courted in literature. The Americas was Utopia, the Garden of Eden where naked savages lived in a state of pristine innocence. According to Davis (1988, 4), the Americas awakened memories of terrestrial paradise and of the Golden Age described by the ancients. Columbus concluded in 1498 that he had arrived on the "nipple" of the earth, which reached closer to heaven than the rest of the globe. This ambivalence was brilliantly captured in the allegory of Robinson Crusoe and Friday.

Some compunction was felt in some European quarters about the treatment to which these peoples were being subjected, as a result of which they were coming to be in short supply in the islands at a time when there was a growing need for massive quantities of manpower. Measures were therefore initiated to replace the indigenous slave labour force with imported African slaves. However, the ambivalence demonstrated with regard to the indigenous peoples hardly existed in the case of Africans and Africa. Life in Africa was viewed as immeasurably and unspeakably miserable, and it was in fact kindness to take Africans away from their native lands and introduce them to the comparative blessings of plantation slavery in the Americas. This was by far the dominant view held at the time, and only a small minority of individual opinions deviated from it.

New World African Slavery: Racism or Economic Determinism?

To equate the conditions under which European serfs were held in bondage in Europe and the Americas with the chattel slavery imposed on Africans is naive. The extraordinary treatment of African slaves would have to be accounted for by the demands for large amounts of cheap (unremunerated) labour for New World plantations, as well as by racist ideas about the spiritual, moral and physical condition of Africans.

The large numbers of slaves required had a clear economic motivation. However, the numbers were a direct consequence of the harsh treatment meted out to slaves. Smaller numbers of African slave imports would have been required if the lives of slaves had been humanely managed. There has never been any assessment of the economic merits of overworking slaves to early death over preserving their health and their lives for longer periods of able-bodied work.

Historians are content to observe that slave owners in certain regions and at certain times preferred the former option (of overworking slaves to an early death). Was the low position in which Africans were placed by Europeans in the racial and ethnic hierarchy an important factor in the selection of that option? In other words, was some vague notion that the former was more economical the only reason? Or was the economic factor – if indeed economics was an active consideration on the part of owners and managers – a rationalization to mask or psychologically suppress another motive, impulse or inclination? That is to say, we may have here another unsolvable case of "push" as against "pull" factors.

It is plausible to conclude that both economic and racist factors were at play in accounting for New World slavery, with racist factors dominant in determining the particular aspect of slavery that has to do with the harsh treatment generally reserved for African slaves. As we shall see later, differences in degrees of harshness may also be partially explained by differences in racial/ethnic attitudes in Nordic Europe as against Mediterranean Europe. The Germanic colonizers are said to have been more brutal than the Latin ones.

It is also significant that Spaniards, while brutalizing the indigenous peoples, were not averse to sexual relations with their womenfolk, and a rash of miscegenation followed in the wake of the conquistadors. By contrast, Anglo-Saxon invaders in North America also brutalized the indigenous peoples but had limited sexual relations with the women, preferring eventually to huddle the populations into reservations.

The lengths to which European apologists of the seventeenth and eighteenth centuries went to rationalize and justify African slavery are an indication of how much they realized that the act for which they were responsible went beyond the pale, and was of a different order from the institution of slavery which their countries had experienced in centuries past. They seized on ideas which were already prevalent concerning Africa and Africans and convinced themselves that what they were doing was justifiable. It was justified by the very act of God Himself – Ham's curse. The enslavement of Africans was the fulfilment of the evangelizing mission of the church and of the civilizing mission of the superior European culture, which by enslaving Africans was really rescuing them from a fate far worse than slavery: remaining in the depraved subhuman context of Africa. They even imagined Africans to be content with slavery, and created one of the several often contradictory stereotypes of the slave: the willing, grateful, submissive partner in his own enslavement. This then confirmed their pre-established, pre-slavery view of Africans as naturally inferior.

This is not to suggest that there was an inevitability about the development of racism in the post-Colombian world. Nuances emerged in different parts of the Americas, as we shall see, based on a number of contextual factors. The timing of the advent of the plantation was one crucial factor. In the initial period of colonization, from 1492 to mid-seventeenth century, attitudes were different from those which emerged later. That first period was reminiscent of the pre-Americas type of slavery, in which there is an individual relationship between slave and master (although the plantation model did exist in Crete, Sicily, Malta and Cyprus and although, as we said above, in Germanic Europe of the Middle Ages, foreign slaves from eastern Europe could be held in the status of chattel). Africans were "listed as servants in census enumerations in Virginia in 1623 and 1624 and as late as 1651. Some Negroes whose period of service had expired were being assigned land in the same way as for white servants" (Fredericton 1971, 243). Attitudes and the system changed after about 1650, giving rise to "chattel slavery", in which the slave was defined as a person with no rights and no claim either to actual or potential equality with other men. "Slave" became virtually synonymous with "African" (completely synonymous, as we shall see later, with *negro, nègre*). The plantation economy was therefore very important in setting the particular pattern of racism, but the basic foundation already existed.

It is still, however, important to examine the first period closely, to gain a better understanding of how much the regime of slavery of that time may have differed from the regime of the ensuing period. Racial attitudes seem to have been quite complex, more complex than is suggested by simple claims for mild treatment of slaves. Comparatively mild treatment extending to paternalism should not be equated with absence of racism. Mild treatment, whether institutional (as is claimed for the Spanish colonies) or individual (as is claimed for Barbados), could be determined by several factors (demographic, psychological, and so on) which may attenuate but do not eliminate the basic foundation of special racial attitudes towards Africans. That is why we alluded in the preface to the crudeness of the formulae which attribute certain behaviours and attitudes to ethnic groups, races, nations and classes. These are generalizations, almost of the nature of stereotyping, which may be beset by contradictory evidence and exceptions.

So that whereas it is true that during the first period (the pre-plantation period, when Spain was the only colonizing power in the Caribbean), the *sociedad de hacienda* that preceded the plantation society meted out similar treatment to Africans and indentured whites, there is evidence that this was not the full picture and that the basic foundation still manifested itself in some special nuances of the picture. Commenting on the situation in Virginia in the first period, Fredericton states that

> some blacks, but no whites, were in fact being held in servitude for life; and there is fragmentary evidence of discriminatory practices which seemed to set black servants off from whites of similar status – for example Negro women, unlike white women, were apparently used for field work, and a Virginia statute of 1640 enjoined masters to provide arms for all their servants except Negroes. (1971, 244)

CHAPTER FOUR

Asia and Africa

India

*I*ndia provides an excellent example of the signifi-
cance of the social historical context in the emergence and development of
racial, ethnic and colour values. The inhabitants of the northern states of India
(Punjab, Jammu and Kashmir, Uttar Pradesh, Rajasthan) tend to be light
skinned, while those of the southern states are more dark skinned. There is a
clear historical explanation for this (see below). There is also some degree of
correlation between caste and colour, which can also be accounted for
historically and is related to the regional correlation. The higher castes in any
region in India tend to be fairer, the lower castes, darker. So ingrained is this
pattern in the psychology of the people (whether or not it is totally consistent
with reality) that it has given rise to several proverbs which identify upper
castes with a light skin and lower castes with a darker skin. Among these
proverbs are the following ones (provided by Beteille 1968, 174): "A dark
Brahmin, a fair Chuhra, a woman with a beard – these three are contrary to
nature"; "Trust not a dark Brahmin or a fair Holeya"; "Do not cross a river
with a black Brahmin or a fair Chamar."

But the overall situation is quite complex. According to Beteille,

> people from the topmost castes are generally fairer than the Harijans. But there
> are numerous intermediate castes, and among these one frequently encounters
> persons who are either darker than some Harijans or fairer than many Brahmins.
> . . . People from the lower castes in North India tend to be, on the whole, darker
> than those of some of the highest castes in the South. (1968, 172)

This shows how caste differences cut across regional differences and also have
their own colour factor. Land ownership is also reported to have a colour
correlation. As Beteille explains,

> non-Brahmin castes tend to be, on the whole, dark-skinned. Where land-owning
> families exist among them, however, their members are often as light-skinned
> as the Brahmins and sometimes moreso. Where members of the aristocratic
> land-owning families also belong to the highest caste, they are likely to be
> particularly fair. (1968, 173)

The corresponding lifestyles of these different castes are also seen as contributing to the colour correlations:

> refinement [sic] of features of the kind valued by the Tanjore Brahmins is
> probably the outcome in part of a certain style of life. In the rural areas Brahmins
> generally lead a sedentary existence and are not exposed to sun and rain to nearly
> the same extent as the average non-Brahmin peasant. (Beteille 1968, 174)

As we noted earlier, there is a well-established opinion in anthropology that
climate has had an important effect on racial/colour differentiation in the
human species. Lifestyle, that is, indoor occupations as against outdoor
occupations, would then be a contributory or reinforcing factor. As we saw in
the case of Europe, a skin tone approaching pallor was highly valued, as it
signified an indoor lifestyle associated with the nobility.

The complex, non-discrete, continuum-like nature of the colour distinctions in India has no doubt prevented polarization, and negated any likelihood
of "race" and "colour" problems in India. Indeed, caste and religion supersede
colour as bases for the structure of the social order and as determinants of
social action. However, a very general feature of Indian society is the high
social value ascribed to skin colour. A very interesting manifestation of this is
the tendency for wealthy land-owning families of darker skin to seek light-
skinned brides, even from among the poorer members of the subcastes, in
order that their progeny may climb a rung higher on the skin-colour value
scale. This pattern is of course also quite commonly represented in the

Caribbean. Matrimonial ads in Indian newspapers show that the most desirable features in a wife are light skin colour and virginity. According to Beteille,

> in many Indian languages the words *fair* and *beautiful* are often used synonymously. . . . The ideal bride, whose beauty and virtue are praised in the songs sung at marriages, almost always has a light complexion. A dark girl is often a liability to the family because of the difficulty of arranging a marriage for her. (1968, 173)

According to one visitor to India, reporting her experiences in a Jamaican newspaper, the *Gleaner* (26 March 1998, A8), skin tone modification is also practised in India. She quotes the following from the beauty columns of a leading Delhi newspaper:

> "I have a daughter who is just 10 years old. She has a dark skin and feels very depressed about it because she is the only dark one in our family. Please advise." The beauty columnist advises thus: "Use a mask like *Chane ke atta* and a little *chandan* powder, a few drops of lime juice and unboiled milk. Leave it on till it dries and then remove by rubbing it off in circular movements in cold water. Your skin will look healthy and glowing and it will look fair eventually."

The same *Gleaner* report notes that "without exception for both males and females, every ad for a potential spouse begins with the number one requirement being: 'Wanted: fair-skinned etc.' ". But it is evident that fair skin colour has much greater weight in choosing a bride than a groom. A dark-skinned son is not so much of a liability to a middle-class family as a dark-skinned daughter, since for the former other qualities such as wealth, occupation, and education play an important part (Beteille 1968, 175). Preferences of this sort recur in several parts of the world, including the Caribbean (see chapter 5).

In the popular folk history Brahmins are seen as originating in North India. They are referred to as "Aryans", dominating the "Dravidian" masses. This view is of course supported by history and by linguistic evidence. The South Indian languages belong to the Dravidian family, genetically distinct from the Indo-European family to which the North Indian languages generally belong. These language families are not "pure", since, as in all the other language families of the world, there have been outside influences due to contact with other language families. But their genetic lineages are easily identified and well established by the proven methodology of historical and comparative linguistics.

The language mixture is a function and mirror of the human biological mixture that has also taken place. In this latter case, too, the categories may have become rather blurred, but the basic pattern survives: the northern peoples are fairer, originated from a particular historical genetic stock, and speak Indo-European languages, while the southern peoples are darker, originated from a different historical genetic stock, and speak Dravidian languages.

The significant historical fact underlying the contemporary race and ethnicity picture of India was the widespread migratory movements of charioteering peoples which altered the face of the world in the second millennium BC. It brought to north-west India an invading people who called themselves Aryas, adopted into English as Aryan. However, this view is contested by some Indian historians, who claim that the Aryans were native to India and that, quite improbably, the Indo-European stock of languages originated in northern India.

The word Aryan has come to be used widely to represent the "white" "race" (in addition to "Caucasian" and "European", the latter designating, properly speaking, the European subset of this "race"). The considerable extension of these migrating peoples may be gleaned from the fact that in addition to the term Aryans in India, the original root exists also in the name Iran, probably also in the names Ireland and Eire. More substantial evidence for this extension is that languages as far afield as Hindi, Iranian, Latin, Greek, German, English, Gaelic and Irish all belong to one genetic family, derived from one single ancestral language in the pre-historic past spoken by the original single ancestral people.

These Aryans, originating most likely in the Steppes of north central Europe, were semi-nomadic tribes who had developed their own phenotypical characteristics, among which their fair skin colour was predominant. They migrated in every direction, conquering peoples in their path, mixing with these populations in some cases, and retaining their culture and phenotype to varying degrees in other cases.

The earliest Vedic hymns of India refer to battles between the Aryas and the Dasas, or Daysus, who evidently represented the survivors of the pre-Aryan Harappa culture of the Punjab and the north-west. The Dasas are described as "dark, bull-lipped, snub-nosed" (Basham 1971, 33). The word *dasa* later acquired the meaning "slave" or "bondsman" in Sanskrit, the ancient language of northern India descended from the original Aryan language. This kind of socialization of an ethnic name has several other examples in other parts of the world and in other historical contexts: *Sclavus* also comes to mean "slave"; *Kuli* comes to mean "person performing menial tasks"; *Congo* in the Caribbean comes to mean "backward"; *Arab* in the Caribbean comes to mean "ragged", "disorderly" (see later). In Sanskrit, by contrast, *aryas* took the meaning "noble".

Though this suggests that many of the conquered peoples were enslaved by the Aryans, considerable other evidence indicates that a great deal of racial and ethnic mixing took place. According to Basham:

> as they settled among the darker aboriginals, the Aryans seem to have laid greater stress than before on purity of blood, and class divisions hardened to exclude those Dasas who had found a place on the fringes of Aryan society, and those Aryans who had intermarried with Dasas and adopted their ways. (1971, 35)

The four major classes (or castes as they are referred to in the case of India) appeared and crystallized during the period of the composition of the Vedic hymns: *brahamana* (in modern English, "Brahmin", priests), *ksatriya* (warriors), *vaisya* (peasants), and *sudra* (serfs, forerunners of today's Untouchables). These divisions have survived up to today with an increased number of subdivisions (subcastes). It is very important to note that the Hindu word *varna*, which has been loosely translated into English as "caste", meant "colour" in Sanskrit, and expressed a "racial" category. Isaacs (1968, 94) notes that "in classical Hindu texts there is an association of colors with the main caste (*varna*) groups – white with the Brahmins at the top, black with the Sudras at the bottom, red or bronze and yellow with the middle groups of Kshatriya and Vaishya". He then claims that "there is enough in the present actuality of Hindu society to make it plain that skin color is related in important ways to hierarchies of status in the Hindu system".

It seems then that in the development of Indian society, earlier hierarchical structures based on race became modified as a result of racial mixing, and evolved into "caste"-based structures that have maintained some relics of the earlier colour stratification. This is remarkably similar to the evolution of Caribbean societies (see later).

The arrival of the British, French, Portuguese and Dutch as colonizers reinforced the "white", "fair" bias of the Indian social order. So that when Indian indentured workers arrived in the Caribbean in the mid-nineteenth century, the ideas they brought about colour were quite compatible with those of the society which received them.

However, it is interesting to note that there is one ambiguity in India that makes colour values, relatively speaking, not as straightforward as in Japanese or Chinese society. This may be due to the presence of so many dark-skinned people in India compared with those two other Asian societies, and to the fact that these dark-skinned peoples pre-dated the arrival of the fairer peoples. There is evidence of positive attitudes and evaluations toward the colour black and negative ones towards the colour white. As in Africa, white is associated with death and leprosy, perhaps historically the most feared of all human conditions. The most interesting evidence, however, is the existence of two very important figures in Hindu cosmology, the deities Kali and Krishna, who are both depicted as black.

China

The case of China presents some difficulties of historical interpretation. China is considered, in the race/colour scheme originating in the Western colonial/imperial system, to be part of the "yellow" world. There is no indication that these "yellow" peoples have fully accepted this characterization of themselves and the pejorative connotations that it has developed among Western peoples (such as is contained in the term "the yellow peril"). They certainly do not seem to refer to themselves as "we yellow people", in the same way that people of African descent, and to a lesser extent Native Americans, have adopted the way in which Europe has represented them and have come to refer to themselves as "black" and "red" respectively. We made allusion in the introduction to the non-commensurability of languages and to the different ways of dividing the colour spectrum among the world's cultures. English makes a distinction between "yellow" and "white". It is not clear that the Chinese make this distinction in the same way.

The Chinese people only underwent what may be termed mild colonization by Europe. They are aware of the colour representation that Europe has wished to impose on them and have had to come to terms with it even while not fully accepting it. Whereas they do not necessarily see themselves as "yellow", they have had to defend themselves by rationalization and redefinition (as "black" people have had to do with the term "black" in reference to themselves). Isaacs cites the rationalization of a leading Chinese scholar in the closing years of the Manchu Dynasty: "Of the five colors, yellow is the color of the soil, and the soil is the core of the Universe. Westerners identify the

Chinese as a yellow race. This implies that from the beginning, when heaven and earth were created, the Chinese were given the central place" (1968, 92). This, by the way, is another example of how the particular ecological conditions, in this case the colour of soil in China, can affect the development of colour symbolization.

The Chinese indigenous colour symbolization seems to have developed in the context of their own extreme ethnocentrism combined with their contact with the people of darker colour towards the south: Malays and Indians. Like the Greeks and Romans, the Chinese considered all non-Chinese to be barbarians, and reserved special contempt for those furthest removed, on the periphery of a world of which China was the centre. Again, like the Greeks and Romans, they created a colourful vocabulary to refer pejoratively to these peoples. According to Davis, "since foreigners were thought to be something less than human, the Chinese had no compunction about enslaving Koreans, Turks, Persians and Indonesians . . . a special contempt was reserved for the dark-skinned barbarians of southern islands whose inferiority was abundantly proved by their nakedness and primitive customs" (1988, 51). (It is to be hoped that Davis's use of terms like "barbarians", "inferiority" and "primitive" is merely a reproduction of the usage of the Chinese themselves, and is not meant to represent Davis's own thinking. Since his prose is unclear, we have to give him the benefit of the doubt.)

How the Chinese perceived themselves colour-wise is not obvious. They evidently recognized their non-dark pigmentation and were able to distinguish themselves from the darker people, though in the colourful vocabulary noted above there is no dominant reference to skin colour. However, Isaacs (1968, 91) claims that skin colour does figure sharply in passages about the "kun-lun slaves" brought from the islands in the South Seas to China by the wide-ranging Chinese traders during the T'ang and Sung Dynasties (seventh to thirteenth centuries AD). According to Isaacs, they were called "devil slaves" or "black devils". Twentieth-century Chinese have expanded the use of colour terms to designate non-Chinese peoples. Pejoratively speaking, Malays are called *bla-chan,* "prawn (brown) paste", and Indians are *tousee-kwai,* "black-bean devils", or *hei-tan* , "black coal" (p. 93).

In the case of Europeans, it seems that the Chinese were unable to see much difference in skin colour between themselves and these colonizers who had conquered them militarily. According to Isaacs (1968, 91), Chinese writers of the nineteenth century describe the British invaders as "green-eyed devils", while the Indian mercenaries accompanying the British were again the "black devils". The primacy of colour in characterizing the other has been maintained in the case of the Europeans, but can no longer be applied to the skin, and is then applied to the eyes.

Isaacs and others speak of a Chinese celebration of whiteness going back to the classical tradition:

> A poet of the fourth century BC celebrated a bevy of beauties for their "black-painted eyebrows and white-powdered cheeks". Of Yang Kuei-fei, the most celebrated beauty in Chinese history, the Tang poet Po Chui-i wrote: "So white her skin, so sweet her face/None could with her compare." Hands and arms of "dazzling white" move gracefully through endless reams of ancient Chinese poetry. The most common metaphor for feminine skin was white jade, and references to all the visible surfaces of jade-colored female skin abound in poets' songs. Chinese folk songs are similarly filled with the whiteness of generations of beloveds: "My sweetheart is like a flower", sings one, "Please do not let the sun burn her black." In story after story Chinese writers of the 1940s were still quivering at the "snow-white" or "pure white" necks and arms of their heroines. There is some evidence that these standards have prevailed not only among effete upper-class Chinese but among rude villagers as well. (Isaacs 1968, 92)

This celebration of whiteness predates the colonial presence of Europeans in China. This seems to be a case of the colour white having acquired high aesthetic (and perhaps erotic, sensual) value, and then of the people striving, by the use of white powder or by avoidance of the sun (with the help of broad-rimmed hats and parasols), to approximate to that ideal colour. However, another highly prized phenotypical feature mentioned for the Chinese is the "high-bridged, pointed" nose. According to Isaacs (1968, 97), citing Cornelius Osgood's *Village Life in Old China: A Community Study of Kao Yao, Yunan*: "the noses of boys and girls were pinched to make the bridges higher, a form which was considered particularly attractive". The high-bridged pointed nose is even further removed from the Chinese dominant phenotype than is white skin. It begins to appear quite mysterious how the Chinese developed such a phenotype value system. The Caribbean phenotype value system also ranks very highly the high-bridged nose, and the same pinching of the noses of black children is known.

Japan

Wagatsuma confirms the non-equivalence between a Japanese term generally translated as "white" and the word "white" in English. He states that

> it might strike some as curious that the Japanese have traditionally used the word "white" (*shiroi*) to describe lighter shades of their own skin color. The social perception of the West has been that the Chinese and Japanese belong to the so-called "yellow" race, while the Japanese themselves have rarely used the color yellow to describe their skin. (1968, 129)

In the Japanese language, *shiroi* is used for "white" in describing their skin colour and is also used to describe snow. The Japanese had the same kind of contacts as the Chinese with peoples of the South Seas. Within Japan, northern tribes were dominant and would have been responsible for imposing a "white" skin bias on the darker tribes towards the south of Japan. Furthermore, Japan was strongly influenced culturally by China, and one would expect similar colour values to exist among the peoples of the two countries.

Both in China and Japan, white powder was freely used on the skin to accentuate the appearance of whiteness. Note that this practice existed among Europeans from antiquity and during the period of the Middle Ages and the Renaissance (when both males and females used it), and continued to recent times. Even black-skinned Caribbean women used it until quite recently, although this was also due to the fact that, in the absence until recently of cosmetics prepared especially for black skins, Caribbean women were forced to use cosmetics imported from Europe and North America.

As with the Romans and European medieval society, it was the social order of China and Japan which prompted such practices. The whiteness, even pallor of the skin, was a sign that the person was not exposed to the sun in some peasant-type occupation, but lived an indoor life of leisure and luxury. The parasol or face hood were also widely used for protection against the rays of the sun whenever it was necessary to go outdoors. It was also in the north of China and Japan that snow was a feature of the ecology, and this must have reinforced the appreciation of extreme whiteness of skin. Numerous quotations from Japanese literature of all ages use as flattery the simile "skin white as snow".

However, the Chinese and Japanese languages have not shown the kind of metaphorical and connotative expansion of the terms black and white that are typical of Greek, Latin and western European languages. The English-Japanese dictionary of Vaccari (1967) records *koroi* as the term for the colour black (as opposed to white), with *koku* used in compounds: *koku-shoku*, "dark complexioned"; *kokushoku jinshu*, "black races"; *koku-jin*, "black man". Apart from *kurai* in the meaning of "dismal", "gloomy", and *haraguroi* in the meaning "black hearted", the dictionary does not record any pejorative semantic expansions of "black". In such cases English "black" is rendered by *sugoi*, particularly in expressions referring to wickedness, cruelty, anger: *sugoi kaotsuki*, "black looks". Other terms are also used to render meanings equivalent to the connotative, pejorative meanings of "black" in English: *yojutsu*, *majutsu*, "black magic"; *yami-ichi*, "black market"; *moteamashi-mono*, "black sheep" (cf. *kuroi hitsuji*, "a sheep black in colour"); *kegasu*, "to blacken" (= denigrate); *kyo katsu*, "blackmail".

As in Western culture, modern Japanese are shifting their models of beauty. According to Wagatsuma, "there used to be a general association among the Japanese of white skin with wealth, black skin with lower economic status" (1968, 141). This was, as we said, prompted by the dominant north being fair-complexioned and the south tending to be dark, the people of the court and the urban sector in general being whiter than the rural folk who toiled in the sun. Wagatsuma further adds that "the younger generation, however, increasingly tend to consider sun-tanned skin as the sign of the socially privileged people who can afford summer vacations at the seaside or mountain resorts". This, and other changes in the Japanese and Chinese models of beauty, again show how these general models, and, in particular, the attitudes to colour, are contextually constructed.

Africa

Africa is of course an important test case for investigating and understanding the history of race, colour and ethnicity and their hierarchical ordering. Africa is the home of "blackness", the antithesis of "whiteness", and, culturally speaking, African culture is widely seen as being antithetical to European culture. The widely used appellation "the Dark Continent" sums up the European view of Africa, where "dark" denotes and connotes a wide range of pejorative meanings.

Interestingly, Africa is also widely understood to be the location of the emergence of the first humans, and they were probably dark brown to black in pigmentation. It is also probable that they remained brown to black because of the relatively low degree of mixing with other types and because of natural selection. There are two main theories of skin colour diversification. One is that dark skin evolved as protection against sunburn and skin cancer. The other (more compatible with Africa as the location of the first humans) is that dark skin came first and that light skin evolved as protection against vitamin D deficiency. As early humans moved northwards beyond the fortieth parallel, they reached the zones where black skin filters out too much ultraviolet. They got rickets. The darkest-skinned young male hunter became crippled and was unable to keep up with the hunt, while the darkest-skinned females died in childbirth because of pelvic deformities. The lighter-skinned survived. The farther north humans went, the more complete was the process.

For those who remained in the south, natural selection favouring a high melanin content would have led to social selection giving blackness the edge over other skin colours. Little or no protective clothing was worn, and to the extent that, by natural selection, unclad persons who were black-skinned were better able to prosper in the environment (they better withstood the effects of pervasive sunshine and heat, were healthier and tired less), they were therefore better hunters and more virile, producing more and healthier offspring. This social, political and economic advantage of black men would then have led to an aesthetic advantage, where "black" would have been seen as aesthetically desirable and handsome.

In the particular region of Africa, the lower region of the Nile valley, where the first humans are thought to have emerged, the soil is also particularly dark in colour, and this would have reinforced the high value placed on blackness. An analogous process of the interplay of natural and social selection in the Nordic regions of Europe would have produced a dominance of light-skinned (including hair and eyes) people, and a social preference leading to a standard of beauty based on whiteness. The presence of snow would have reinforced the high value placed on whiteness.

The association of blackness with virility has persisted up to today and has crossed the middle passage to the Americas. It has also entered the psyche of Europe and has affected the relations of white males with black males. There has always been, from New World slavery to the present time, an uneasy, often unspoken, tension based on the supposed attraction of white females to the virility of the black male; and there is today the perception that white females who come to the Caribbean in search of sexual experiences choose partners who are particularly black.

There is therefore every reason to believe that very early in the history of the human species, "black" was highly appreciated as skin colour in sub-Saharan Africa. This would have remained quite consistent throughout the ages. In the course of time, colour symbolism and values became more complex. White was introduced as an important colour in the frame of perception of these Africans; and, particularly in the case of cloth appearing in sub-Saharan Africa as a result of the influence of Islam, white, the colour of the clothing of priests, became in some areas a colour carrying religious meaning.

Africans, on encountering "white" people for the first time, had the same kind of cautiousness and disdain that are generally reserved for "strange" foreign people. But there is no evidence that this disdain descended into contempt. The gross ethnocentrism and cultural arrogance recorded for the Europeans and Chinese are not recorded for African peoples. Reporting on his experiences in African villages previously unvisited by Europeans, the explorer David Livingstone wrote that the moment a child met them he would "take to his heels in agony of terror" and that the mother, alarmed by the child's wild outcries, would rush out of the hut and dart back again "at the first glimpse of the same fearful apparition" (Snowden 1983, 74).

The fifteenth-century Venetian explorer Alvise da Cadamosto, reported that the Negroes in a Senegalese village "touched my hands and limbs and rubbed me with their spittle to discover whether my whiteness was dye or flesh. Finding that it was flesh they were astounded" (Snowden 1983, 133). Hoetink (1967) mentions an African myth in which "the negro regards himself as perfectly cooked and the white man as underdone because of a defect in the creator's oven where people were fashioned from clay". In the Caribbean, there still exists the notion that white people seem "raw"; and among the Rastafari of Jamaica, a pejorative designation for white people is "pork". Davis (1988, 453) quotes Peter Heylyn, a seventeenth-century historian, that "Negroes were so in love with their own complexions that they painted the devil white!" And he also cites Sir Thomas Browne that "standards of beauty were a matter of custom: the African was happy with his color and considered the European's less attractive". Finally, according to Simons (1961, 6), in Swaziland, parents frighten their children with talk of a white bogeyman.

At the contemporary period, there are few examples in African languages of pejorative semantic expansions of "black" and of positive expansions of "white"; similarly for pejorative expansions of "white" and ameliorative expansions of "black". The Luganda language provides the greatest number of examples of the positive connotations of "white". The root *tuku* appears in the adjective *tukutuku*, "white", and also in the verbs *tukula*, "to be clean", "to be clear (of weather)", *etukuza*, "to purify oneself", and in the derivative adjective *tukuva*, "holy" (Murphy 1972).

Hausa has *baki*, referring to deep colours in general: black, very dark blue, very dark green, very dark red. It is used in expressions such as *baki kirin*, "jet black", *bakar fata*, "black person", and *bakata*, "to blacken" (= to make black). But *bakata* has not been expanded to mean "denigrate". Other pejorative English expressions based on "black" have no analogous expressions in Hausa. For example, "blackmail" is *yi wa sharri*; "black market" is *kasuwar shunku*. It is also interesting to note that in Hausa the adjective "white" is *fari*, but "white person" is *jar fata*, in which *jar* is not related to *fari*, "white".

In Dyula, we find *hlain*, "black", and *ka-hlainen*, "to blacken"; but *kabuden*, "to denigrate", based on a root *bud*, which also appears in *budn*, "to abort", "to spoil". However, Europeans and white people in general are referred to as *kululum*, of which the root, *lul*, also occurs in *luli*, meaning "shining", "polished", "educated".

In Zulu, *mnyama* refers to the colour black; but, first, a separate term, *nsundu*, is used as equivalent to English "black of skin"; and, second, there are no examples of pejorative semantic expansions. For example, *ubuthakathi*, "black magic", *ihlungandlebe lomuzi*, "black sheep", *ukudixa*, "blackmail".

In Bobangi, *boyindo* means "black (colour)", but the word for blackmail is *ekota*. Note here that the root, *ndele*, occurs both in the term *mondele*, "white man", and in *ndelengene*, "to be insincere", "to be a hypocrite".

Generally speaking, Europeans seem not to have been perceived by Africans as representing or exemplifying the colour white in nature. All the African languages studied for this book use a term other than the colour term "white" to refer to Europeans. In addition to the Hausa example cited above, there is Bobangi *mondele*, "white man", but *eyengo*, "white (colour)"; Zulu *umlungu*, "white man", but *mhlophe*, "white". It seems that it was not the colour of the skin but rather the moral and social characteristics that formed the basis on which Africans perceived and designated Europeans.

Africa has not been without its colour symbolism weighted in favour of "light" skin. At the present time, it is evident that the effect of European colonialism and imperialism has been to propagate to some degree notions of the high value of whiteness and of Caucasoid phenotypical features. Unfortunately, there have been few studies of African aesthetics of the human body, but there is copious evidence to suggest that, for example, plumpness and a well-formed bottom are much more highly appreciated in women than slimness and flat bottoms. Certainly in the pre-colonial period, and still existing to a large extent, Africa developed an endogenous aesthetic of the human body that included, for example, so-called scarification, elongation of the neck and flattening of the forehead.

Even before the advent of European colonization in Africa, and contemporary with it, some parts of Africa had experienced domination by lighter-skinned peoples from the east and north. The area of Moslem domination was extending southwards and westwards when it was interrupted by European colonization which, ironically, put an end to a long history of Moslem enslavement of sub-Saharan peoples. Smith reports that

> in Sokoto in Northern Nigeria where a Moslem Fulani aristocracy had conquered the local Hausa in the first decade of the nineteenth century, a social significance is given to colour distinctions; value is placed on lightness of skin as an attribute of beauty . . . and a host of qualitative terms reflect this interest, such as *ja-jawur* (light-copper skin), *baki* (dark), *baki kirim* or *baki swal* (real black). The Fulani rulers of Zaria distinguish on racial grounds between themselves and their Hausa subjects, stressing such features as skin colour, hair and facial form, and also make similar distinctions among themselves, since past miscegenation has produced wide physical differences among them. (1965, 138)

Abdalla supports Smith. He shows how the colour value system of the Hausa changed with the advent of Islam:

> The Maguzawa [non-Moslem Hausa] divide the *ishoki* into two main categories; the *gona* or farm, hence "tamed", spirits, and the *daji* or bush, hence "untamed", spirits. It is generally believed that tamed spirits are easy to manipulate, and hence potentially more friendly to man than untamed bush spirits. In the Maguzawa cosmology, *gona* or farm spirits are not necessarily white, nor the *daji* or bush spirits necessarily black. The identification of "white" with good spirits and "black" with dangerous spirits does not seem to be a cardinal belief among the Maguzawa in pre-Islamic times. But it is so among the Hausa of Northern Nigeria today. The Maguzawa tamed/untamed dichotomy has apparently coalesced with the Muslim white/black dichotomy commonly found in many Muslim societies. The new interpretation has been further refined as it is assumed that white spirits are generally Muslim, live in villages or towns, and

cause only minor ailments. Black spirits, on the other hand, live in the bush, are usually non-Muslim, and often afflict their patients with serious illnesses or misfortune. (Abdalla 1990, 43)

CHAPTER FIVE

The Caribbean

Racism and Slavery: The Chicken and the Egg

*W*e have outlined the race and ethnicity picture of the world at the end of the fifteenth century when Christopher Columbus arrived accidentally in the Caribbean, and in the ensuing two centuries when the foundation of present-day Caribbean societies was laid. The essential fact is that basic sociopsychological structures which had emerged in Europe from antiquity through to the Renaissance were transferred to the Caribbean, and to a large measure they defined the path that the new societies in the Caribbean would take. Needless to say, the peculiar social and economic circumstances of these new societies would lead to new dimensions of race and ethnicity. These new circumstances are quite complex, and they have led to equally complex social, psychological and linguistic (lexical, semantic) representational structures projected onto race and ethnicity. But it is still naive to say that New World slavery created racism.

It did, however, produce a race and ethnicity picture that was much more complex than anything that preceded it. On the one hand, the model of slavery

practised in the Caribbean, determined by excessive greed and competitiveness among Europeans for capital accumulation, produced a new dimension
of racial polarization in the world. But, because of the small size of the societies
and the scarcity of white women, it also produced a probably unprecedented
physical closeness between the races that led to the blurring of phenotypical
and cultural boundaries. (However, India is probably another case.) Some of
the resulting psychological structures have been adumbrated above. There is
also the effect on the white male of having been nurtured in childhood by a
black "nanna" and the effect on him of seeing the alter ego of his suppressed
sexuality so close to him. But there is still a considerable amount of work to
be done in this area.

The major fact is the enslavement of Africans and the genocide, partial in
some cases and complete in others, of the indigenous populations. The
question emerged, and is still debated, as to the precise cause and effect
relationship between racism and slavery (the usual chicken and egg dilemma).

Did slavery and the particular plantation modality of it create the new
dimensions of racism and heightened ethnic arrogance? Or did pre-existing
racism and ethnic arrogance lead first of all to the choice of Africans to replace
the indigenous peoples in the supply of slave labour, and then to the excesses
of brutality and inhumanity reserved for the African slaves?

How significant was the timing of New World slavery, coming closely on
the heels of the final victory of European Christian forces over the African
Moors in the reconquest of Spain?

Did the condition of slave foster the development of the extremely low
esteem in which Africans and their descendants came to be held, and the
pejorative stereotypes and generalizations which were ascribed to them? Or
did these stereotypes already exist prior to the period of New World slavery
and facilitate European rationalization and apology for the practice?

Indeed, did the wealth and power which underlie European racism and
ethnic arrogance already exist in the fifteenth century before the conquest of
the Americas? Or was the conquest of the Americas the springboard for
European wealth and power, which then fuelled racism and ethnic arrogance
(ironically reserved particularly for the group – Africans – the exploitation of
whose labour led to this wealth and power)? When Pizarro, the Spanish
conquistador, a man of a low level of culture, confronted Atahualpa, a man
of some cultural and intellectual achievement, what thoughts crossed Pizarro's
mind and led to the brutal humiliation of the Inca king? Was it simply excessive

greed, the prospect of extraordinary wealth that led to Pizarro's excessive inhumanity? Or was it an already learned inability to recognize the humanity of Atahualpa and his people?

These are questions that will continue to be debated, and are perhaps unresolvable in the categorical terms in which they are often posed. These questions will not be explored in any detail in this work. The position taken here is that New World slavery and its particular plantation modality simply added a new dimension to an already existing mental condition in Europeans. It will also be noted that New World slavery itself had different versions and operated under different material and psychological conditions, and that these have led to different race and ethnicity structures in different parts of the Caribbean, albeit within a common framework.

The Sociopsychological Effects of Slavery

Perhaps the most direct effect of slavery was in the corruption of the minds of those African slaves who came to accept the race and culture hierarchy (later transformed into a colour hierarchy) imposed by their European masters, and reinforced by the objective conditions in which the Africans found themselves. In this hierarchy, Europe and Africa were placed at opposite poles of a human and cultural scale. White and black were the visible, front-line symbolic representations of this scale. Some blacks escaped the effects of this mental conditioning, and continue today to engage in the struggle for rescue and redemption. The obvious examples are those who resisted slavery in several different ways, especially those who escaped from slavery and were able to set up free autonomous "Maroon" communities. In these communities, the race, ethnic and colour hierarchies built by European power did not take root. But these dramatic examples are not the only cases. Caribbean descendants of Africans have been struggling not only for political independence and economic survival but also for mental liberation. This was poignantly expressed by Bob Marley in the well-known song lines: "Emancipate yourselves from mental slavery / None but ourselves can free our minds."

Even the colour hierarchy which came to be so typical and characteristic of these Caribbean societies had already existed in the mentality of Europeans prior to the establishment of slave societies in the Americas. European military and economic dominance had already begun to shift from the Mediterranean to north-west Europe, and, as we saw, near approximations of the colour white and even of pallor began to triumph as an aesthetic ideal over the "olive" complexions of the Mediterranean. In the period of antiquity, colour gradients had been recognized, from the white European through the brown complexions of Egypt and Mesopotamia, to the darker complexions of the Kush peoples of the Lower Nile, and finally to the little known "black" peoples deeper into Africa, towards the source of the Nile and south of the Sahara desert.

The overall preference (interspersed, however, with hostility – see later) shown by the white elite in the New World for the emerging lighter-skinned persons produced by miscegenation, who were closer to the European phenotype, was not merely a recognition of their paternity in the issue of such persons but the result of a higher evaluation of this shade and phenotype already existing in the European mentality. This is not to suggest that there was always something sinister about this preference. It would seem natural (although it has not always been the case) that people are more willing to accept others who are closer to their own norm, and more hesitant to accept those furthest removed phenotypically from their norm.

In the circumstances, both before and after the establishment of New World slave societies, this evaluation was based on a simple assumed correlation between race/colour/ethnicity and moral, cultural and aesthetic values. But in the New World, it was the erotic/sexual dimension that was the most complex. White men had no hesitation in having sexual relations with black women. Indeed, it has been suggested that white males in Caribbean sugar colonies had a special weakness for black women. One case which was reported in a planter's own diary shows the planter's obsession with having intercourse with black women wherever he found them; he had a particular predilection for the wives of his slaves (see Hall 1989).

When intermediate colours/shades were added to the pigmentation scale, it was consistently a case of males mating with females of shades/colours darker than themselves, as an expression of the power relations based on a colour hierarchy. The reverse, of a male mating with a female closer than himself to the white peak of the hierarchy, was not typical. However, cases (rather exceptional, it seems) have been reported of black male/white female sexual encounters even during slavery, especially where there was a fair number of female European indentured workers living in similar conditions to slaves. This ended with the seventeenth century, at least in the British colonies, when white women were forbidden to work in the fields.

For the African man, white was the forbidden fruit. For the African woman, white was the avenue through which her offspring had a chance for a better life. And this must have made rape or other degrees of non-consensual sex more palatable and acceptable, although suicide and abortion were also practised. It was only when, in more recent times, Caribbean men of darker shades gained some measure of economic power that such men were able to aspire to mating with women of lighter shades than themselves. Indeed, it became, and continues to be, a clear pattern for successful black male professionals or businessmen throughout the Caribbean (and the Americas) to marry women of lighter complexions than themselves.

Africans who were brought to the Americas had no previous experience of this cultural and racial (colour) hierarchy and had to learn by force the hierarchy and its scale of values. Africans had to internalize a schema in which white was power, privilege and dominance, while black was poverty, slavery, subjection and submission. This schema was, however, only one part of a very complex structure of race, colour and cultural values and identities that the peoples of these societies created to organize their lives.

The Sociohistorical Background

It is now time to examine the sociohistorical background to the formation of present structures of race and ethnicity in the Caribbean. It is not easy to take a global view of the area. There are indeed very generalized factors present, but, for each of these, it must be noted that there are nuances in the way they operate, and exceptions, in form or degree, in the way these factors apply. The idea of "unity in diversity" may be very appropriate in capturing the sociohistorical essence of the Caribbean. "Unity" refers to a number of common features in the way in which race and ethnicity are played out in the region. "Diversity" accounts for the very particular manifestations in each subgrouping and ultimately in each individual territory.

It must be further admitted that we are making here a weak claim about the cause/effect relationship between sociohistorical factors and the race/ethnicity picture. It is not always clear how a particular factor applies, especially when it does not seem to apply in the same way in all cases. We are often confronted with an intersection of a variety of factors; and of course we are not always sure that we have grasped their full extent and their full effect.

The first important sociohistorical fact is the relatively large number of different ethnic groups thrown together in relatively small physical spaces (in some cases less than one hundred square miles) and therefore unable to avoid one another. In addition to the indigenous peoples, there were Europeans of different nationalities, ethnicities and sub-ethnicities, Africans of different ethnicities, Indians (also diversified), Chinese, Arabs, Jews, Japanese. In many or most cases (Trinidad, Jamaica, Suriname and Guyana, for example), all these different groups were significantly represented in these small spaces.

The Indigenous Peoples

It is very well known that the indigenous peoples fared very badly. They were first of all enslaved, overworked and generally maltreated. Their forced interaction and intercourse with Europeans exposed them to new diseases which ravaged their populations. In a matter of decades their numbers were so drastically reduced in the Greater Antilles that they ceased very early to constitute groups that could preserve and transmit their ethnicity through generations.

There are some notable exceptions to this. In Dominica, a Carib community exists which preserves in some measure the racial phenotype of its ancestral stock. This phenotype is becoming less and less distinctive as more and more miscegenation with the non-Carib population takes place. According to Lowenthal, "a visitor in 1878 reported twenty 'uncontaminated' Carib families in Dominica and half a dozen in St Vincent. By 1940, only a hundred inhabitants of Dominica's Carib Reserve – one fifth of the total – appeared or believed themselves to be full-blooded Indians" (1972, 178, citing Taylor 1951). Dominican Caribs are, culturally, relatively well integrated into Dominican rural society. The community has not preserved the Carib language, but speaks the French-based creole language, the mass vernacular of Dominica. It is Roman Catholic by religion, with no traces of syncretic forms. Cuisine and craft (basket weaving and canoe building) may, however, be the best preserved links with the ancestral culture and are at the moment the artefactual forms of Carib ethnicity.

Owen (1975) observes that the Caribs of Dominica base their ethnic identity on four main symbols: territory (the reserve), legends and stories, chieftaincy, and physical traits. At the level of affective identity, there remains a strong feeling among Dominican Caribs of ethnic separateness, which is nurtured both by the awareness of their historical distinctiveness and by their marginalization in Dominican society.

In Belize and Honduras, there exist communities variously referred to as Black Carib or Island Carib, or, more properly, as Garifuna. They are the descendants of Carib people who were removed from islands such as Martinique to allow unfettered colonization there, and were taken to the island of St Vincent. There they were joined by Africans, and the result was a racial mixture showing phenotypical features taken from both races. They were finally moved to Central America when St Vincent's turn came for exploitation. The best preserved forms of the ancestral language and culture of the islands (Lesser Antilles) are thus now to be found in these communities on the Caribbean coast of Central America.

The Garifuna people are relatively homogenous in colour and culture, and have been protected from the colour and ethnic hierarchy typical of the outside world. However, they are coming more and more into contact with Belizean society, and it will be interesting to observe whether the differentials in social and moral value ascribed to colour and forms of culture by the wider Belizean society will lead to the construction of new systems among the Garifuna.

Trinidad also has a Carib group. There, the Caribs do not have a very distinctive, recognizable phenotype, although some Trinidadians may claim to be able to identify them by some features of hair colour and texture and of facial structure. The group has a geographical identity, being associated with the town of Arima. They only come to life in any significant way once a year at the Santa Rosa festival, which is a Roman Catholic observance they particularly adhere to. They are completely integrated into Trinidadian society. Their language, religion, music, cuisine and craft are non-distinctive, and membership or participation in the group is by geographical tradition and by affective collective association.

The recognition of the indigenous peoples in the ethno-history of the Caribbean has taken on another interesting form, especially, but not only, in the Hispanic islands. The elimination of these peoples as a well-defined observable group has made the category of "*indio*" or "Carib" available for exploitation in the systems of racial phenotypical representation. Although the indigenous peoples were savaged and humiliated by the European conquerors, we have seen that they were also romanticized by European writers as representing, *par excellence*, the pristine innocence of the human being. Their life and their lands were thought to be the mythical Elysian Fields imagined by Greek antiquity or the Utopia of Sir Thomas More.

Their phenotype was perceived to be in some respects closer to the European norm than was that of the African. Their hair was long and straight, and their skin pigmentation, although difficult to represent (it was sometimes and in some places "red", and in others "yellow"), was seen as lying somewhere in between the polarized categories of white and black. Eguchi (1997, 370–71) cites a North American traveller of 1925 who found the women "rather comely". He reported that "they [the Caribs of Dominica] are more attractive-looking than the black people and more clean. Their colour, if uncontaminated by negro blood, is a golden bronze or copper." The imagined *indio* or Carib phenotype (black straight hair, copper to dark complexion, high cheekbones) now carries a relatively high social and aesthetic value, and many persons are attracted to this category and may claim it for themselves. (This is discussed in more detail in chapter 6.)

In other areas of the Caribbean, for example Trinidad, Martinique and Jamaica, Carib, Arawak and Taino do not constitute a phenotypical category, but remain an available source for racial/ethnic ancestral reference. For ancestral reference, there is, throughout the Caribbean, some measure of avoidance of black/African (especially among mixed origin persons); but there is also a reluctance to claim white/European ancestry (for fear of being thought "pushy") or Chinese and Indian (from India) since these categories are not absolutely prestigious. Persons who wish to avoid self-classification in any one of these categories may claim Carib (Trinidad, Martinique) or Taino (Jamaica) ancestry.

There is a growing awareness throughout the Caribbean of the pre-Columbian peoples. Museums, archeological digs and historical research are producing more knowledge about these peoples and making it available to the public. The occasion (in 1992) of the five-hundredth anniversary of Columbus's landing was exploited to examine critically the significance of that event, and everywhere in the non-Hispanic Caribbean, the judgment was antagonistic to Spain and sympathetic to the cause and memory of the indigenous peoples. Several formulae were suggested to replace "discovery" in reference to the event. "Landing", "invasion", "accident" were proposed. The opportunity is taken everywhere to identify the contribution of the indigenous peoples. In this respect, in many places and among many persons, especially in the upper socioeconomic strata, there is much less hesitation and ambivalence in recognizing this contribution than in recognizing the African background and contribution.

Africans

While Africans were being engaged to operate this race/colour schema, and while there is no clear evidence of any particularly high aesthetic or moral value that Africans placed on the colour black (in other words, no clear evidence of any particularly heightened racial and ethnic arrogance), there is copious evidence that Africans held on to their ethnicity. Whether in a relatively pure form as in the case of the Maroons, or in a modified, contextualized, syncretized form as in the case of those who remained in the context of slavery, ethnic cultural forms were highly valued, persisted and grew, in some cases, despite the strong hostility and depreciation of the European/white elite. Language, religion, music and dance were/are the most expressive manifestations of this ethnicity. The social thus came to be quite separate from the ethnic. This has persisted to the present time. Today, women can bleach their skin and straighten their hair and at the same time participate fully in expressions of non-white ethnicity.

It is evident that the ethnicity which developed outside the Maroon communities is not everywhere an "African" ethnicity. However, some cases do exist. The Rastafarians, originally of Jamaica and now spread virtually throughout the Caribbean, are a case of "African" ethnicity, although this is, in many respects, a reconstructed ethnicity rather than a continuity from the earliest arrivals of Africans in the region. There have also been other attempts to reaffirm or reconstruct ethnicities based on the notion of Africa as the motherland, and on a recognition that "we are Africans" – for example, the Garvey movement of the 1930s, the *Négritude* movements of the 1940s, the Black Power movement of the 1960s. But these have not prevailed or succeeded in binding people together in a sustained common pursuit of cultural or political interests. There are also cases of "sub-ethnicities" based primarily on religious practices, which are recognized by the practitioners as being "African". The Lucumí of Cuba and the Shango of Trinidad are examples of a Yoruba ethnicity. The Kumina people of Jamaica and the Vaudoun people of Haiti recognize their religious affiliation to "Africa", without necessarily being able to pinpoint the exact African modality with which they are ethnically linked.

Among the general Caribbean population of African descent, the picture is very complex and ambiguous. This population has come under the severe assaults of the race and ethnic hierarchy of which we have spoken, and it has emerged extremely scathed. They have been unable to construct and define freely their own identities, and have had to accept definitions of themselves imposed from outside. Europeans had, immediately on the founding of these post-Columbian societies, seized the prerogative of naming, and thereby of defining, of symbol creation and of setting the normative semantics of Caribbean experience, and indeed, to some measure, that of the world. Even aspects of the natural environment came under this prerogative of naming. Thus many fruits in the Caribbean are named on the basis of how they were perceived in relation to some other European fruit (golden apple, otaheite apple, custard apple, avocado pear, pineapple, grapefruit, naseberry, coolie plum), and these names have been accepted by the non-European populations as part of the colonial heritage.

The earliest and perhaps most dramatic example of this assault on identity was the naming of the people. Ethnic African names were quickly abandoned in favour of the all-encompassing "negro", which had been earlier (at least as early as the period of antiquity) constructed to refer to the skin colour of peoples of the African continent, and which had later come to represent these people racially and ethnically. We should note here that the indigenous peoples also came under this all-encompassing naming by colour. They were represented as "red". They were also rather ridiculously named *Indio* (Indian) by Columbus, thereby forever enclosing their identity in a Spanish/European world.

Another example is the semantic pejoration of one of the names of the indigenous peoples of the Caribbean (*Caribali*) to produce the term "cannibal". Fortunately, the phonetic distortion that the term underwent (*Caribali* to cannibal) means that the formal link between "cannibal" and "Carib" may no longer be perceived.

As has been noted above, this control of names and meanings is not confined to the Caribbean experience. It is worldwide, as can be seen in the semantic distortion of words like "jungle" and "tribe", which came to refer primarily to African realities and have come to take on very negative, pejorative connotations.

This prerogative of naming and of symbolization is an important perspective in understanding the issues of power and identity in the Caribbean. The significant symbols in the Caribbean are generally Eurocentric, and this includes the form of language itself. They help to perpetuate the trauma of inferiority, alienation and anomie in Caribbean people. As we have seen, one startling example of this is the symbolization of black and white, which already is recorded for the Graeco-Roman period of antiquity, and which has come down to us as a standardized area of English (as well as of French and Spanish) semantics.

The use of colour terms to refer to so-called races began already in the period of antiquity. These colours had already developed meanings, connotative and metaphorical, which carried clear sociopsychological values. Applying them to "races" was a master strategy of psychological control to which so-called white, black/Negro, red and yellow peoples are still subject, and from which non-white peoples are still trying to escape. "White", with its extremely positive connotations, was co-opted by Mediterranean Europeans who are in fact the least white of "white" peoples; while "black", which as a colour was afflicted with very negative pejorative connotations, was assigned generally to the peoples of Africa. Not all the peoples of East Africa or sub-Saharan Africa have a skin pigmentation that can be reasonably associated with the colour black. The Xhosa and Zulu of South Africa tend to be more brown than black. And these are not the "coloured", that is, mixed race, South Africans, but indigenous peoples who have no modern known history of racial mixing. There are also ethnic groups in West Africa who tend to be brown to dark brown rather than black.

Even where some attempts are made to correct the absurdity of these significant symbols, they often fall short of what is required. Thus "black" in the Jamaican flag was officially recorded to be, not an ethnic symbol recognizing the majority ethnic group, but a symbol of "hardships faced". In 1997, the Jamaican government set up a special committee to re-examine the national symbols and their meanings. There is therefore the feeling that there may be a need to create new symbols within a different tradition, but there is no certainty as to what these might be.

There is also the important area of onomastics (the study of the formation of names), which in the Caribbean was controlled by masters and resulted in African slaves acquiring new, often mocking and ridiculous Eurocentric names. Given the important role that the word, and the name in particular, plays in the African world view, this control of personal names was another masterful strategy for psychological control: for control of identity, for control beyond the simple control over life and death. This led as usual to resistance, in this case in the form of a proliferation of nicknames to which only the community was privy, and more recently to a fashion for non-western European, and particularly for African or African-sounding names. Caribbean peoples of African descent have continually struggled to reject such external definitions and to reappropriate the prerogative of self-defining.

Aimé Césaire, confronted with, and reacting to, Shakespeare's portrayal of Caliban as the monumental representation of the primitive in humanity, sought, in his play *Une Tempête*, to rescue Caliban, or sought to have Caliban rescue himself, by recasting a conversation between Caliban and Prospero in which Caliban declares that he will no longer be called Caliban. The name Caliban, indeed, is either an unwitting or a very clever corruption on the part of Shakespeare of the word "cannibal", itself a distortion of one of the variant names (*Calina, Carina, Caribali, Calibali*) of the indigenous people of the Caribbean region. Shakespeare's Caliban is in fact nearer the form of the original word, and, as well, is less of a semantic and humanistic degradation than is implied in the phonological and semantic distortion "cannibal". Césaire's Caliban rejects the name; nor will he accept the other name which Prospero suggests: Hannibal (Césaire's cynical approximation to "cannibal"). And here Césaire is alluding, whether consciously or unconsciously, to the tendency of some Africans and African Americans to attempt to rescue their humanity by evoking and invoking great African heroes of the past, of whom Hannibal is one. Césaire rejects this in favour of a process by which ordinary "primitive" individuals can rescue their own humanity by reappropriating the prerogative of naming and, therefore, of defining. Caliban renames himself X, by which Césaire expresses the importance of naming and language in the process of self-appropriation, the reclaiming of one's self; but he also expresses the bind in which Caliban, and Caribbean people in general, find themselves, due to the absence of a language in which this renaming and reclaiming can be communicated. It is the Caribbean dilemma. And it is interesting to observe how Malcolm X relived Césaire's Caliban in another time and another place.

The languages developed in the Caribbean by African slaves became another important area of racial and ethnic pejoration. The emerging language of slaves was called "*patois*". Properly speaking, the term referred then to the rural dialects of France, which were falling into disuse and becoming moribund. These French dialects were losing speakers as younger generations abandoned them in favour of more socioeconomically valuable language forms; and they were becoming degenerate and non-viable as language systems. They had no important communicative function and did not have a strong ethnic identification. It was the regional dialects of France (as distinct from the *patois*) which served the purpose of identifying a particular regional or ethnic division (Picardy, Normandy, Provence, and so on). The language of slaves was drawn into this conceptual framework and the foundation for the future negative evaluation was set, even though, objectively, the language of slaves shared few, if any, of the functional or structural (linguistic) characteristics of the patois.

These Caribbean languages are in a rather peculiar position, quite analogous to the position in which the cultures are, *vis-à-vis* the official elite cultures. Caribbean cultures, for example, are rather ambiguous in terms of identity. They are new cultures unable to attach themselves to any old continuous tradition when compared with the evolution of other cultures. The tradition to which they may have been attached is the African, and of course there have always been and still are ideological movements that are founded on this link. However, this is not entirely a part of the perception and consciousness of the general population, although objectively the forms of Caribbean popular and folk culture can be linked with Africa through complex processes of continuities, discontinuities, syncretisms, reinterpretations, calques, and so on.

The problem is compounded by the fact that many Caribbean societies are plural, and although there is a tendency even in these plural societies and cultures to consider the African tradition as the majority tradition or the national tradition, or even the indigenous tradition, this is being seriously challenged by other ethnic groups ("East" Indians in Trinidad and Guyana, for example).

The Graeco-Roman tradition is very evident in the democratic traditions and legal systems. It is evident also in the general intellectual, philosophical, artistic and aesthetic norms. This belongs, however, to the area of exogenous norms, which are now coming under some serious questioning in the search for a distinct identity, even at the level of high culture, to which standard languages belong. Concepts of creolization (or *créolité*) and hybridity are now being experimented with, in an attempt to find a new understanding of identity that avoids the so-called essentialist concepts of African and European (see the conclusion).

As a general rule, Caribbean languages continue to be seen as not belonging to the African tradition; they are judged by the general population against the

Graeco-Roman norms of language structure, according to which, for example, inflections are the essential part of the ideal language structure; they are thought to have "no grammar". These so-called creole languages have remained in the shadow of this tradition, and have attracted to themselves perhaps the highest degree of stigmatization of all of the world's languages. The pernicious effect of living in the shadow is well illustrated by the fact that those creole languages which no longer have existing side by side with them, and are therefore not existentially overshadowed by, the European languages to which they are related through their lexicons, have most successfully escaped the stigma and the negative evaluation, and have progressed or are progressing to the status of official and national languages. This is the case of Papiamentu in the Netherlands Antilles, and Sranan in Suriname. Haitian, although related lexically to French, has also managed, to a large degree, to escape the strangling dominance of French. The reasons for this are to be found in the particular sociocultural history of Haiti.

However, there are Caribbean groups/communities in which the role of language is not ambiguous or ambivalent, but where language has been called upon to serve the "national" interest of the groups. In both cases, the groups have no ambivalence about the tradition to which they belong, and both cases provide excellent examples of a very general marronnage which language has been called upon to sustain and of which language is a major expression. The first case is again that of Maroon communities of Jamaica and Suriname, which show considerable linguistic complexity. We shall see later (chapter 8) how the African language (Twi-Asante), preserved by the Maroons of Jamaica, played, and continues to play on a lesser scale, an important role in achieving freedom and in preserving and asserting a separate Africa-based ethnicity and identity.

The other case is that of the Rastafarians of Jamaica and of other parts of the Caribbean to which the movement has now spread. The language of Rastafarians is not "African" in form, although, based as it is for the most part on Jamaican creole, it has a number of syntactical, phonological and lexico-semantic features derived from African languages (chiefly Twi-Asante; see Alleyne 1980). However, Rastafarians have transformed Jamaican creole both in form and function. Their language is now a powerful force, copied by persons all over the world to assert an identity and an association with a certain philosophy, religion, world view and lifestyle. It is interesting that these two cases (Maroons and Rastafarians) are Jamaican phenomena. (They will be discussed at greater length in chapter 8.)

There has been some controversy surrounding this question of African ethnicity in the Americas, and many interpretations have been proposed. These range from the "stripping" of Africans of their culture and ethnic identity to the continuity of African culture(s), in some cases virtually intact, with "normal" processes of evolution. It is becoming more and more evident that one single theory of African American culture cannot encompass all the different cases that exist in the Americas, and indeed we shall see that the three modalities examined in depth in this work (Puerto Rico, Martinique, Jamaica) each present a particular case as far as an African-based ethnicity is concerned.

There are groups or individuals for whom it might be argued that they were stripped of their African culture, or at least of some aspects of it. There are other groups and societies who have preserved and consciously recognize an African culture and ethnicity, although it is obvious that this culture has undergone some measure of change and is not simply an intact survival. Indeed, even on the African continent, there is no culture that is an intact survival of the African cultures of the sixteenth century.

As we said above, the most notable case of a group which has preserved and consciously recognizes an African ethnicity is that of the Maroon societies of Jamaica and Suriname. The life span of these groups has stretched from the inception of these New World societies to the present time. They have undergone change in the context of migration, though they are still dominated by isolation and limited contact with other groups. Even within these groups, there are differences in the degree and form of African ethnicity, due to the different degrees of isolation and contact with other groups across the internal frontiers.

One particular Suriname group, the Saramakka, has been quite isolated and has only recently (within the past three decades) begun to have any significant contact with other Suriname groups, and with the international world (through visiting anthropologists, missionaries and migration to Holland). They recognize their African ancestry and have preserved an African language for special purposes. Their religion is not characteristically syncretic, nor is their music. However, they have as a vehicle for everyday interaction, a "creole" language. Whereas more than 80 per cent of the vocabulary of this language is of English and Portuguese origin, the phonology has a number of African phonemes: *mb, nd, ng. kp. gb,* as well as lexical tone. The syntax of this language is also replete with structures and grammatical morphemes that are West African in origin. Together, these features make Saramaccan a unique language within the "creole" category.

The Saramakka people also give their children names from the days of the week (though the children are also baptized in church). Each person has two souls: the *akra*, which is born and dies with the individual, and the *jojo*, which leaves the body at death and roams in nature as the *yorka*. *Akra* and *yorka* are of Twi origin; *jojo* in Ewe means "guardian". Thunder and sky deities are called *Tap-Kromanti* (*Kromanti* being the term which the Saramakka and the Jamaican Maroons use to refer to themselves, synonymous with Ashante). One of these deities is *Bada*, who seems to be the *Bade* of the Ewe.

The other Maroon societies have been engaged in more significant societal relations with the other non-Maroon groups. But there is evidence that they (like the Saramakka) have remained unaffected by the racial and ethnic hierarchy that became established in the outside "creole" societies. Maroon society, generally speaking, is homogenous with regard to language, race, ethnicity, and so on. The general phenotype is African, that is, dark skin, short "woolly" hair, flat nose, and these features do not carry the low social and aesthetic values that they may have in the outside societies. The terms for black do not carry any particular connotation, either pejorative or ameliorative.

In the non-Maroon societies of the Caribbean, the African was a slave and became a "negro" in English and Spanish, and a *noir* or a *nègre* in French. His descendants have become "West Indian", "Caribbean", "creole". They are the only racial group who are no longer simply identified by their ancestral origins. In Caribbean societies, there are Europeans (including Scots, Irish, French, British, German, Portuguese), Indians, Chinese, Javanese, Caribs, Lebanese, Syrians. But there are no "Africans". Individuals may, on a purely personal level, assert an African identity and call themselves "African Jamaican", "Afro-Cuban", and so on. In some territories, Barbados for example, such individuals are a rarity, and the term and concept "African Barbadian" virtually does not exist.

These individuals asserting an African identity have in some cases formed themselves into groups based on that identity, but such groups (including the Maroons and Rastafarians) have remained minorities and somewhat marginalized. However, as we shall see in the chapters dealing with the special cases of Jamaica, Martinique and Puerto Rico, the role of Africa in the construction of Caribbean identities differs in nature and importance in different Caribbean territories. In Jamaica, for example, it has always been fairly significant and is likely to become more so in the future.

Slavery confirmed the absolute pejoration of black. Although the indigenous people were also enslaved, their early disappearance erased that particular stigma from the collective consciousness of the emerging societies. The developing category of mulatto, especially those examples which tended towards the black pole, had an uncertain social value since, in spite of all efforts to conceal, it would be known that there was an African (slave) element somewhere in the ancestry. Many people, especially in the Hispanic islands, sought to circumvent this by claiming indigenous ancestry. In the Hispanic islands, this went beyond individual claim and became rather well stabilized into a racial phenotypical category to which a person could assign himself or herself, but, more importantly, to which he or she could be assigned by the general societal categorization. Needless to say, there is some inconsistency in the assignments. The same individual in Puerto Rico or Cuba may classify himself or herself as *indio,* but may be classified as something else by others. In the Dominican Republic, the category *indio* is firmly established, and has virtually replaced "mulatto" as a phenotypical category. It may even incorporate phenotypes that in other Caribbean countries would be classified as black/negro/African; indeed, it has assumed the proportions of a national identity category.

As we shall see later, this often has to do with the need to avoid the classification "negro", a need experienced both by the individual person wishing to enhance his or her self-image and social standing, and by his or her outside classifiers, that is, the society itself, wishing to remove the "black" stain from the national carpet and enhance the national image. This belongs to a generalized system of attenuation (in contrast to the pejoration of black), a social consensus to "denegrify" the society, which is well established in the Dominican Republic and to a lesser extent in Puerto Rico.

The Other Groups

The other major groups arriving in the Caribbean – Europeans, Jews, Indians, Chinese, Arabs – all brought with them a basic colour hierarchy that put white or "clear" complexions at the top and black or "dark" complexions at the bottom. The ethnic hierarchy is more complex, and we have to distinguish here between the general recognition and experience of European military and economic power on the one hand and the forms of European culture on the other. We have seen that the period of the Renaissance confirms the military, technological and economic power of Europe. This is also the beginning of the age of European colonial and imperial expansion, and this power begins then to be felt across the entire globe, especially in the Caribbean.

The societies from which the non-European groups came also experienced this European imperial power. While they may not have accepted the comparative and hierarchical ordering of world cultures in the form that Europe wished to present it (all of them recognizing and cherishing their long cultural tradition and possessing confidence in the intrinsic and acquired worth of their own cultures), the conditions under which they came to the Caribbean made them experience the imperial power of Europe in a direct and overwhelming way. Whether it was African slaves or Indian and Chinese and African indentured workers, or Arab migrants, they all came from countries under European colonial imperial control or domination; they travelled in European ships controlled by European merchants and captains, and arrived in the Caribbean to societies that were the epitomes of European hegemony.

Europeans

The white group is western European in origin and presents another example of the Caribbean axiom of "unity in diversity". There are many common features of the white presence in the Caribbean, but important differences can be observed, not only in the precise origins of Europeans, but also in their social relations, social status and group coherence.

A very important difference in the social and ethnic status of whites can be observed between the Hispanic islands and the Anglo-Saxon ones, with the French islands lying in between. It has to do with the demographics, and also with the national character and with colonial policy. Whites have a much stronger numerical presence in Cuba and Puerto Rico than in the other islands, and are the political ruling class in both.

Throughout Latin America, whites very early acquired and appropriated the designation *criollo*, and even laid claim in some cases to the status of "native", in contradistinction to their racial congeners, the *españoles* of Spain. Not only has their language, Spanish, become the official language but it claims to be the national language as well. The *criollo* identity became very important, a vital factor in the struggle for independence from Spain. By contrast, in the Anglo-Saxon islands, it was the mulatto class, articulating the revendications of the black masses, which led the independence movements.

The Spaniards (and the Portuguese) seem generally to have implanted themselves psychologically as well as materially in their colonies, and to have considered these colonies to be "home". Similarly, the colonial policy and attitude were not to view these territories as external colonies but as extensions of the motherland. North-western Europeans (British, Dutch, Danes), by contrast, had no great interest in developing lasting roots. They were to a large extent absentee owners, or people who came intending to make a quick fortune and return home to Europe. Cuba, Puerto Rico and Hispaniola became home to a large number of Spanish migrants even before the north-western Europeans came on the scene just before the mid-seventeenth century.

This psychological state distinguishing Iberian Europeans from Nordic Europeans seems to have had some kind of symbiotic interaction with absenteeism. British landowners were notoriously absent from their plantations in the Caribbean. Even where they lived in the Caribbean, the plantation was, generally speaking but particularly in such locations as Jamaica, a place where a fortune could be made that would enable the owner to return to England to live a life of comfort. In turn, their absence and lack of commitment prevented the development of an elite class, analogous to that which emerged in the Hispanic colonies, which could nurture a psychological attachment and commitment to the colony and challenge the economic and political authorities in the home country.

Another interesting manifestation of this is that the British allowed the emergence of a cadre of local people, mulattoes and blacks, to occupy relatively high levels of the colonial administration. This resulted in there being many more blacks in middle-class positions in the British and former British islands. The British also found it easier to give up their colonies than the Portuguese and Spanish (or French).

The most general pattern in the Caribbean is that persons representing themselves as white (*blanco*, *blanc*) and represented in this way by others, occupy the position of a social and economic elite, although they almost everywhere constitute a clear minority. Haiti is one exception, since the white group was virtually eliminated by the Haitian Revolution; Puerto Rico is another, since white persons are numerically very significant. Lowenthal sums up the demographic situation as follows:

> whites number 4 per cent in Barbados, only 1 per cent in Martinique and in Jamaica. Other islands with small white elites are Trinidad, St Kitts, Antigua, St Vincent, Guadeloupe, and Curaçao. Societies lacking white Creole elites are Haiti and the US Virgin Islands, as are the Commonwealth Windward islands of Grenada, St Lucia and Dominica. Coloured Creoles, not white, today comprise the Windward elite. (1972, 85)

White minorities occupy elite positions regardless of the political arrangements in any particular territory. The different political systems in Jamaica (independence), Puerto Rico (Commonwealth of the United States of America) and Martinique (Department of France) have not altered this historical and contemporary position of the white group. On the other hand, its cultural position is rather problematic. Given the extremely dynamic nature of Caribbean cultures, it is not easy to say which group (racial, ethnic, social) is the most powerful focus in this area. A distinction has to be made between the "high" culture, exogenous and somewhat stagnant and non-creative, and the "low" (in other words, popular) culture, aggressive, creatively dynamic. In some territories (Jamaica and Trinidad for example), the popular culture is very compelling and competes for the status of national culture. This popular culture has not altogether won the approval and recognition of the elite classes, but given the exogenous nature of the "high" culture and its association with the white elite, the popular culture is really the only serious claimant for the status of national culture. It is one of the dilemmas of Caribbean society: how to foster the evolution of "classical" forms of the popular culture in order to elevate its status and enhance its claims as the national culture.

In Jamaica, the very aggressive popular ethnic culture is assuming the proportions of a national culture, with Bob Marley coming to be accepted by all as the strongest, most positive icon of Jamaican culture, and reggae music as its strongest and most positive expression. There are parallels, to a greater or lesser extent, in the majority of the other Caribbean territories. European culture, though still prestigious, is becoming marginalized, and the persons historically associated with this culture are themselves becoming culturally marginalized.

Puerto Rico is the only Caribbean country where a radio station is dedicated to the playing of classical (that is, European "high culture") music throughout its daily broadcasting. Concerts featuring classical music (including the Casals festival, one of the biggest classical music festivals in the hemisphere) and peninsular Spanish plays of all centuries run side by side with local Puerto Rican music concerts and local plays. In Jamaica such classical concerts and plays from the British theatre are a relatively rare occurrence and attract very small audiences compared with local music concerts and local theatrical productions.

The area of culture that is most clearly dominated by the white groups everywhere in the Caribbean is language. As the inheritors of the colonial language, and by virtue of their historical access to education at all the levels, the white group everywhere possesses "natively" the official standard variety of the colonial language. This has enhanced their advantages, already inherent in the prestige of their race and colour, in the social and economic spheres.

Beyond language, the situation is more complex. First of all, in some cases, particularly in Martinique, the white group is historically attached to the land and the countryside as large landowners, only recently entering the areas of commerce, banking and insurance, thereby becoming more urbanized in culture. As rural people, they have shared some of the features of Caribbean rural culture: food and some musical genres. In Martinique they are reputed to be among the best and most frequent speakers of the creole language.

Rich Whites, Poor Whites

Although there are social divisions within the white groups everywhere, they do not affect the ethnic coherence of the groups. Nor do they affect the dominant socioeconomic position that the group as a whole generally enjoys. The most important division is between the "rich" whites and the "poor" whites, and this occurs more conspicuously in Guadeloupe, Martinique, Barbados and Puerto Rico.

The demographic history of the Caribbean has given rise to this social/ethnic/racial category known as "poor white". They are called *Blanc Matignon* in Guadeloupe, *Petit Blanc* in Martinique and *Redlegs* in Barbados. Wherever there was a numerically strong group of indentured servants from Europe, or Europeans contracted for agricultural work in the post-emancipation period, some of their descendants have not made sufficient economic progress to escape the category of "poor whites". The epithet "poor" may have had some literal meaning in the past, but today as a group, the members tend not to be very poor. Many have, from the earliest times, made considerable economic advancement. Some became large land and slave owners, and in modern times others have become prosperous through commerce.

In Barbados, Guadeloupe and Martinique, they are numerous enough to constitute an historical and contemporary subclass of the white ethnic group. They have tended to be as zealous as their more privileged brothers in preserving their ethnic separateness through a high degree of endogamy. This separateness is emphasized much more *vis-à-vis* blacks than mulattoes, with whom intermarriage may be tolerated (preferably a poor white female with a mulatto male of higher economic status – the male contributing his economic status and the female her social/ethnic/racial status). This demonstrates the continuing significance of race/colour as an organizing principle in these societies.

There is relatively little left of a separate culture (as opposed to race/colour) in this group. Poor whites organize themselves chiefly on the basis of race. Their cultural behaviour is virtually undistinguishable from that of blacks of the same economic standing. They speak the same mass vernacular, enjoy the same cuisine, share the same religious practices. They may differ in world view, although in Barbados there has been considerable levelling in world view between blacks and whites, manifesting itself in very generalized features such as discipline, thrift, orthodox Christianity with some belief in a spirit world. However, the influence of Jamaican and North American black youth culture affects black Barbadian (and to a lesser extent black Martinican) youth quite strongly. Though it does reach white Barbadian and Martinican youth, its influence here is not as strong. Therefore, the area of musical taste presents perhaps the largest cultural difference between blacks and poor whites.

In Puerto Rico, the independent peasant class is composed of white persons who may be considered poor. As we shall see, this group originated in nineteenth-century migration, building on earlier settlement in the country-side where land was plentiful. They now form the nucleus of the *jíbaro* category, which is a strong competitor for representing the national image and personality of Puerto Rico. Certainly the *jíbaro* is romanticized in poetry and other forms of literature in a way reminiscent of the treatment of the *guajiro* of Cuba and the *gaucho* of Argentina.

The poor whites are just as tenacious of white ethnicity and identity as their rich brothers and sisters; their endogamy has been as absolute, even though, because of their economic position, they have to live closer to the other racial/ethnic groups. They may therefore engage in more sexual relations with non-white women than their rich counterparts, but the incidence of marriage with such women is as infrequent as in the case of their rich brothers.

As a general rule the rich whites are the descendants of the large estate owners and other economically prominent persons of the slave plantation period, whereas the poor whites are the descendants of indentured Europeans (*engagés* in French) who were contracted to work. Some of the indentured Europeans eventually became rich landowners and slave owners, and the division was therefore not impermeable. There may also have been some cases of rich whites falling into hard times and joining the ranks of the poor whites.

(Sub-)Ethnic Divisions among Whites

Ethnic or sub-ethnic divisions are also a feature of some of the white groups. These divisions are either minor or virtually non-existent for Martinique and Barbados, but are quite marked in Trinidad and to a lesser extent in Jamaica and Puerto Rico. In Martinique, the white group accepts a French ancestry and makes no distinction in terms of regional sub-ethnic origins in France or or in terms of origins elsewhere in Europe. The group was originally composed of a majority of Normands, with significant minorities of Bretons and persons from the central provinces of France. These divisions are no longer recognized. Similarly, Barbadian whites recognize themselves as "English" (rather than "British"), although their ranks were built up of persons originating in all the major regions of the British Isles, including Scotland, Wales and Ireland. The dominant region seems to have been the south-west of England, in Somerset.

The white group in Jamaica is predominantly of British ancestry; but there are other components which, though sharing social and economic dominance, are ethnically differentiated. There are Jews belonging both to the Sephardic and Ashkenaze sects. Syrian-Lebanese may in some cases be ranked as white on the basis of their hair texture and skin colour, depending on how well their ancestry is known (through their names, for example) and on whether they are perceived to have the phenotypical features associated with Arabs. A person of Middle Eastern origin, but who does not have the marked pheno-typical traits associated with an Arab, who has undergone a change of his or her name from Arabic to European, and who is Christian by religion (particularly Roman Catholic), will most likely be viewed as white. Where these conditions do not hold, the person will be classified as a "Syrian" or "Syrian-Jew". There is still a high degree of endogamy among Jews and Arabs, but increasingly common class and economic interests may be leading to more miscegenation and intermarriage between Christian whites, Jews and Arabs.

Persons of known Syrian/Lebanese ancestry do not have as high social status and prestige as Christian whites or Jews, because of the perceived low international standing of their region of origin and the surviving memory of the conditions under which they came to Jamaica. In order to "put down" Syrian/Lebanese perceived as "uppity", African and mixed-race Jamaicans may recall a past when these people or their parents "walked the streets carrying suitcases on their backs peddling cloth from house to house". This is reminiscent of the Puerto Rican "put down": "*dónde está tu abuela?*" (where is your grandmother?), said to "uppity" mulattoes.

In Trinidad, white is also a racially, ethnically and socioeconomically complex concept and category. The very top socioeconomic stratum is occupied by three different ethnic (or sub-ethnic) white groups: one Anglo-Saxon and Anglican (Episcopalian, Church of England), the second British/Irish and Roman Catholic, and the third French (Creole) and Roman Catholic. The separate ethnic identities are becoming less distinct as common class and economic interests become stronger, leading to a reduction of endogamy and a weakening of religious devotion and separateness. There is still, however, a strong perception in the general population of a rivalry among these groups. In the past, this rivalry manifested itself, for example, in the creation and practice of separate football (soccer) clubs and private social clubs. Up to the 1950s, the football rivalry between Shamrock (Irish, Roman Catholic), Notre Dame (French Creole, Roman Catholic) and Casuals (the non-ethnic whites) was as strong as that between these (the "white" clubs) and the "brown" and "black" clubs. Football clubs were finely differentiated by race, ethnicity, colour and class, but in the characteristic Caribbean tradition of that time, the rivalry never descended into violence.

People of Portuguese origin may be "white" or a special "non-white" category depending on how brown or white their skin shade is (or has become from the type of work engaged in), and depending on their current socioeconomic standing. There is usually a correlation between the type of work engaged in, the socioeconomic standing, and skin shade. People of Portuguese origin came originally as indentured workers in the immediate post-emancipation period, and later were widely identified as small shopkeepers of low social status. This low status is reflected in the term *Potigee* (instead of Portuguese) used in the Trinidadian mass vernacular to refer to them. This form reflects the replacement of the vowel *u* by *i*, typical of the French-based creole language of Trinidad, as well as a back formation of a singular form (really a numberless form) derived from "the Portuguese" viewed as a plural form (on the analogy of *bees* [plural] – *bee* [singular], and so on). The vowel ending was also strengthened by the existence of similar class/race designations – *chinee*, *coolie* – all pejorative and connoting low social status. Many *Potigee* families (that is, non-white, low social status) have become "white" as a result of economic mobility. These are of course excellent examples of the social construction of race as well as of the growing importance of class *vis-à-vis* race in the ordering of Trinidadian society.

The Representational System

A series of innovations and semantic shifts in the terminology of race and ethnicity in the Caribbean has resulted in a contemporary lexico-semantic structure of extraordinary complexity. Some of the terminology and meanings and the practice of identifying peoples by skin colour had already been developed from the earliest times of Greek and Roman antiquity, and these terms, their denotations and connotations, formed the nucleus of the developing representational structures in the Caribbean. The structures are based on a series of different axes. For denotative representation, the axes are colour, race, class, ethnicity. Connotation then intervenes in the representational system and is based on two axes: pejoration and amelioration. Colour, class and ethnicity became more complex as these societies evolved through history, and the representational structures accordingly became more complex.

We begin with a simple tripartite division into white and black, with *indio* as a third, fading, category. The first two are denotatively colour terms which had already acquired connotations, one positive, the other negative, before the colonization of the Americas. They had already also acquired racial and ethnic references: *white* = Caucasian as race; Spanish, French, British, and so on, as ethnicity; *black* (or *negro*, *noir*) = Negroid as race; African (with hardly any subclassification) as ethnicity. In Central and South America, where the indigenous peoples survived, *indio* referred to race and to ethnicity without subclassification (as in the case of *black*). As soon as societies were established in which whites and blacks interacted in the Caribbean, the virtual immutability of the social status of each group led to further semantic expansion by which the terms came to refer to castes: white = high, black = low.

The first terminological expansion took place when other European powers (British, French) followed the Spaniards and Portuguese in their forays into West Africa and in their colonization of the Americas, and borrowed the Iberian word *negro*. In Spanish, *negro* was originally an adjective for the colour black. But adjectives in Spanish can readily be used as nouns, and *negro* was used as both: *un hombre negro* (a black man); *un negro* (a blackman). The same applies to *blanco* (white).

Negro and *blanco* were both colour terms and racial/ethnic terms. Only *negro* was borrowed, and the word entered English and French as a noun with a racial/ethnic meaning: a negro, *un nègre* (compared with a black man, *un homme noir*).

Another major early development caused by the peculiar social status of blacks was the further semantic expansion of the noun *negro* (*nègre* in French) to mean "slave". The colour terms black and *noir* also came to mean "slave". Thus the pejoration and the socialization of the meaning of black and negro (*noir* and *nègre*) was complete.

Similarly, in some places (Haiti, Mauritius), *blanc* came to mean "owner", "boss" (in addition to "white person"), undergoing a similar socializing of meaning. Conversely, other terms like *béké* and *bakra*, which originally (in their African source languages) meant "owner", "boss", came to refer to white people in terms of their race/ethnicity.

There seems to have been a focus on the representation of blacks, because *white* did not follow the terminological development of *black*. Not only was *blanco* not borrowed into English (which was logical since white people were not, as it were, a new, foreign object introduced by the Iberians, whereas negroes were), but *white* never became fully an ethnic noun in English. Thus English has "a negro", "(the) negroes", "two negroes", but not "a white", or "the white" (although "(the) whites", "two whites", have become marginally acceptable in English).

The nouns *negro* and *nègre* then underwent a further development. They acquired a neutral meaning in the Hispanic and French Caribbean and are used to express the idea of "fellow" (that is, without regard to race or colour):

un negro delgado, un nègre mince, "a thin fellow". In Martinique and Puerto Rico, *nègre* and *negro* are used as forms of address and are now applied irrespective of the race of the addressee, somewhat like English "mate". This evolution went further and resulted in an interesting affective amelioration of the terms. They are used to mean "friend", "sweetheart", "darling", and the like. It has also been attested in another French-influenced territory, Mauritius, where *mon noir* is equivalent to *mon ami* (my friend).

This development did not take place in the English Caribbean. It may be significant that this affective development took place in the Latin countries, but not in the north-western European countries (Germanic), and may say something about the different racial attitudes in the two European modalities. Pitt-Rivers (1968, 272) provides an interesting explanation for the affective use of *negro* and *negrito* in the Hispanic Americas. He claims that intimacy is opposed to respect; because these forms are basically disrespectful, they are used to establish or emphasize a relationship in which no respect is due (but see later).

The existence of the two forms (*black* and *negro*, or *noir* and *nègre*) as a result of the borrowing of Iberian *negro*, allowed the splitting of meanings. One term could be used for neutral reference as a colour term and the other for affective (pejorative) reference: French *noir* (neutral) and *nègre* (affective, pejorative); English *black* (neutral) and *negro* (in its particular vernacular forms: American *nigger*, Jamaican *niega*, both from sixteenth-century English *negger, nigger,* itself a borrowing of French *nègre*). In Spanish, *prieto* was used for the colour black, while *negro* expresses race or ethnicity.

Other kinds of splitting took place in order to achieve the semantic distinctions between colour, ethnicity and class. For example, we shall see (chapter 8) that in Jamaica, the expression *a black man* may mean either "a man of black complexion" or "a man belonging to black ethnicity", depending on the stress and pitch placed on *black*. In the hispanophone and francophone Caribbean, the splitting gives rise to apparent redundancies or hyperbole: *un negro prieto, un nègre noir* ("a black-skinned fellow").

An analogous development took place with the emergence of double forms for "white": *blanc* and *béké* in Martinique; *white* and *bakra* in the British territories. The first mentioned member of the pair refers to the colour white, while the second member (*béké* and *bakra*) refers to ethnicity, and then to upper socioeconomic status. *Bakra* and *béké* came to mean (or retained the meaning) "owner", "boss". This gives rise to expressions such as *a black bakra, un béké noir*, made possible after emancipation by the rise of some black-skinned persons to positions of owner and boss.

The white group also was subject to complex forms of representation, including the socialization, amelioration and pejoration of meaning. This shows that blacks were involved in the construction of representations. This involvement is apparent in the evolution of the meaning of white to "owner", "boss". But this and the other positive connotations of "white" are later developments. We saw in chapter 3 that African languages do not record representations of Europeans on the basis of the colour of their skin. In the initial period of European/African contact in the Caribbean, it seems that Europeans were not represented by colour but by African terms such as *mbakara* (Igbo), *mbeke* (Bambara), *uburoni* (Twi), the semantics of which did not contain any colour component. These terms meant basically "stranger" (*mbeke, uburoni*) and "one who surrounds, governs" (*mbakara*). Indeed, the current form, *brouni*, still used by the Maroons of Jamaica, still means "stranger". These Maroons use this term not only in reference to whites but to designate all non-Maroons. Thus the word retains intact the meaning of the African antecedent *uburoni*.

In some of the French territories, *béké* became generalized as the ethnic term (and later as the social class term) for "white" and was adopted also by the white group in reference to themselves. *Bakra* had a similar development in the British territories. However, a very significant difference exists between usage in the French territories and usage in Jamaica. Whites of Anglo-Saxon origin in Jamaica have not (do not) use the term *bakra* in reference to themselves. And the term had (has) a fair degree of pejoration (cynicism and mockery) when used by blacks in reference to whites. On the other hand, Martinican whites refer to themselves as *béké*. They categorically refuse to accept any representation of themselves as "*blanc*" (white).

Needless to say, it was the poor whites who were viewed with the greatest contempt, not only by blacks but by the white elite. Williamson (1817, 27) has this to say about the "redlegs" in Barbados: "a race of people transported in the time of Cromwell . . . tall, awkward made, and ill-looking fellows, much of a quadroon colour; unmeaning, yet vain of ancestry; a degenerate and useless race as can be imagined". In the extraordinarily ambivalent situation which developed, there emerged side by side and within the same individual both positive and negative connotations of "white", and both ameliorative and pejorative representations.

Blacks had difficulty in representing their own ethnicity, their own race and their own colour. All three of these identities came in for savaging in the circumstances of Caribbean slavery, and in particular plantation slavery. Pulled out of Africa where their ethnicity, race and colour were not existentially challenged, Africans arrived in the Caribbean to a situation of extreme personal angst, where all the objective conditions were designed to humiliate them and to discredit their race and colour. They were told, literally and indirectly, that their culture, race and colour befitted them only for the kind of work and civil status in which they found themselves, and that their masters by these same tokens were befitted to rule over them.

This has resulted in personality complexities represented by the two extremes of the *sambo* (the United States) or *quashee* (Jamaica) (the cringing, submissive, docile slave willingly accepting his or her condition), and the rebel (historically, the resistance fighter, Maroon, constantly resisting his or her condition, in contemporary Jamaica, the Rasta, the "rude boy", and in Trinidad, the "bad John"). In between these two extremes, there was considerable ambiguity and ambivalence in the general African population. The process of psychological reconstruction and rehabilitation continues up to today, and an essential part of this process has been the struggle to represent ethnicity, race, colour and self in appropriate ways.

The term "negro" has never proved acceptable to the African populations. It was a European invention and it became synonymous with "slave". According to Cassidy and Le Page, *nayga* (the Jamaican vernacular form, cited above in the form *niega*) "is avoided by whites, and resented by negroes if used of them by whites. As used among negroes, it is a term more or less derogatory, commonly implying extra blackness, backwardness, laziness, stupidity" (1967, 317). These are the qualities built into the stereotype of Africans created by Europeans. Africans had to accept this partially, but everywhere they also partially rejected it by a process of "denial" which took (and takes) several forms. In Jamaica, the term *nayga* was reserved for persons other than one's self, for persons whom one wished to insult. The distancing was (and is) also in terms of time; *nayga* is often preceded by the adjective "old", referring to persons of times gone by (during slavery, for example) who, it is felt, fully fitted the derogatory stereotype. In Puerto Rico and the Dominican Republic, negroes are considered not to exist as a national category, the category being reserved for migrant Haitians in the case of the Dominican Republic, and, ironically, for migrant Dominicans in the case of Puerto Rico.

The history of the struggle waged by Africans to represent themselves terminologically is well known. This writer has had considerable difficulty in representing them. "Negro" is of course totally unacceptable; "black" is the product of a European obsession, going back to Greek antiquity, to refer to people by the perceived (often strangely perceived) colour of their skin. "African", which would have been more acceptable, especially given the elimination or fusion of specific African ethnicities (see Alleyne 1988), is not generally used or recognized by the people everywhere in reference to themselves (except, as we said above, in particular cases). "Creole" is being proposed, but its reference is too uncertain. It originally referred to persons (and other biological species) of European descent born in the New World. This was/is more the case in the Hispanic colonies, to a lesser extent in the French colonies, and only marginally in the British colonies. In Jamaica, the term was never used to refer to blacks. In Trinidad, which was under Spanish rule and under French effective colonization before it fell to the British, "creole" tends to mean local, Trinidadian, but it is not used to refer to persons or forms of culture that exhibit the perceived African (or Indian) prototypical phenotype.

It is the people of African descent in the United States of America who have been most active in the search for appropriate ways of self-representation.

Once brought to the New World, Africans lost their ethnic individuality as Yoruba or Ewe or Kikongo, and lost their regional cultural identity as Africans, and became simply blacks, *negros*, *nègres* or *neger*. At the next stage of evolution, black, *negro* or *nègre* became synonymous with slave. And later, designations such as negro and coloured were employed as euphemisms to avoid black and African. None of these has ever met with total acceptance by all the individuals concerned.

Black has been revived in anglophone Afro-America; so has African, particularly in the United States of America where the term African American is the latest in the history of such representations. But why is there still a preference for black over African? There may be simple psycho-linguistic reasons. Identity entails popular definitions of "Who am I?", "What am I?" In some political circumstances (such as existed or exist in the Caribbean), self–other definitions become specified by colonial classifiers. Europe had seized the prerogative of naming and of symbol creation with their meanings and values.

Perhaps the major achievement by Europe in this regard has been to seize the positive connotations of the colour white (whether these connotations are natural/universal or themselves contextually constructed) and to apply this colour and its connotations to themselves. Whether by a process of antithesis, or through some natural universal association, or whether contextually constructed, Europe assigned negative connotations to the colour black, and when Africa was "discovered", the colour black was used to represent Africa.

The Europeans who are first recorded as using colour terms to refer to people are the Greeks and Romans of antiquity. But they, quite amazingly, are the Europeans furthest removed from the colour white, and they held the more truly white Europeans from the north in contempt. Many Africans are far from black, particularly the first Africans encountered by the Greeks and Romans. But there was this obsession with naming people by colour.

Interestingly, as was already noted above, the Chinese and Japanese, at home or in their diaspora, have not accepted the colour characterization of themselves as yellow, also negative in its connotations; they certainly do not refer to themselves as "we yellow people". Similarly, the indigenous peoples of this hemisphere do not generally refer to themselves as "we red people". The evidence that all this is contextually constructed is that the Chinese and Japanese, if they are forced to represent themselves by a colour, will use white. But African diasporic people have now largely accepted black and seem to prefer it to African.

Of course, in the highly conflictual reality of the world and the post-Columbian Caribbean, it has become an act of defiance for African diasporic peoples to use the term black to refer to themselves. Indeed, there are many other cases where a group triumphs psychologically over a pejorative label by accepting it and using it defiantly. The use of "nigger" as a term of endearment is one example. The use of "Yankee" by northern Americans to refer to themselves is another.

In addition, in trying to account for the current preference for black, we must note that black has been undergoing redefinition and is no longer a simple race/colour/ethnic category. There has been an ideologizing of black which now endows it with ideological features lacking in African; and this makes it more appealing than African. For example, by using black rather than African to represent themselves, Black Power leaders in Trinidad and Jamaica were able at least to invite Indians to join the movement. It is true that the attempt failed, obviously because the Indians saw black not as an ideological or class signifier but as a racial, ethnic category. But inviting the Indians to join a black movement stood a much better chance of success than inviting them to join an African movement.

Finally, for those who wish to avoid African, whether because they are uncertain about their origins, or because they do not wish to be associated with the stereotype and media image created about Africa, or because representing themselves as African would be, in their estimation, an act of disloyalty to their present national affiliation, black appears more acceptable. Nevertheless, there remains some semantic overlap between black and African.

The Caribbean dilemma has been how to reconstruct an identity, while avoiding a representation and definition imposed from outside. This process has been complicated by the arrival of populations from Asia, which have now become the majority in some societies, and added to the racial mixing.

One of the options of reconstruction has been to use, as one of the foundations, the reappropriation of a large, vague geo-cultural identity based on Africa, given the complete impossibility now of reconstructing or reappropriating a more particularistic identity based on a specific ethnic group. Let us note in passing that this last option may be impossible for the general populations (since we cannot all do what Alex Haley did), but it is a reality for certain sub-ethnic groupings of Caribbean people: The Maroons of Jamaica have no doubts about their Twi-Asante (Coromante) ancestry; Cuban and Trinidadian groups similarly proclaim their Yoruba ancestry; Haitian Vaudoun faithfuls are becoming more aware of their Ewe-Fon links. These are continuous, unbroken links of identity for which there really is no need for reconstruction and reappropriation. The dramatic case of reconstructing and reappropriating is that of the Rastafari, who have built an identity around a perceived Ethiopian ancestry.

New Mixed Categories

The creation of new mixed categories made it necessary to find new forms of terminological representation. The first two categories arose from the crossing of white males with indigenous Carib/Arawak females, and with African females; and the naming of these two categories is very instructive. In the first case (white male with indigenous female), the term used in Spanish was *mestizo*, derived from a reconstructed **mixticius* which would have emerged in the vernacular variety of medieval Latin. It was based on the past participle *mixtus* ("mixed") of the verb *miscere* ("to mix"). The ending *-icius* is used in Latin to derive adjectives from past participles. It does not have a precise and consistent meaning. But it is interesting to note that it has an association with the notion of "acquired". It occurs most frequently in the language of law to designate persons acquired in various ways: *adoptaticius* (adopted child), *adscripticius* (enrolled, as citizen or soldier), *conducticius* (hired, mercenary), *dediticius* (civil status of those having surrendered). It could also denote things acquired: *advecticius* (imported, foreign). In the language of commerce it came to be used in the description of various types of goods: *panis depsticius* (bread made by kneading).

In the second case (white male with African female), it is again a Spanish term *mulato*, derived from *mulo*, "mule", which was introduced. The sufix *-ato* is derogatory, and the word inherits the pejorative connotations both of the root, "mule", and of the ending. The naming of the first category (mestizo) belongs to a period of great curiosity in the "discovery" of new lands and of new "strange" people. By the time the second category had to be named, curiosity had waned and been replaced by contempt and derision. Ideas about purity had interested European people and thinkers from as far back as Greek antiquity. These ideas were strengthened during the Renaissance and became an obsession in the eighteenth century, the Age of Enlightenment.

The mulatto, like the mule, was viewed as an aberration of nature. These initial attitudes displayed in the naming of the category changed to more positive ones as Caribbean slave societies developed and stabilized. It was realized that the mulatto group was a buffer between the whites and the rebellious blacks. And although relations between the mulattoes and the whites were never completely easy and cordial, their status corresponded to the ethnic, racial and colour middle position they occupied between the two extremes of black and white. The females of the category became especially favoured as sexual partners; and some of the males were favoured by their fathers, and were even sent to Europe to be educated.

As we know, the mulatto eventually gained considerable social value. Among the French, the association with mule was lost and the name lost its pejorative ending, *-ato*, and became *mulâtre*. The word thus acquired a new ending, *-âtre*. This ending is one which in French is typically added to colour terms (equivalent to the English ending *-ish*); cf. *jaunâtre*, "yellowish", *rougeâtre*, "reddish"). Thus the amelioration of the mulatto was completed in

French by its incorporation into the colour representation of race and ethnicity. It may also be further evidence of what we referred to earlier as the European obsession with naming peoples on the basis of their colour. Among the British, it is not evident whether this association with mule has been lost, but in the (former) British territories of the Caribbean, the term is not in regular popular usage. The Jamaican form *malata* shows the loss of any perceptual link with mule.

.

CHAPTER SIX

Puerto Rico

Ethno-Demographic History

*C*olumbus reached Boricua (or Boriquén), to which he gave the Spanish name San Juan Bautista, on his second voyage in 1493. It was estimated that there were then on the island fifty to sixty thousand inhabitants belonging to a racial/ethnic group whose most widely used name is Taino. By 1511, the Spaniards had conquered and enslaved the island's peoples. But in 1544, when Bishop Don Rodrigo de Bastidas carried out the order of Charles I to free the "Indians" (*indios*, as they came to be called by the Spaniards), the Bishop estimated that there were only sixty "Indians" left. This figure probably did not represent the number of native inhabitants still alive on the island. It is obvious that the governor meant that only that number bothered to come to hear the reading of the decree.

Some Caribs may have been brought to Puerto Rico from the other islands to increase the labour force (Sued Badillo and Lopez Cantos 1986). Brau (1956a) reports that Governor Manuel de Lando's census of 1530 recorded the number of *indios* as 1,148. The 1771 census counted 1,756 "pure Indians", that is, 2.5 per cent of a population of 70,210 inhabitants; and the one taken in 1778 found 2,302 Indians on the island. Given the settlement of the island in small rural farms, these census estimates are not reliable. After the decree ending the enslavement of the native inhabitants, landowners probably lied about the number of natives allotted to them as serfs. In this way, they could force the importation of Africans. In later censuses there is no separate indication for "Indians" who apparently are put together with *pardos libres* (free mulattoes).

It is often said that black Africans were brought to the Caribbean to replace the Indians as slave labour. However, the fact is that Africans began to arrive with the conquering armies of Spain. Slavery had been an old tradition in the Old World. In the fifteenth century (at the end of which Spain had begun its colonization of the Americas), Jews, Moors, Berbers, Arabs and eastern Europeans were still part of the slave labour force of the Mediterranean world. From 1440, the Portuguese began bringing sub-Saharan African slaves to Europe via direct Atlantic sea routes (rather than overland as had been done before). By the 1650s, only the Iberians still actively practised slavery in western Europe and only non-Christians were being enslaved.

By the second half of the fifteenth century, sub-Saharan Africans became the predominant group in the western Mediterranean slave labour force. Between 1450 and 1505, 140,000 slaves from Africa were brought to Europe (Verlinden 1955). Some of these African slaves made up half or more of the armies conquering the New World.

In accordance with official provisions in force, the only blacks who were allowed to enter the new colonies in the New World were peninsular blacks. These were referred to as "*(negros) ladinos*", "*negros de Castilla*", "*negros de Portugal*", and they came chiefly from Seville, Lisbon and the Canary Islands. These were urban slaves in Spain, and were brought to do mining and agricultural work in the Caribbean colonies. According to Sued Badillo and Lopez Cantos (1986, 173), these *ladinos* were intractable and became a social problem, as they corrupted the Indians and sowed the seeds of discord and rebellion among them.

In 1503, the governor, Ovando, recommended a halt to the immigration of *ladinos* into Puerto Rico. As early as 1506, the Crown ordered the expulsion of all black slaves from the island. Many also left with their owners for more promising lands in the New World. And in 1519, the first Royal Licence was issued for blacks (*bozales*) to arrive directly from Africa. There was some resistance to introducing *ladino* slaves or *bozales,* as white immigration was preferred, especially in Puerto Rico (Figueroa Mercado 1974, 249). Puerto Rico was poor and could not afford to buy slaves as easily as other, wealthier territories. Traffickers preferred to take their cargoes elsewhere.

Up to the third decade of the sixteenth century, some sugar was being cultivated in Puerto Rico, but there followed a sharp decline as many Spaniards left, lured by the greater fortunes that the Central and South American mainland promised. Although importation of Africans ceased after a rebellion by blacks in 1527, the census of 1531 showed that there were seven times more African slaves than white Spaniards.

During the sixteenth century, the gross number of slaves continued to diminish, some having been taken to the more economically active islands of Cuba and Hispaniola. This prompted a request to the king in 1579 to send one thousand Africans for work in sugar cane cultivation and gold mining. At the end of the sixteenth century, whites were again the majority ethnic group. This changed once more in the following century when, by 1673, even the city of San Juan had more blacks and mulattoes than whites. In 1693, Governor Arredondo asked for whites to be sent from the Canary Islands or from anywhere else for fear that blacks might too grossly outnumber whites. The census figures for 1771 and 1778 show the dramatic turnaround:

	Year 1771	Year 1778
Whites	31,951	46,756
"Indians"	1,756	2,302
Free Coloured	24,164	34,867
Free Negroes	4,747	7,866
Mulatto slaves	3,343	4,657
Negro slaves	4,249	6,603

Sociopsychological Conditions of Slavery

It is generally accepted that the Hispanic Caribbean experienced a set of sociohistorical conditions that distinguishes it from the rest of the region (Hoetink 1967, 1973; Mintz 1996; Duany 1985; Safa 1998). There is evidence to suggest that this was certainly the case for Puerto Rico, and that the status and social conditions of Africans there may have been somewhat special. The number and percentage of free blacks throughout the pre-emancipation history of Puerto Rico were significant. The census figures presented above show higher numbers for free blacks than for enslaved blacks. For example, from the mid-seventeenth century, runaway slaves from the neighbouring islands who took refuge in Puerto Rico were declared free by the decision of the Council of the Indies if they accepted baptism and swore loyalty to the Spanish king. This news "attracted all would-be fugitives, so that it became necessary to supply a place for them to establish themselves. The Negro colony in San Mateo de Cangrejos was a result of this and the refugees became some of the most faithful defenders of the Spanish flag" (Figueroa Mercado 1974, 105).

Under a formula called *coartación* (that is, the purchase of freedom in an instalment payments plan), slaves could work for wages during their free time, put their savings in the hands of their owner (charged by law to be its faithful custodian) and eventually purchase their freedom. The free slaves could also buy the liberty of their kinsfolk by this process. In 1848, Governor La Pezuela opened another door to freedom (even if the motive was really to demotivate slaves from rebellion). A lottery was held among the most disciplined slaves from all the *haciendas*, giving the winner his liberty as the prize. A slave who informed about a conspiracy among his fellow slaves was also given his freedom.

The result of all this is that at the date of Emancipation in Puerto Rico (1873), there were only 30,000 enslaved persons needing to be freed. This compares with Martinique where, at its date of Emancipation, there were 85,000, and with Jamaica where the number was 311,000. There is no more dramatic index of the differences in the race/ethnicity pictures in these three Caribbean territories than these comparative statistics.

Free blacks in Puerto Rico participated in public and religious ceremonies. Similarly, according to Diaz (1953, 173–75), all social classes took part in the diversions engaged in by slaves on holidays and Sundays as well as on religious feast days. "On the haciendas, the owners and the *mayorales* (overseers) were present and in the Capital the feasts were held outside the walls until the curfew sounded" (Figueroa Mercado 1974, 235).

More social mixing thus seems to have taken place between the different groups on the island than is considered to have been the case in other areas of the Caribbean. This led to a spread of cultural forms through the different ethnic (and social) groups, resulting in a Puerto Rico which is more culturally homogenous than other Caribbean societies. Figueroa Mercado reports that "groups of free mulattoes danced in the Cathedral without their hats during Corpus Christi, even though the Holy Sacrament was in view" (1974, 100). Though this was suppressed in 1684, it is significant that an obviously African feature of linking dance with religion was already practised by mulattoes and even brought to the very centre of European ethnicity – the cathedral.

The Roman Catholic Church had a different attitude towards slaves than the Protestant churches. In the Spanish colonies, the slave had to receive the catechism, be baptized, married by the church and buried in holy ground. It was forbidden to separate marriages or families under penalty of a fine. The Spanish and Portuguese remained longer under the influence of the church than other European countries, and this affected their political and economic development. According to Little:

> The capitalist spirit, the profit-making motive among the sixteenth century Spaniards and Portuguese, was constantly inhibited by the universal aims and purpose of the Church. This tradition in favour of the old religious criterion of equality is in contrast to the objective, capitalistic attitude of Anglo-Saxon and Germanic countries, such as Britain, the Netherlands, and the United States. (1971, 166–67)

In these Anglo-Saxon and Germanic countries, there was a separation of church and state that contributed to their capitalist industrial and mercantilist development.

For these (and other) reasons, the slaves in the Hispanic Caribbean are said to have been better treated than in the territories under other colonial powers. Those in Puerto Rico are considered to have had especially mild circumstances. This was not altogether for humane, religious or philosophical reasons. The economic situation seems to have contributed and this becomes apparent when Cuba and Puerto Rico are compared. Puerto Rico, as we said above, was always a poor colony, unable to afford many slaves. The owners therefore had a motivation to preserve those they had. Cuban liberal landowners, who agitated for independence, opposed abolition, while their Puerto Rican liberal counterparts supported freedom for the slaves. However, even while sympathetic to slaves, the three leading Puerto Rican liberal abolitionists, José Julián Acosta, Francisco Mariano Quiñones and Segundo Ruiz Belvis, presented to the Spanish Court in April 1867 a report recommending abolition, but which contained the following negative stereotype about blacks:

las gentes de color libres representan en Puerto Rico, al par que uno de los elementos más vigorosos de la población, el elemento de fuerza que auxiliado por la inteligencia, iniciativa y los capitales de los blancos, más grandemente contribuye al bienestar material que hoy disfruta la provincia.

the coloured people represent in Puerto Rico not only one of the most vigorous elements but also the element of strength which, backed up by the intelligence, initiative and the capital of the white people, contributes most grandly to the material well-being which the province enjoys today.

This shows the deep ambivalence of the ruling classes in Puerto Rico. At every point, the economic situation, including the mode of economic production, determined one set of relations with blacks: relatively close interaction, relatively greater opportunities for freedom, milder treatment, support for abolition, and so on. But what could never be superseded was the stereotype of black people related to the notion of their innate inferiority, a notion which we have seen goes as far back as Graeco-Roman antiquity.

The above picture had its countervailing aspects. The Roman Catholic Church may have been liberal when compared with the Anglo-Saxon Protestants, but "records [of whites and blacks] were kept separately and the Negroes and their descendants were called of 'bad race' " (Figueroa Mercado 1974, 255, n. 394). Although the number of freed slaves was relatively high, from 1551 both slave and free black were forbidden to carry arms day or night, as a reaction to slave rebellions. This suggests that either there had been collusion between slaves and free blacks, or there was fear of it. It suggests that there was some consciousness on the part of Africans, or a perception on the part of the white establishment, of a common African ethnicity rising above differences in civil status.

Rebellions continued in the ensuing centuries, though to a less prevalent degree. Following the Haitian Revolution, the pace of rebellions stepped up considerably in the nineteenth century, provoking the following outburst by the mayor of San Juan (Don Pedro Irizarry) which, in the opinion of Figueroa Mercado, "indicated the opinion held by whites of the Negroes" (1974, 256):

The slaves if always free and independent . . . will never stop being bad citizens internally, poor devils and traitors, invisible domestic enemies of their masters, of the native land and the State, astute, vigilant and resolved to commit the most infamous deeds, the most horrifying crimes and the most scandalous perfidies. . . . Just as it is impossible to change their black color to white, it would not be less impossible that their vicious and corrupted hearts should be innocent in

their captivity. He is kept under control, it is true, by force while his numbers
do not exceed or are equal to the free men, but as soon as that terrible moment
arrives, misfortune also ultimately results, and the destruction of the whole island
. . . (Diaz 1953, 212)

Comparative Social History

A general comparison between the Hispanic and the non-Hispanic Caribbean
in terms of their socioeconomic histories is instructive. There is, first of all,
the length and the intensity of the Spanish colonial presence. The Dominican
Republic gained independence in the mid-nineteenth century, and Cuba and
Puerto Rico had their colonial ties with Spain terminated in 1898. Up till then,
these islands experienced the unbroken presence of Spain, although militarily
occupied for brief periods by other European powers. The other powers began
their colonizing adventures in the other islands in the mid-seventeenth century, almost 150 years after the Spaniards had started theirs.

The Spanish came early to Puerto Rico and established their first real
colony in the Americas there. But the plantation, which came to be the basis
of Caribbean societies, remained relatively weak in Puerto Rico until the late
eighteenth century. From 1509 to 1860, only approximately sixty thousand
slaves came to the island. Perhaps 80 per cent of these came after 1800. But
in 1836, slaves accounted for only 11 per cent of the total population.
Censuses between 1765 and 1865 record an average of 10 per cent slaves. In
1860, the importation of slaves ceased, and at emancipation in 1873 only
about 5 per cent of the population were still slaves. On the other hand, after
1830 whites became the largest racial/ethnic group. In 1776, 45.5 per cent of
the population was classified as white; by 1834 this rose to 53.8 per cent. In
1815, a *Cedula de Gracias* (or Royal Decree) encouraged European migration,
bringing to Puerto Rico a large mass of free but impoverished whites. There
has been, therefore, a progressive whitening of Puerto Rico.

There was also a considerable "browning" of the population. In addition
to the forced miscegenation of white males and indigenous and black females,
Spanish laws, as we saw above, favoured manumission which allowed for more
free and consensual mating of persons from different racial groups. The
Hispanic Caribbean in general, and Puerto Rico in particular, may have had
a greater incidence of mixed unions. The fact that there were so many
injunctions against such unions suggests that they were in fact taking place.

The *Código Negro Carolino* (late eighteenth century) ordered that all means should be sought to ensure that black and mulatto slaves marry blacks and mulattoes of the same condition and that white persons could not engage in matrimony with their black and mulatto slaves. It must be noted that all the cases presented as examples of mixed unions (Sued Badillo and Lopez Cantos 1986, 281) are of white males marrying mulatto females, and that the military officers involved were punished by being relieved of their commissions.

On the one hand, there existed in Puerto Rico a real obsession to maintain the purity of the white race, and a great fear that there would no longer be persons eligible to fill certain official (civil and military) and clerical positions reserved for pure white persons. On the other hand, according to Sued Badillo and Lopez Cantos (1986, 282), in spite of these regulatory injunctions, "unequal" marriages (that is between persons of different races/colours) continued and "*la población puertorriqueña se pigmentó poco a poco, pero de manera inexorable*" (the Puerto Rican population darkened gradually, but inexorably).

Interracial social interaction was also facilitated by the existing dominant socioeconomic system (small agricultural holdings, mining, urban commercial activities) which, unlike the plantation system, could not impose rigid controls over the lives of people. Thus the "free coloured" population (*pardos libres, gente libre de color*) constituted from the beginning a much larger percentage of the total population than was the case in the British colonies. This group also grew rapidly in the nineteenth century. In 1860, it accounted for 41.33 per cent of the population (Duany 1985).

The other factors are more controversial, and their impact on the race and ethnicity picture is less clear. Hoetink speaks of "a difference between the Hispanic and non-Hispanic Caribbean in terms of the rhythm of economic evolution" (1985, 58). Mintz suggests that "convincing historical interpretation of any Caribbean social phenomenon will have to be systadial ('same stage') rather than synchronic ('same time'), in character. . . . Jamaican society was escaping from a period of frantic plantation expansion at the start of the nineteenth century, just as Puerto Rico was entering into such a period" (1996, 47). Hoetink develops this idea further:

> Ultimately, virtually all Caribbean societies have witnessed the introduction of modern, large-scale sugar plantations producing for the world market and dependent on black labor, but the paths followed by the two areas [Hispanic and non-Hispanic] in this regard were different. It was not the fact that the

modern sugar plantation was introduced relatively late in the Hispanic Caribbean that made the difference; other societies (Trinidad and the southern United
States) were also latecomers. It was rather that the Hispanic Caribbean had two
periods of booming plantation economy, with a lengthy dividing interregnum
between . . . The first period started immediately after the conquest and lasted
about three-quarters of a century. Many slaves were imported then, and these,
together with the remnants of the aboriginal population, had to work in the
modern sugar mills of the day. In the long period of economic decay that
followed, blacks, Amerindians, and whites were heir to abundant lands and,
away from the cities, they were out of sight and control of metropolitan power
. . . Culturally, it was syncretic, adopting Amerindian and African-derived
cultural objects and ideas, but it retained Spanish as its language and its own
brand of Catholicism, centered on the worship of saints and on private altars,
as its religion. Genetically, it was an interweaving of European, African and
Amerindian strands. These multiple influences were reflected in a local conceptualization in which physical traits ranged from "dark" to "light", different
"types" of which could well manifest themselves within a single family. "Pure"
types gave way to a racial continuum in which, however, the higher social
prestige of "light" color did not disappear. (1985, 58)

Sued Badillo and Lopez Cantos confirm a first period when sugar dominated the socioeconomic life of Puerto Rico. According to them, "the economic sector that moved the slave regime during the second half of the 16th
century was that of the sugar producers" (1986, 111). This was in spite of the
difficulties caused by an insufficient availability of slave manpower. On the
other hand, Duany does not mention a first plantation period for Puerto Rico
and Cuba. He claims that "the islands [Cuba, Española, Puerto Rico] did not
produce [sugar] commercially for the world market until the nineteenth
century. Until then the islands were predominantly settler colonies of strategic
military importance for the defense of the Spanish imperial system" (1985,
101).

Duany mentions only a diversified peasant economy of mixed farming,
cattle raising, and smuggling for Puerto Rico before 1750. This, according to
him, favoured the constant assimilation of "coloured" people into the white
sector and the rapid growth of a fundamentally hybrid, mulatto society. He
adds that

the general poverty and stagnation of the islands socially equalized the majority
of settlers, preventing the formation of the two-class racial structure typical of
plantation societies. A stratification system could not be founded on the clear-

cut opposition between "racial" groups, one Negroid, one Caucasian, if only because a large sector of the population was genetically mixed. (Duany 1985, 101)

Duany's highly cosmetic view of Puerto Rico omits essential details having to do with the way in which power wore a racial cloak. Regardless of the particular economic relations, social relations (urban versus rural, occupation, and so on) or demographic relations, race accounted for a large part of the social order. For example, much is being made by Duany of the emergence of the mulatto class in the Hispanic Caribbean. It is true that, as we have said, the socioeconomic system existing in Puerto Rico produced a relatively large proportion of racially mixed individuals, and that they may have enjoyed relatively higher status in the Spanish colonies than in the British colonies. However, in the first place, this class emerged everywhere in the Caribbean and the Americas, wherever Europeans and Africans came together; indeed, this class became quite significant in the post-emancipation period of the plantation colonies of the British and French (Haiti especially), because of the numerical weakness of the white group (creole and metropolitan). As we have said, it was everywhere seen as a useful buffer between the white masters and the rebellious slaves.

In the second place, the major pattern everywhere was of white males mating with black females. Although the higher percentages of free blacks and mulattoes in the Hispanic Caribbean and particularly in Puerto Rico suggest that the mating was more consensual on the surface in the Hispanic colonies than in the British, French and Dutch, the power relations within the racial/cultural hierarchy meant that there was no marked incidence in the Hispanic colonies of black men mating with white women.

Much of what Hoetink says (cited above) applies to the rest of the Caribbean (and even to the United States), except that, as we have said, the "light" coloured individuals are much more numerous in Puerto Rico and they spread throughout the social strata, even constituting a large part of the independent peasant class (the *jíbaros*). Such a class of independent peasants exists in the non-Hispanic, anglophone Caribbean, but it is mostly black (and Indian in Trinidad and Guyana), has no particular designation (the most frequently used being "country man"), and is not particularly romanticized in the literature, music and art as its members are in Cuba and Puerto Rico.

In the Hispanic Caribbean, the colour hierarchy is, as a schema, the same as in the non-Hispanic Caribbean, but it is true that, again, the numerical significance of the colours/shades is different. In the Spanish colonies, the colours/shades intermediate between black and white rose rapidly and became numerically dominant; whereas in the non-Hispanic Caribbean, with the steady importation of African slaves and insignificant immigration of whites (and probably also given certain psycho-cultural differences between Nordic and Mediterranean Europeans which impacted on degrees and modes of social and sexual intercourse with blacks), it is the black end of the continuum/hierarchy that prospered numerically (with Martinique being a slight exception; see later, chapter 7).

Hoetink's description of the schema for the Dominican Republic fits the Caribbean in general (with some nuances which should be recognized): "Whites (and especially those from the metropolis) were clearly favoured socially over blacks. . . . A color continuum developed within which subtle differences in skin color, hair texture, and facial features were noted and essentially catalogued in an extensive vocabulary, with all its social implications" (1985, 61).

Hoetink later admits that caution should be observed in making any causal connection between the sociohistorical factors and the race/colour/ethnicity picture because

> a continuum like that in Santo Domingo also developed in northeast Brazil, where an export-oriented sugar economy had been established at an early date. Furthermore, some small islands in the archipelago, such as Curaçao, were characterized by socio-racial stratification like that in Saint-Domingue but proved to be unfit for export agriculture; their economy was based on commerce rather than crops, and slavery, though it existed, could not be considered a pillar of their economy. These cases may serve to remind us that, even though economic development seems to exert a strong influence on racial structures and relations, it is not the only shaping force. (1985, 62)

It is evident that the major sociohistorical factor which distinguishes Puerto Rico is that its history is marked by the relatively slow numerical rise of the African population and by the relative numerical strength of the white and mulatto populations. The low demand for African labour is well documented. The free peasant class had developed throughout the seventeenth and eighteenth centuries. So that when the large sugar cane plantations began to develop in the early nineteenth century, largely on the southern plains of the island, "the population density and the general poverty in the rural areas were such that the need for cane cutters could be filled largely by the island's own labor force" (Hoetink 1985, 13).

Racial/Ethnic Constructions in Puerto Rico

Puerto Rico lies at the extreme European pole of an African/European racial/ethnic continuum in the Caribbean. At the other (African) pole are the Maroon nations of Suriname and Jamaica. Puerto Rico occupies this position on the basis of a series of phenotypical, physiognomic, psychological and cultural features. Somatically speaking, the absence, or relatively low levels of melanin dominate. In addition to which, there are more instances of straight hair, thin noses and thin lips than are to be found in other Caribbean territories. Feminine hips are wider in the Caucasian manner (but, interestingly, bellies and bottoms may be pronounced and protrude in the African manner).

There are more claims of European ancestry (Gallego, Canarias, the two Spanish regional sources most frequently espoused) in Puerto Rico than elsewhere. The adjective *hispánico* is also frequently used in reference to Puerto Rican culture. This contrasts with Jamaica, where claims of Scottish ancestry, which used to be proudly made up to four or five decades ago, are hardly ever heard now. And there is no adjective analogous to *hispánico* that any Jamaican uses to refer to his or her historical ethnicity. Possible analogous adjectives (Anglo-Saxon, British, Britannic) are rarely used, and then only guardedly, although one intellectual cynically coined the term "Afro-Saxon" to refer to a particular sociocultural ideological type in the English-speaking West Indies.

The little that is left of cultural traits inherited from Africa (when compared with Jamaica or Haiti) is not enough to support an active Africa-based ethnicity in Puerto Rico. The kind of ethnic/cultural hierarchy that exists in plural Jamaica in the form of a continuum with class, colour, culture mutually reinforcing themselves, does not exist in Puerto Rico. In fact, in Puerto Rico, cultural features inherited from Africa are to a large extent absorbed into the national popular/traditional culture, and are practised and appreciated without regard to race/colour. For example, although it may be the case that the *bomba* as a musical genre originated among the Africans of Puerto Rico, today it is played and enjoyed by Puerto Ricans of all colours.

The Africanness of Puerto Rican culture is particularly recognized in the musical forms *bomba* and, to a lesser extent, *plena,* and in the general appreciation of the drum as a music source. But these forms are not the exclusive property of phenotypically African Puerto Ricans, although *bomba* players may be in the majority dark-skinned persons and the genre is still geographically associated with the southern part of the island, where the large sugar plantations were located and where the majority of dark-skinned Puerto Ricans are still to be found. (It should be noted that, as in other parts of the Caribbean, in Puerto Rico dark-skinned persons are heavily represented among traditional and pop musicians.) Appreciation of and interest in the traditional *bomba* and *plena* are as much determined by variables such as age, ideology and personality (adults, nationalists, conservatives, as opposed to modernistic youths). Foods such as *mofongo* (crushed plantains, frequently called *fu-fu* elsewhere in the Caribbean) and *mondongo* (tripe stew) may be African in origin, but are no longer the particular province of phenotypical Africans.

Africa has always been a controversial factor in the construction of Puerto Rican identity. In the current dynamic situation, there is some support for the notion of the African basis of Puerto Rican culture, and there are groups of artists and musicians who openly proclaim an African identity and an African inspiration for their work.

The iconography of Puerto Rico is predominantly white. The images that are presented in the newspapers, on local television and in outdoor advertising are predominantly white, and reflect the racial homogeneity of the ruling classes. However, other racial images appear in the popular iconography and present an interesting picture of the racial and ethnic problematic of Puerto Rico. Amidst the great variety of Catholic icons, Puerto Rican popular craft artists have taken a special interest in two figures of African origin (although, particularly in the case of one of them, phenotypically transformed to conform more to the Puerto Rican dominant type).

The first is one of the Three Wise Men. Babin (1973, 84) considers them to be "*lo entrañable de nuestra tierra*" (the beloved of our land) and "*soberanos indiscutibles de Puerto Rico*" (undisputed sovereigns of Puerto Rico). Their feast day (6 January) is perhaps even more observed than Christmas day. The Three Kings have been elevated by Puerto Rican wood (and plaster of Paris) carvers to the status of saints (referred to collectively in Puerto Rican folklore as *Los Santos Reyes* [The Holy Kings, The Saint Kings], although individually they do not carry the title *San-* (Saint). The popular Puerto Rican imagination has transformed Melchor into a black king, while Balthasar, the Moorish king in the European tradition, becomes a fair-skinned image. Melchor often appears in a commanding position. He is almost always the one for whom the distinction of being mounted on a white horse is reserved. In addition, he is the main standard-bearer of the national symbols: the flag and the Puerto Rican *cuatro* (a four-stringed instrument).

The Virgin Mary is perhaps most frequently represented in Puerto Rican iconography by the Black Madonna. Among these representations, perhaps the principal one is that of the Virgin as she appeared in the miracle of Hormigueros, which took place in Puerto Rico at the beginning of the seventeenth century. The carvings of Puerto Rican popular art portray the white peasant (*jíbaro*) being saved from a wild bull by the *Virgen de la Monserrate* (as the Black Madonna is called in Spain where she first appeared). In these carvings, the Virgin is dark-skinned but with longish straight-looking hair.

There have been different interpretations of the significance of these two figures – *Los Santos Reyes* and *La Virgen de la Monserrate* – in the folk iconography of the Puerto Rican people. Zenon is at a loss as to how to account for "this special passionate cult of black and brown saints in Puerto Rico" (1974, 225). As we said earlier, Bastide believes that the Black Madonna represents a sorceress, a worker of miracles, a mysterious goddess endowed with extraordinary powers (1968, 38–39). If this is so, it is in keeping with the general stereotype created about Africans.

Brau, assessing the different sources of the Puerto Rican character, attributes to Africa the "resistance, the vigorous sensuality, the superstition and the fatalism of the Puerto Rican" (1956b, 128). (The Indian's contribution is "indolence, a taciturn nature, disinterest, and hospitable sentiments", and Spain "inculcated its chivalrous seriousness, its characteristic haughtiness, its festive tastes, its austere devotion, constancy in the face of adversity and love of country and independence".) Diaz Soler echoes Brau in his assessment: "The African brought with him to these lands [Puerto Rico] the mysterious and sensual rhythms of his music, impregnated with spiritualisms from the heart of Africa, his traditions and customs" (1953, 8).

As we said earlier, the Three Kings were depicted at first in European Christianity as white men. They later came to represent the three great continents: Europe, Asia and Africa. Bastide observes that Balthasar was depicted behind the other two, sometimes kneeling closest to the Christ Child, but never between the other two – "that would have been equivalent to ignoring his color" (1968, 39). We have seen that the transformation in the Puerto Rican folk imagination made Melchor the representative of Africa and gave him the prominent role. There seems to be no other interpretation than that, in the ethnic and cultural and psychological history of the island, Africa is seen as an important, valuable contributor.

On the other hand, there have been some attempts to promote the notion of a white/*indio* binarity in the Puerto Rican cultural and racial heritage, and to deny the African element. There seems to be some influence from the Mexican concept of the *mestizo* representing the racial, cultural and national identity of Mexico. This has remained a romantic myth of a few persons. Zenon cites a number of literary expressions of this myth. For example, a 1939 poem of Clara Lair talks of *Español de América!/ Indioespañol!/. . . Que tus dos semirazas hiervan en mi almirez!* (Spanish of America!/Indio-Spanish!/. . . How your two semiraces boil in my mortar!) And another poem of the same year written by Julio Enrique Inguina proclaims: *Tengo yo sangre india y sangre de español/Nieto soy de una india. . . que dió su corazón a un guapo capitán* (Indian blood have I and blood of a Spaniard/Grandson am I of an Indian woman who gave her heart to a handsome captain). (Note again that in this encounter, the male is white/European and the female non-white.)

As we said earlier, the more common treatment of the concept of *indio* is to redefine it as one of the replacements of the discredited concept of *negro*. Zenon provides a series of excerpts from Puerto Rican writers to show how they have attempted to eliminate *negro* from the Puerto Rican historical identity in favour of an *indio-español* identity (1974, 53–73).

The Language Factor in Ethnic Constructions

Culturally speaking, Puerto Rico has no other language but Spanish, and the notion of a Puerto Rican "language" offering an ethnic or national challenge to Spanish does not evoke any interest. In fact, owing to a perception that the Hispanic culture and language are threatened by English, there is a marked interest or anxiety for the preservation of the "purity" of the Spanish language in Puerto Rico. A short column entitled *Dígalo así* (Here's how you should say it) appears in one of the daily newspapers, in which the columnist regularly inveighs against anglicisms that occur in Puerto Rican usage and strongly advises adherence to a Castillian norm.

This linguistic homogeneity is a very important feature that distinguishes the Hispanic islands generally from the rest of the Caribbean, where there is typically a linguistic and cultural divide between the elite and the masses. This may range from a complete multilingual situation such as exists in Suriname (where the elite official language, Dutch, is not related to the "creole" mass vernacular) to what is called a "(post-)creole continuum" such as is claimed to exist in Jamaica. (Opinion is divided as to whether the Jamaican situation should be interpreted as a continuum or as bilingual. Although there is no clear categorical separation in usage between the official language, English, and the mass vernacular, there is other evidence to support the notion that two languages do exist in Jamaica.) The "French-speaking" territories (Haiti and the French Overseas Departments) lie in between (see Alleyne 1985).

The language issue in the Hispanic islands is often simplistically stated in terms of "there being no creole language there". This statement fails to recognize that in the wider concept of the Caribbean, which includes the South and Central American littoral washed by the Caribbean Sea, a creole language does exist in the form of *el palenquero,* spoken by the descendants of Maroons in a community called Palenque de San Basilio in northern Colombia. And the language Papiamentu spoken in the Netherland Antilles (Curaçao, Aruba, Bonaire) is lexically based on dialects of the south-west of the Iberian peninsular. At the time when Papiamentu was being formed, the apparently clear distinction between what are now called Spanish and Portuguese did not exist. "Spanish" and "Portuguese" are the result of the standardization of specific regional dialects of the peninsula. Papiamentu is historically based on the dialects of the south-western region of the peninsula, that is, neither exclusively on what is now called Spanish (or *castellano*) nor on what is now called Portuguese.

The more fruitful way of posing the question is to ask what factors have led to the relatively advanced linguistic assimilation of Africans in Puerto Rico, compared with the continuing language-based ethnicity of the descendants of Africans elsewhere in the Caribbean and in San Basilio. We have already stated what some of these factors might be. There are still today a number of linguistic features occurring in the speech of Puerto Ricans which may not be restricted to persons of African descent, but which may be survivals from an earlier period when Africans in Puerto Rico did have a distinct dialect (Alvarez

Nazario 1961). In some parts of the former colonial world, local norms have emerged to challenge the colonial standard language norm in an assertion of new national identities. The United States is a good example of this. Norway is another example, having rejected Danish in favour of its own local variant, now called Norwegian. Both English Canada and French Canada are in the process of trying to define national language norms.

The picture in Latin America is quite different. There is a marked effort to preserve the unity of the Spanish language and not to recognize highly idiosyncratic regional features (especially, in the case of Puerto Rico, anglicisms). Latin American countries are represented on the Academia Real de la Lengua Española (Royal Academy of the Spanish Language), the regulatory authority for monitoring the Spanish language. This has been very effective in preventing the fragmentation of Spanish into several official national languages.

More on Racial/Ethnic Construction

There is other evidence of a strong cultural orientation in Puerto Rico towards Spain and Europe. There is at least one radio station that plays "classical" music almost twenty-four hours a day every day. European Christianity is universally adhered to, with Roman Catholicism dominating (but with a growing presence of Protestant churches which have come to the island as a result of the influence of the United States). There are no syncretic religions in Puerto Rico of the kind found in Jamaica (Pukumina, Revival), Haiti (Vaudoun), Trinidad (Shango) and other Caribbean societies. There are some practices under the name *Santería*. Although these are related to the Cuban practices, the Puerto Rican phenomenon in no way constitutes a religion. There are also practices which harness the spiritual forces for the purposes of carrying out acts of health management, social problem solving, and so on, known as *brujería* (witchcraft), or *espiritismo* (spiritism). These may be remnants of religious beliefs and practices brought by Africans to the island.

In spite of these objective socioeconomic and demographic factors that make Puerto Rico a special case in the Caribbean, or at least place it at one end of a race/ethnicity continuum, some of the essential features that characterize the Caribbean, historically and at the contemporary period, are quite evident.

The racial hierarchy has been and still is intact. From the inception of Puerto Rican post-Columbian society, the colour hierarchy inherited from Europe and reinforced by slavery was established. The cleric Fray Inigo Abbad y Lasierra (n.d.) is clear about the particularly low position occupied by blacks in the hierarchy. He mentions the two categories of slave and free, but makes no distinction in terms of their condition:

> . . . con todo no hay cosa más afrentosa en esta isla que el ser negro o descendiente de ellos. Un blanco insulta a cualquiera de estos impunemente con las expresiones mas vilipendiosas; algunos amos los tratan con un rigor indigno, recreándose en tener siempre levantada la vara de tiranos, de que resultan la infidelidad, deserción y el suicidio.

> . . . all in all, there is nothing more insulting on this island than to be a negro or the offspring of one. A white man insults anyone of them with impunity using the most humiliating expressions; some owners treat them with unworthy harshness, taking delight in always raising the tyrannical rod; the result is disloyalty, desertion and suicide.

There is throughout the Spanish colonial period ample evidence of the harsh treatment meted out to black slaves. Even if it can be established that it was milder compared with the treatment reserved for slaves under the Nordic Protestant regimes (English and Dutch), there is no doubt that Puerto Rican slavery was neither benign nor gentle. Whether or not racism started out as an economically determined superstructure is debatable. What is a fact is that it was a hostility directed at the very person of the slave, not at his condition.

The *Gaceta del Gobierno de Puerto Rico* of 3 June 1848 published the *Bando de Prim contra la raza Africana* (The Proclamation of [Governor] Prim against the African race). It speaks of the *"ferocidad estúpida de la raza africana . . . sentimientos que le son naturales [son]: el incendio, el asesinato y la destrucción"* (stupid ferocity of the African race . . . their natural inclinations [are]: arson, assassination and destruction). This was one of a series of *bandos* which prescribed severe penalties for free or enslaved Africans. These laws were more draconian than any other slave laws.

As in other parts of the Caribbean, the major change in the schema over the years has been the evaluation of the mulatto. We have seen that the naming of the category reflects the low esteem in which "mixed breeds" were held. But the dominant pattern was one of ambiguity and ambivalence. The cleric Fray Inigo Abbad y Lasierra in the first (or earliest surviving) written history of Puerto Rico (n.d., *c.* late eighteenth century) expresses quite favourable opinions on the qualities of the mulatto, whom he describes (predictably) as the issue of a white man and black woman (*hijo de blanco y negra*):

> *Altos y bien formados . . . [entre ellos] hay muchos expeditos y literales para discurrir y obrar. . . se han distinguido en todos los tiempos por sus acciones y son ambiciosos de honor.*

> tall and well built . . . [among them] are many who are prompt and literate for speaking and working . . . they have distinguished themselves at all times by their actions and they are zealous about honour.

However, the cleric goes on to describe the mulatto's colour as *oscuro desagradable* (unpleasantly dark). And, according to him, the local whites (*los blancos criollos*) treat the mulattoes with contempt.

The Hispanic legislation covering slavery, which is contained in the document entitled *El Código Negro Carolina* of the late eighteenth century, does not distinguish between blacks and different degrees of mixture. They all have the same status *vis-à-vis* the white population. The legislation prescribes that

> *se hace necesario establecer la subordinación y disciplina más severa de ella [la población negra] hacia la población blanca, como base fundamental de la política interior de las colonias de agricultores del Nuevo Mundo. . . . Por tanto, todo negro esclavo o libre, pardo, primerizo, segundón o tercerón y en adelante será tan sumiso y respetuoso a toda persona blanca como si cada una de ellas fuera su mismo amo o señor del siervo.*

> it is necessary to establish the most rigid subordination and discipline of the black population toward the white population, as the fundamental basis of the internal policy for the colonies of farmers in the New World. . . . Therefore every black whether slave or free, every "*pardo*", etc. [different degrees of racial mixture] will be as submissive and respectful to every white person as if each one of them were his own master and lord.

Reporting on the legislation, Sued Badillo and Lopez Cantos state that the law considered every coloured individual, without regard for his greater or lesser degree of pigmentation, as an inferior person (1986, 245).

One apparent unique feature in the Hispanic colonies was the way in which legal rights and restrictions were doled out to different fragments of whiteness in the population. The Hispanic system of *castas* was an attempt to regulate a system that emerged and existed by convention and consensus in the British and French colonies. This caste system operated in different forms in different

Hispanic colonies. In the Caribbean, where there was no substantial indigenous population to regulate, there were fewer *castas*, terminologically distinguished, than in South and Central America. Basically, Puerto Rico had *blanco* (white), *mulato*, *pardo* (a degree removed from *mulato* in terms of whiteness) and *negro*. In South America, membership in a particular caste determined one's standing within the pecking order and one's relations with the other castes (Jimenez 1966, 12).

Puerto Rico was minimalist in the execution of this system, retaining the essential feature of privilege for whites and discrimination and restrictions for the rest, whether free or slave. Free blacks, and *pardos* (*mulatos* and other *castas*), as descendants of slaves, were legally and socially discriminated against. They were restricted in the work they could do, in their freedom of movement, the places they could attend and live in, whom they could marry, the bearing of arms, their access to institutions, the clothing they could wear – in short every aspect of their lives was carefully regulated (Jimenez 1996, 13). The *blanco* caste was most rigidly guarded and the most earnestly sought after, and the practice of "passing", now viewed as a characteristically North American phenomenon, was very early practised in the Hispanic colonies, where the forging and fixing of documents to assert whiteness was prevalent.

On the other hand, as we suggested earlier, social interaction between races and colours seems to have been less restricted in the Hispanic colonies than in the British colonies (with the French colonies lying in between). Manumission was a more common practice, particularly by Hispanic slave owners of their mulatto children. Cross-caste marriages were discouraged, but they nonetheless occurred with much greater frequency than in the British colonies.

The "race" towards whiteness, which was a feature of all societies in the Americas, was perhaps more pronounced in the Hispanic colonies and especially in Puerto Rico, where relations were more fluid because of the particular sociohistorical circumstances. Mid-eighteenth-century visitors reported that Puerto Rico had "a lack of families of refined and pure ancestry", and that even among the scant white families there were few "without mixture of all types of bad blood" (Jimenez 1996, 13). The system of mating seems to have been quite complex, influenced by several factors. In the anxiety to "*mejorar la raza*" (improve the race), deserting white sailors were assured a warm welcome by the inhabitants, who offered their daughters for wives even if the suitors had nothing to recommend them other than their whiteness and pure Spanish ancestry. The titles of white and Spaniard were rich property in themselves (Abbad y Lasierra n.d.).

Then there was the scarcity of white women, coupled with the perceived greater sexual attractiveness of the mulatto women. The Spanish patriarchal system allowed a child to inherit the condition (caste) of his or her father. According to Jimenez:

> In 1757, for example, clerics were instructed in how to register births, marriages . and deaths in the two parish ledgers, one for blancos and another for negros and pardos, free or enslaved. In the event of a cross-caste marriage between a blanco and a pardo whose parents were free, it was to be registered in the "white" ledger. If either parent had been a slave, and the pardo was male, the marriage would be listed in the "black" ledger; if it were the female, then the marriage would be in the "white" book. Any children of the marriage would then be classified according to the ledger in which the marriage had been registered. These regulatory prescriptions suggest a certain receptivity to pardos legalizing their unions with blancos and can be seen as both an accommodation to the popular preference for "colored" women as (fetishized) sexual partners (a preference which had much to do with their numerical preponderance), and as indicative of the greater value placed on the male's racial caste position. (1996, 14)

Puerto Rico has been caught up in a struggle throughout its history to manage its racial and ethnic condition, and to construct and define its racial and ethnic identity. On the one hand, Puerto Rico's historical circumstances permitted a degree of assimilation that has resulted in a degree of ethnic and racial homogeneity unknown elsewhere in the Caribbean. Puerto Rico does not have the wide diversity of cultural forms, in religion, language and music, that is to be found in Jamaica. It has not had its initial plural society compounded by the arrival of any significant numbers of people from Asia.

Though it does have a colour/class pyramid of social structure of a pattern typical of the Caribbean, there are some special features in the Puerto Rican pyramid. Blacks occupy the bottom of the socioeconomic scale, but they are not alone there and do not even dominate. In fact, as we have said, all colours are to be found there. Relatively few blacks have moved into the higher socioeconomic brackets. Geographic mobility has also been restricted. There are concentrations of blacks that preserve the settlement patterns of previous centuries going back to the period of slavery. Loiza Aldea, for example, is a black town with a black ethnicity. And the south and south-west coastal regions, where the large sugar plantations were established, have a greater number of darker-skinned persons than other regions.

Interpretations of Puerto Rican Society and Racial System

There have been several interpretations of Puerto Rican society in terms of the role which race plays. The general Latin American myth of racial and cultural assimilation, and of psychological assimilation manifested in the alleged absence of racial prejudice, is very strong among the general population. It is true that there is no publicly sanctioned institutional racism in the form of the exclusion of blacks or any other groups from the institutions of the society. However, it is still the case that certain important institutions are not frequented by many blacks. This is the case, for example, with the main campus of the state university, where Puerto Rican blacks are grossly under-represented.

The Latin American myth of assimilation is the national, official, public position. The vast majority of persons will overtly articulate the opinion that racism does not exist, and even that separate races do not exist in Puerto Rico. "We are all Puerto Ricans" expresses a dominant ideology, a subjectivity that is based variously on the noble desire to have one unified nation and identity, on the fear of being lumped together with the United States as a racist society, and on the desire to preserve a status quo which benefits the ruling classes.

The objective situation may be otherwise. There has been an ongoing debate in academic circles, in the press, and among the population at large, in which the counter position is forcefully presented. Evidence, in the form of personal testimonies, is sometimes adduced. It is not the aim of this study to pronounce definitively on this issue, however important it may be. Suffice it to say that it depends on how we define racism and racial prejudice, and what degrees of feeling and behaviour must exist before we can say that we are dealing with a pathological, hostile racism prejudicial to the victims, rather than mild controlled colour-centrism.

The other complication is the general one, typical of the plantation societies of the Caribbean: the extent to which we are dealing with class prejudice (classism) rather than race prejudice (racism). As we noted, there is certainly in Puerto Rico some degree of the correlation between colour/race and social class that is to be found generally in the Caribbean. As in other parts of the region, the correlation is not absolute and categorical, in the sense that some persons near the black end of the colour continuum have moved into the upper echelons of society. But these are still viewed as remarkable exceptions; they are individuals who have made it in spite of the system of preference and privilege which favours persons near the white end of the continuum; they are few enough that their names are well known and remembered.

More significantly, the lower echelons of Puerto Rican society are populated by persons of light complexion. In fact, a *jibaro*, the Puerto Rican peasant, may be blue-eyed and have blond hair, owing to the particular historical demographics of the country. The picture, therefore, is that the majority of darker-skinned persons belong to the lower socioeconomic strata and the less dark to light-skinned population is distributed throughout all the strata. This picture is reinforced by the presence of a large number of migrants from the Dominican Republic who, by residence and occupation, belong to the least privileged stratum and enhance the correlation between dark skin tone and low socioeconomic status.

Whether or not racism exists, and whether or not it is a more powerful theory of Puerto Rican society to see it as class-based rather than race/colour-based, the significant fact is that there is a social, aesthetic, and even moral value hierarchy corresponding to skin colour (and other phenotypical features such as hair texture, shape of nose, shape and size of lips), regardless of the fact that some – relatively few – individuals of dark skin, woolly hair, flat noses and full lips may have achieved middle-level social status.

There is a general agreement among Puerto Ricans that, even if it is the case that racism does exist in Puerto Rico, the racial system is different from that of the United States. The American system has been described as biological, that is the racial categories have a biological (now, more properly, a genotypic) criterion, however irrational the criterion of one drop of blood may be, and however difficult or impossible it is to apply it in all cases. On the other hand, the Caribbean is said to have a system in which categories are socially determined. Puerto Rico (and the Dominican Republic), as we shall see, would be a special case, and the reverse of that of the United States, in that one drop of white blood makes you non-black; so that there are virtually no "blacks" recognized in Puerto Rico (especially if other phenotypical features such as straight hair, thin noses and lips are present).

These views are simplifications of both systems. The American system is a biological one, but the frontiers between the categories are blurred and indeterminate, since they are beyond the perception of ordinary people; hence the prevalent practice of "passing". Persons consciously and deliberately pass, and others have been passed by parents who keep their genetic history secret. The criterion is specific to whites and blacks and has no applicability in the case of other groups. One drop of Native American blood matched with Caucasian blood makes you white, or at least mixed; and one drop of black blood matched with Native American makes you Native American, or at least mixed; and so on – the categories are quite arbitrary. In this sense, the American system is a socially constructed one.

In addition, there is a colour/somatic hierarchy in the United States by which the closer one approximates to the Caucasian norm, even while being classified as black, or mixed, or whatever, the higher one's social status and the greater the preference and privilege one enjoys. This holds both for the white reference group and for the Negro reference group. Within the latter, children learn from an early age that "if you white, you right; if you brown, stick around; if you black, stand back". In Charleston, for example, there were different churches for light- and dark-skinned African Americans, and traces of this still exist.

Although, as in the Caribbean, there was some degree of correlation between social class and skin colour, in the past skin colour superseded class as a more powerful determinant of church affiliation. And although today class may have gained more diagnostic power, there are still significant traces of the determining role of skin colour. Among African Americans, as among Caribbean peoples in general, there is still a marked tendency for successful dark-skinned males to choose lighter-skinned females as mates, responding in this way to the "light" bias in the aesthetic and social value systems.

In the white reference group, it is sufficient to look at the iconography of mass media advertising to know that a light complexion, long straight hair, thin lips, thin noses and flat bottoms are compulsory for African American models. Vanessa Williams, the African American Miss America and a successful film personality, epitomizes those features. An American Broadcasting Corporation (ABC) news special broadcast on 17 April 1997 reported the results of an enquiry into the persistent role of "skin tone" (as it was called) in the American social order. It reported on matters such as the enormous size of the skin bleach business; that dark models do not get much work; that light-skinned African Americans earn more than their dark-skinned counter-parts and that employers believe that if they employ a lighter-skinned African American, he or she would be more acceptable to clients and other persons (black or white) with whom the company has to deal. It reported also on a specific study in which white respondents were shown different photographs of the same African American person with light and dark skin tone. They were asked to assess the different images on a scale of "happy", "sociable", "smart", "successful", and "moral". The lighter skin tone was consistently rated more highly.

This is no different from Puerto Rico and the rest of the Caribbean, and the rest of the non-African world. It is based on the socialization of perception and on social value consensus. To the extent that institutional racism may now be absent from both the American and the Caribbean societies, the two systems may be moving quite close to each other.

The United States, therefore, really has two systems. One is a binary system based on an alleged biological purity but yet, in the final analysis, socially constructed. The second is a continuum system based on a colour hierarchy with a range of social, economic, aesthetic and moral values about which there is consistent consensus across the two components, black and white, of the binary system. Puerto Rico may be unique in the Caribbean insofar as it lacks the binary system or at least tries to deny its existence. In any case it certainly is not based on an overall notion of "one drop of black blood".

In Puerto Rico, there are also in reality two systems interwoven. On the one hand, a kind of one-drop-of-black-blood system exists, especially in small rural communities where everyone may know everyone else's background and where, for example, marriages have been forbidden on racial grounds because the racial ancestry of one of the partners is known to contain some degree of black. There is in this case some anxiety over the possibility of recessive genes appearing in the offspring. In the other subsystem, especially in modern Puerto Rico, anonymity (including ancestral anonymity) may result in physical appearance being the only criterion of social evaluation. In the process of denial, one drop of white blood makes you a non-Negro in Puerto Rico. So, as we said above, there are virtually no "negroes" in Puerto Rico; no person is willingly and unhesitatingly assigned to this binary category, especially if he or she has "good hair". This denial was officialized in 1930, when the census changed the racial categories in its surveys by removing the category "negro".

However, the categories in Puerto Rico and their terminological representation are more complex than in the United States, with different phenotypical features intersecting, reinforcing or cancelling one another. For example, in Puerto Rico, straight hair (or *pelo bueno*, good hair, as it is called) can virtually nullify dark skin (but not too dark skin), while light complexion may not have an equal effect in nullifying negroid-type hair (*pelo malo*, bad hair). The value of hair texture may be higher in Puerto Rico than in the United States. Even within the category of "good" hair, there are different levels of social value, in addition to aesthetic preference.

The Puerto Rican and North American racial systems are not independent of each other. There are two ways in which the latter has influenced and continues to influence the former. First, the United States occupied Puerto Rico in 1898 and exercised direct political control. There has been some lessening of political influence, but the American presence is still very strong, especially at the level of corporate business activity. According to Zenon (1974, 128), American business executives tried to install North American-type racism in the enterprises they controlled in Puerto Rico.

The second avenue of American influence is the experience of Puerto Ricans in the United States, which may be causing some shift in their interpretation of the island system. This is extremely complex and difficult to grasp. On the one hand, American Black Power has found no resonance in Puerto Rico. Stokely Carmichael, who visited Puerto Rico in the 1960s, was extremely disappointed with the muted response he received. Even Martin Luther King Jr could not arouse Puerto Ricans to the cause of civil rights for blacks on the island. On the other hand, Puerto Ricans in the United States are confronted with that binary subsystem. While some, not having been accepted as white by the US system, continue to reject this system and opt for a special ethnic/racial categorization as Hispanic or Puerto Rican, others (the more dark skinned) may accommodate themselves to it, falling in with either the African American or the West Indian reference groups.

The presence of Puerto Ricans (and other Hispanics) in the United States has affected the binary, bipolar subsystem there by forcing the creation of another special category, intermediate between black and white. By rejecting the classification of Puerto Ricans as white, the bipolar subsystem reinforces the colour continuum subsystem by focusing on the intermediate zones. However, the influence of the United States leads Puerto Ricans to perceive and to think in binary bipolar terms. It is among Puerto Rican scholars at

North American universities, and among returning migrants to the island, that one is most likely to hear an open representation of the Puerto Rican system as bipolar, and the open articulation of the opinion that racial discrimination and prejudice exist in Puerto Rico with blacks (both Dominican and Puerto Rican) as the victims.

There have been different interpretations of the race situation in Puerto Rico in the sociological literature. Seda records a number of them, some of dubious scientific credentials proposed by North American journalistic visitors to the island, who claim that racial categories do not exist and that therefore there is no racial prejudice (1976, 196 sqq.). This interpretation also claims that the racial criterion in the social structure of Puerto Rico is superseded by the criterion of social class, and that therefore there is social prejudice rather than race prejudice.

Duany offers a Marxist interpretation of Puerto Rican society that arrives basically at the same conclusion as that noted above. According to him,

> since populations become culturally differentiated as a result of their economic and social adaptation to different environments, ethnic boundaries are linked to competition for scarce resources . . . ethnic relations cannot be conceptualized outside of class relations . . . Puerto Rico blurs the distinctions between black and white to stress the importance of property in ethnic relations. (1985, 18)

He concludes that "upper and lower strata of [Hispanic] societies were not rigidly divided along racial lines . . . Physical differences did not emerge as stigmas that could transcend similarities in class positions and occupation" (p. 18).

This view is supported by Mintz (1974) and Knight (1970). However, it fails to recognize that the negative connotations of black inherited from Graeco-Roman antiquity, and the stigma of black and other associated phenotypical features coming from the equating of black with slave, remain in Puerto Rico up to today. Puerto Ricans have done a lot to remove this stigma, but they have done so by virtually removing "black" from the national symbolization.

Duany provides a highly informative account and analysis of the social history of Puerto Rico and Cuba, and relates this in very insightful ways to the question of race and ethnicity. In contrasting Puerto Rico with Cuba, Duany proposes that "in the Cuban context, impurity of blood came to mean bad race, African origin was slave status. Slavery was regarded as a stain that contaminated a slave's descendants, regardless of the actual physical appearance." He adds that "such a pigmentocracy based on the principle of descent did not evolve in a society dominated by the free wage-earning laborer as was Puerto Rico" (1985, 19).

Duany re-emphasizes this point repeatedly:

> In Puerto Rico especially, the distinction between black and white never over-rode the distinction between landed and landless. Considering that more than one-third of the island's propertied persons in 1860 were black, one can see that social class – not skin color or family origin – was the crucial cleavage in Puerto Rico's mixed society. . . . Class served as the single most important category for social interaction in Puerto Rico. The Puerto Rican masses did not generally adopt race as the idiom for expressing differences in power, prestige and property. (1985, 22–30)

He does not make a working distinction between race and ethnicity, and between categorial elements of social structure and social values. What he says about the blurring of boundaries and the subordination of ethnic relations to class relations is valid for ethnicity. As for race, we have proposed that biological or genotypic race has given way to a phenotypical continuum whose poles retain the bipolarity of black and white. Duany is very categorical in his conclusions rather than nuanced, as the Puerto Rican situation, past and present, seems to require.

Duany does, however, seem at least to recognize the correlation of black both with low social status (in the social structure) and with low value in the psychological value system, that is, regardless of the social status of the individual. He says that "Puerto Ricans seem to have developed a creole ethos tolerant of the mulatto group but scornful of the black sector, which continues to be placed in the lowest social category of all" (1985, 29). In this, he seems to agree with Lewis (1963) and Hoetink (1967). He adds that "it is not so much the social treatment of the negro as that of the mulatto which came to distinguish the Puerto Rican from the Cuban racial classification system" (1985, 30).

Other scholars present a different picture of race in Puerto Rico. They talk of racial awareness, racial prejudice and even racial discrimination. Seda (1961, 1976, 1980) and Zenon (1974) are among the best-known writers, and both mention a host of others who attest to the existence of this phenomenon. Seda (1976) reports and analyses the responses of a group of Puerto Ricans to fourteen cards containing photographs "representing every possible racial type" in Puerto Rico. They were asked to group photographs of persons belonging to the same race. He reports a high level of consensus in the identification of two racial categories *blanco* and *negro*. Almost 60 per cent of the black and white interviewees reported that there were two "races" in Puerto Rico. Only 30 per cent of the "intermediate" (mixed) interviewees reported the existence of two races. Seda concludes that there is a perceptual tendency towards racial bipolarization (with an intermediate category which is blurred) and he attributes this to North American influences.

This seems to contradict the view presented above, that the category of *negro* is denied in Puerto Rico and that it is redefined as "*trigueno*" or "*indio*". But in fact we may be dealing here with different conceptualizations of *negro* (and of *blanco*): racial, ethnic, colour, class. The difference in conceptualization may also be in terms of *negro* as an active structural component of the contemporary Puerto Rican society, as against *negro* as an historical strand in the building of Puerto Rican race and culture. Persons may either admit or deny the existence of *negro* depending on the nature of the conceptualization which is involved. Puerto Ricans are strongly aware of their African background and the possibility of African blood in their veins (and African features in their phenotype). Different reactions are possible: among them, hide it, deny it, admit it only as one part (of varying significance in the opinion of different persons) of the "heritage", admit it as the fundamental basis of Puerto Rican ethnic and cultural identity. The *abuela* (grandmother) is both hidden (with constant fear of her existence being revealed) and admitted.

There is indeed some degree of racial bipolarization. Social problems debated by intellectuals, scholars, journalists and others, are often posed in terms of discrimination against *negros* (blacks) in Puerto Rico, or in terms of the monopoly enjoyed by *blancos* (whites) in the upper echelons of government and the private sector. For example, in an article appearing in the San Juan daily *El Nuevo Dia* (12 May 1997, 50) and entitled *La Marginación del Negro*, the author says the following:

> [P]ara propósito de discusión solamente, se pueden obviar las dificultades que existen para clasificar a una persona por etnía y trabajar con rasgos genéricos observables que describen al negro. Los individuos situados en categorías marginales con características de más de una etnia, no se consideran.

> [F]or the purpose of this discussion only, we can skirt the difficulties which exist in the classification of persons on the basis of ethnicity and work with observable

generic features which describe the black person. We shall not consider those individuals who are placed in marginal categories with characteristics from more than one ethnic group.

The author goes on to complain that the twenty-eight cabinet ministers are all *blancos*. He asks: "Is there in Puerto Rico no black person capable of carrying out these responsibilities? Why has no one, white or black, asked for an explanation of such an obvious reality?" He advises *negros* to respect themselves and demand their rights:

> *Esto debe ser la consigna y actitud de los negros, sin utilizar el eufemismo "de color", para alterar variables claves en la toma de decisiones sociales a nivel macro.*

> This should be the duty and stance of black people, without using the euphemism "coloured", in order to alter the key variables in social decision-making at the macro level.

The author recognizes the phenotypical diversity in Puerto Rico but superimposes on this, or abstracts from this, a bipolar structure of black and white. It is, however, interesting to note that in a rejoinder some days later, another commentator used the sole community of Loiza Aldea to represent the black community in her pleas for the end to racial discrimination.

As long as Loiza Aldea remains as a community with a high degree of endogamy (probably forced, since its members are not particularly sought after as mates by other groups), with the most appreciated Puerto Rican festival, and with a generally recognized African-based ethnicity actualized by its music, cuisine, and especially its Santiago Festival, there will be a focus for the assertion of the notion of an active "black" racial/ethnic pole in a fundamentally bipolar Puerto Rico. To the extent that this is reinforced by the presence of black Dominicans holding low social status positions, and associated in the popular prejudicial stereotyping with crime, drugs and prostitution, overt racism will continue and strengthen in Puerto Rico.

The Representational System of Race and Ethnicity

Race, colour, class and phenotype are the parameters used in the construction of the representational system in Puerto Rico. These are woven into a very complex lexico-semantic structure. Colour is the main parameter, the structure being built chiefly around terms referring to this. But the terms do not remain semantically stable. They shift constantly in meaning when other features, such as phenotype, class, and even the psychological state of the speaker, enter into the construction and representation of the "other". Thus the same person may be referred to variously by virtually all the terms, depending on how the relevant parameters are perceived by the person doing the representation; similarly, one's representation of one's self may differ completely from that made by other persons.

In other words, the system of representation has, as a point of departure, the perceived skin colour of the individual. The perception then shifts to other phenotypical features, such as hair texture and colour, nose, lips, eyes. This may lead to some adjustment of the classification. If the person's social class status is perceived, that may lead to a further adjustment. And finally, if the person's nationality or country of origin is known, it may lead to a classification *negro* in the case of Dominicans and persons from the Lesser Antilles, or *blanco* in the case of Europeans and white Americans. The other motivating factor is psychological: if one wishes to flatter, there may be further adjustment. Finally, different ideologies in the speaker (conservative, nationalist, radical, and so on) may lead to still further adjustment.

All the terms may be used, and indeed are frequently used, as forms of address, with strong affective connotations. Ironically, only the term *blanquito* (the diminutive form of *blanco*) has a pejorative connotation as a form of address (cf. "whitey" used in Jamaica, other parts of the Caribbean and in the United States of America). By far the most frequent in use is *negro*, preferably in one of its diminutive forms *negrito, negrín*, which enhances its affective value. Both the range of these basic colour terms and their use as forms of address distinguish Puerto Rico (and the Hispanic islands) from the rest of the Caribbean.

Historically, at the birth of the Columbian era, the terms used to refer to race and ethnicity in Puerto Rico are *negro, blanco, africano, español, ladino, indio*. There is some use of ethnic names from Africa in the official records of the slave trade, and there is evidence that slave owners were aware of ethnic differences among Africans and of the stereotypes associated with them. However, these ethnic names – Congo, Yoruba, and so on – did not survive for very long in Puerto Rico. They were subsumed under the one generic term, *africano*. However, two such names have been immortalized in Puerto Rican oral culture: "*El que no tiene dinga tiene mandinga*" (If you don't have Dinga, you have Mandinga) is a "wise saying" referring to the presence of

African blood in all Puerto Ricans: If you do not have it from one ethnic group (Dinga), you have it from some other (Mandinga). Mandingo is a major ethnic group from the area of Mali and was well represented among slaves reaching the Caribbean in the first period of the trade.

Negro first of all acquired (or had already acquired) an ethnic meaning: African. The term *africano* ceased very early to be used as a form of address and as a form of third person reference, replaced in both cases by *negro*. *Negro* then acquired a social meaning: slave. This was facilitated by the removal of the *indios* from the condition of enslavement. *Esclavo negro* (black [colour/race] slave or African [ethnic] slave) was simply reduced to *negro*. The process of de-ethnification of Africans had begun, as well as the final "denigration" of blackness. Africans and their descendants had to embark on a process of re-ethnification, which, as we have said, continues up to today.

We have here also the beginnings of a class structure that was to dominate the Caribbean and wherever else Africans were taken as slaves, that is, the correlation of race and class: of *negro* with lower-class status. This is presented often as a problem in sociological analysis, but it is really more importantly a problem of social injustice which is still only slowly being corrected.

In Puerto Rico (as well as in Martinique and Haiti, in the case of *nègre*), *negro* underwent an enormous semantic change. It assumed the neutral universal meaning of "person", "fellow", for third person reference. As a form of second person address, it was used as a universal (that is, non-racial-, non-ethnic-specific) term, and further acquired a connotation of affection and endearment. In this universal meaning, "fellow", it is used almost exclusively in the masculine form (reflecting the male bias of language). But as a form of affection and endearment, it is often used in the feminine form.

Ironically, in its universal meaning, the term *negro* is used least frequently and most hesitatingly in addressing or in reference to black-skinned persons. This is presumably because it could then be misinterpreted as a racial/colour term and cause offence. That is to say that the original meaning, "black", is still latent. In cases such as this (that is, when a black-skinned person is being addressed), it would most likely be replaced by the euphemism *trigueño* (wheat-coloured). "*Ay, negrito, ven acá!*" (Hey, pal, come here!) can thus be used to beckon anyone except a black-skinned person. For a black person, "*Ay, trigueñito, ven acá!*" would be preferred.

It is plausible to assume that the semantic shift begins with expressions such as *mis negros, nuestros negros, sus negros* (my, our, your slaves). When used in addressing, or in reference to, younger persons, or in a domestic context by the master or mistress of the house, the term would have expressed a paternalism and patriarchy which, together with brutality, were part of the contradictory structure of slave society. There is still a tendency in Puerto Rico for *negro* and *negrito* to be used, particularly in reference to persons younger than the speaker. From paternalistic condescension to sarcastic, hypocritical affection and to real affection are short steps. Why these steps were taken in the Hispanic and French colonies but not in the British ones, is not easy to determine. There was an incipient use of *nigger* as a term of affection, but this was confined to African Americans and was more a cynical adoption of an opprobrious term by the victims than a real semantic shift. "Darkies" also emerged in the United States but did not survive. In this area may lie the best evidence of a difference between the Latin/Mediterranean peoples and the Germanic peoples of north-west Europe in their psychological attitudes towards slaves.

The semantic drift of *negro* left a space open for a term which could neutrally express the colour black. This space was taken by *prieto*. *Prieto* refers only to colour and has none of the negative (nor affective) connotations of *negro*. It is not used in reference to negative things in the outside world such as blackmail, blacklist, and so on. These are still reserved for *negro*. *Prieto* does not express race or ethnicity. The semantic evolution of *negro*, and the existence of the non-racial, non-ethnic term, *prieto*, represent the psychological exclusion and denial of the existence of ethnic and racial black Africans in Puerto Rican society. The expression *un negro prieto* may seem tautological, but, as a result of these different developments, the expression is quite possible and logical, and is frequently used in Puerto Rico. It either means a dark-skinned fellow (that is, *negro* in its neutral, universal meaning) or it refers to a black Dominican or West Indian or North American (*negro* in its racial/ethnic meaning). As we shall see, this has also occurred in Martinique and Haiti where *un nègre noir* means a dark-skinned fellow.

After *negro* had become synonymous with slave, it posed a problem for the representation of freedmen in those areas, like Puerto Rico, where freed slaves were quite significant in number. Those who had been born of miscegenation were already being represented as *pardo* and *moreno*, the former tending towards lighter and the latter towards darker skin colour. *Gente libre de color* was the generic term used to refer to freedmen. Even if the official language continued to use the term *negro*, it became inappropriate to represent the special social category of freedman. After emancipation, the developing social order also sought to distance itself from the pejorative connotations of *negro*. In an interesting psychological *tour de force*, the traditional prejudices against "black", and other phenotypical features that co-occurred with blackness in the African remained, while at the same time euphemisms were created to "avoid direct contact with the contaminated object" (Seda Bonilla 1976, 207). In addition to *prieto*, which, as we said, occupied the space for the neutral meaning of black, three main euphemisms were introduced to avoid *negro*: *trigueño, moreno, indio*.

Moreno (brown) had already existed from Graeco-Roman antiquity as a concept intermediate between white and black in the colour hierarchy. As the category at one remove from *negro*, it was a natural candidate for the euphemistic representation. Alvarez Nazario (1961, 351) has placed the euphemistic usage of *moreno* as far back as the sixteenth century, where it was used to mean black. This usage has also been reported for Spain prior to the colonization of the Americas. It occurs in the *Lazarillo de Tormes* of the sixteenth century. Fernando Ortiz (1954, xx), the Cuban anthropologist noted for his work on Cuban culture and in particular on the African contribution, also uses *moreno* to refer to blacks when he praises the African contribution to Puerto Rican culture in his prologue to Ricardo Alegria's *La Fiesta de Santiago Apostal en Loiza Aldea*: "*pero sin duda, en su música, en su vocabulario, en su psicología, la isla recibió la huella amorosa y cultural de la gente morena*" (but without doubt, in its music, its vocabulary, its psychology, the island received the amorous cultural imprint of the brown [that is, black] people).

In a newspaper article "La Sociología de los Santos de Palo" (*El Nuevo Dia, Revista Domingo*, 29 June 1997, 4–7), in the course of several references, the Black Madonna is never called *negra*, but rather *de tez oscura* (of dark complexion), *morena, parda, trigueña, oscura*.

Blanco was the term used to represent the ruling elite. If it was a purely racial/ethnic concept at the beginning, it very early acquired a social meaning from its close association with the ruling classes. As we said earlier, a particular feature of the social history of some Caribbean territories is the existence of "poor whites", of whom Puerto Rico has perhaps the largest number, both in gross terms and as a proportion of the population. According to Kinsbruner (1990, 436), the caste system in Puerto Rico did not insulate whites from downward [social and economic] mobility or ensure them high social status. *Jíbaro*, which had at first referred to peasants who could be of any colour and may have been mostly mixed, came during the nineteenth century, with the heavy influx of white immigrants, to be closely associated with white, rural, independent, highland. This allowed *blanco* to fully take on the social meaning of "ruling elite". It may even have acquired some degree of connotation of "foreign", both from the Spanish colonial period and the period of North American occupation and influence. As such, while it represented power, prestige, privilege, high social and economic status, and was and is still sought after (perhaps much more during the era of the *castas* than today), it also evoked resentment. It therefore came in for its own pejorative representation, most commonly by the term *blanquito*. The group is also commonly represented by the more offensive *come mierda* (shit eater).

A Puerto Rican may consider himself or herself racially as *blanco* or *blanca*, but may not be ready to state this openly. This is, first of all, because *blanco* is not only a racial category but, more importantly, a social/ethnic category with the suggestion of "foreign" or at least of not representing the true Puerto Rican identity. If the person does not have the appropriate social status, representation by the term *blanco* would be inappropriate. Second, as we said earlier, there has been some influence of the North American racial bipolarity. Puerto Ricans have been placed in a non-white category, both by North American officialdom and by the popular North American construction.

All this creates considerable anxiety, inconsistency and indeterminacy in the Puerto Rican representational system. There is on the one hand a desire to whiten, which goes back to the system of *castas* when the *mulato/pardo*, lying just below the whites in colour and socioeconomic status, sought to buy into the white ruling elite. They may wish to forget their partial coloured ancestry, but they are fearful of being discovered and of being constantly reminded of it (especially during neighbourhood altercations). There is therefore a reluctance to classify oneself openly as *blanco*. It is enough to proclaim ancestry chiefly as *español* or *gallego* (much less often as *canario*, although this is the dominant Iberian modality of ancestry). There is therefore a tendency for people who would pass as white in any other Caribbean territory to call themselves *mulato* and to be referred to by others by a series of terms representing the intermediate phenotypes between *negro* and *blanco*.

The current intermediate terminology is conspicuous by the absence of gross pejorative connotations. This expresses the normative value of the intermediate category in the Puerto Rico of today. However, the category has had mixed fortunes in Puerto Rico. It was despised at first for being impure, a stigma already present in the etymology of the word *mulato*. Given the extreme stigma attached to negro blood, the higher the percentage of this blood in the mixture, the deeper the contempt and the fewer the privileges in the system of *castas*. An assortment of offensive terms has been recorded in history, based in many cases on the names of animals. The Puerto Rican vocabulary up to the nineteenth century was rich in this regard, though not as rich as the one recorded for Mexico. Here are the two systems of *castas*, with their origins as recorded for the nineteenth century and presented by Zenon (1974) and Seda Bonilla (1976, citing Babin 1958):

Mexico
    Spaniard and Indian = *mestizo*
    Mestizo and Spaniard = *castizo*
    castizo and Spaniard = Spaniard
    Spaniard and Negro = *mulato*
    Spaniard and mulatto = *morisco*
    Spaniard and *morisco* = *albino*
    Spaniard and *albino* = *torna atrás* (turned behind)
    Indian and *torna atrás* = *lobo*
    lobo and Indian = *sambayo*
    sambayo and Indian = *cambujo*
    cambujo and mulatto = *albarazado*
    albarzado and *coyote* = *barzino*
    barzino and Indian = *chamiso*
    chammiso and *mestizo* = *coyote mestizo*
    coyote and mulatto = *ahí te estás* (here you are)

Puerto Rico
    Spaniard and Indian = *mestizo*
    mestizo and Spaniard = *castizo*
    castizo and Spaniard = Spaniard
    Spaniard and *negro* = mulatto
    mulatto and Spaniard = *morisco*
    morisco and Spaniard = *salta atrás* (jump backwards)
    salta atrás and Indian = *chino*
    chino and mulatto = *lobo*
    lobo and mulatto = *jíbaro*
    jíbaro and Indian = *albarazado*
    albarazado and Negro = *cambujo*
    cambujo and Indian = *sambaigo*
    sambaigo and mulatto = *calpan mulato*

This terminology did not survive the collapse of the system of *castas* and the changes in the Puerto Rican social order in the twentieth century that resulted in the valorization of the intermediate categories. The dominant racial/ethnic identity of Puerto Rico is now based on these intermediate categories. Avoiding the two poles of black and white as essentialist representations of race and identity, Puerto Rican people prefer to be identified within the broad category of *mestizo* or *mulato* (mixed), with a strong bias toward white. A number of variants of the mixed category exist, and they are based on skin colour and tone, although, as we have said, their actual value and meaning are also determined by other factors: phenotype and class, in particular. These terms are: *moreno, trigueño, quemaito, jabao, cano, colorao, jincho*. Of these, only *jincho* has any negative connotations, referring as it does to a fair complexion that contains some degree of pallor that gives an unhealthy look.

The national ideology (or myth) of Puerto Rico rejects race as an underlying principle of the organization of Puerto Rican society. The belief is that so much mixing has taken place that distinct socially meaningful categories based on race and colour are no longer observable: "We are all Puerto Ricans." However, the reality may be otherwise. Poles of black and white still exist, maximally separated in every respect: phenotype, wealth, social status, evaluation of intrinsic worth. A continuum of phenotypical features exists between the poles. This constitutes a hierarchy in which European-type phenotypical features are generally valued higher (but see below), while African-type features are valued lower. This is the general Caribbean scenario. Woolly, short hair is called *pelo malo*; African-type lips and nose are described as *bembón* and *nariz chata*, respectively, the former a word of probable Bantu origin and the latter probably of an African source as well; they both are pejorative expressions. On the other hand, straight or curly long hair is called *pelo bueno* (good hair), while there is no particular expression for Caucasian lips and nose, since these are viewed as the norm.

However, the aesthetic value system does indeed include some distancing from the poles and an appreciation of the middle ground. This is, to some degree, in consonance with the national ideology. We have seen that the features associated with the African pole suffer pejoration. A degree of pejoration also affects some features associated with the European pole. A person with too-white skin is described as *jincho*, a pejorative term that expresses the unappreciated nature of the skin colour. However, as we said earlier, this is a worldwide phenomenon, contrasting with the Middle Ages and the Renaissance when pallor was the hallmark of beauty. In Puerto Rico today, it is now preferable to have some coloration in the skin going as far as dark brown (provided that the hair is "good"). Hair that is too straight is described as *pelo muerto* (dead hair), and it is preferable to have some degree of curl (provided that the hair is long). A flat-bottomed person is described pejoratively as *chumbo,* and it is preferable to have some fullness in that part of the body.

The social construction of race and colour is particularly evident in Puerto Rico. The general features, including the socially restricted meaning of "black", recur elsewhere in Latin America. According to Pitt-Rivers,

> in Barranquilla, Colombia, color is qualified by other social factors, and the term *Negro* confined to the slum-dwellers of the city. In the modern housing developments where no one is to be seen who would not qualify as a Negro in the United States, one may be told: "Only white people live here." The definition of Negro varies from place to place, and, of course, from class to class. A man may be defined as *negro* in one place, but simply as *moreno, trigueño, canela,* or even white in another. A man who would be considered Negro in the United States might, by travelling to Mexico, become *moreno* or *prieto,* then *canela* or *trigueño* in Panama, and end up in Barranquilla as white. The definition of Indian presents a comparable problem once the word no longer refers to a member of an Indian community. Different places and classes use different criteria. (1968, 270)

CHAPTER SEVEN

Martinique

*M*artinique holds a position intermediate between Puerto Rico and Jamaica in terms of its racial and ethnic history and its current situation. There are some rather remarkable similarities between Martinique and Puerto Rico. Africa has been largely rejected as a focus for ethnicity. Black has been redefined; it has been split into a colour (*noir* in Martinique, and *prieto* in Puerto Rico) and a race/ethnicity (*nègre* in Martinique, *negro* in Puerto Rico). As a race/ethnicity, it has become marginal as a native category in the consciousness of both peoples and has become assigned to particular groups viewed as not belonging fully to the national scene. These groups are made up of darker-skinned migrants (African indentured workers in Martinique in the post-emancipation period, Dominicans and Lesser Antilleans in Puerto Rico) with more pronounced African phenotype who enter both places and assume the vacated space of black phenotype and ethnicity. Most remarkably, in both places, the term for black as a noun (*nègre, negro*) also undergoes an ameliorative semantic development and comes to mean fellow, person; it may also be used in both places as a term of endearment.

Sociohistorical Background

After a few tentative operations in the New World in the sixteenth century, mostly of a piratical nature, France set up its first colony in Saint Christophe (St Kitts) in 1627 with a contingent of Norman emigrants. About 1630, the colonization of the western part of Hispaniola began; five years later (in 1635) Guadeloupe and Martinique were occupied. This was the starting point for a type of settlement that was based principally on a system that would continue up to the third quarter of the eighteenth century: *l'engagement*, that is, indentureship, by which Frenchmen were contracted to work in the new colonies, usually for a period of three years (later reduced to 18 months). The emigrants, including also Frenchmen from Bretagne, the south-west and the Parisian region who arrived later, came in three categories: free colonists, the *engagés* (the "indentured" workers, who could become colonists after their contracts had expired), and forced *engagés* (condemned men and Protestants sent to the colonies to work out their penalties).

This initial colonization was based on small holdings, with small numbers of African slaves and *engagés* working together. According to Horowitz,

> during this early colonial period, lasting roughly from 1635 to 1670, the main lines of social organization were established, for the colonists brought with them not merely their tools, farming techniques and language, but also a social tradition based on the *ancien régime* seigneurial system with its relationships between the lord and the peasant laborer, its notions of elite endogamy, and its rather relaxed concern for peasant marriage and the legitimacy of their children. (1960, 802)

After an initial élan, there followed a period of stagnation when the colonies did not flourish. In 1664, a new impetus was produced by a change in the controlling company and by the arrival of Sephardic Jews fleeing religious persecution in Brazil. The Jews brought the techniques and technology of sugar cane cultivation and sugar production, as well as capital. The result was the sugar revolution, the massive importation of Africans, and the consolidation of ethnic and racial diversity typical of the rest of the Caribbean. The pattern of small holdings gave way, after 1664, to the large plantation devoted to sugar cane, and to a lesser extent to coffee.

From that point, the African population begins to catch up with the French and eventually becomes the majority. In the first census of 1660, Martinique had 2,587 whites and 2,720 black and mulatto slaves. In 1682, the figures recorded are 4,505 whites and free coloured, and 9,364 black slaves. The changes are significant not only for the shift in the racial majority, but also for the linking of free coloured with whites. It reveals a shift in the status and representation of this new group of free coloureds.

These different categories of French immigrants (independent colonists, military, administrators, and the like, and *engagés*) have not persisted in Martinique to the same degree as in Guadeloupe (and Barbados, in the case of British immigrants there). In Guadeloupe, the *Blancs Matignons*, and in Barbados, the Redlegs, are the direct modern descendants of the white *engagés*: rural, poor, agricultural workers. In Martinique, although there is a concept of a distinction between the *grand béké* and the *béké gouyave* (in the historical literature, *grand blanc* and *petit blanc*), the latter (the descendant of the *engagé*) is, at the present time, not rural, agricultural and poor, but rather enjoys a socioeconomic position just below that of the *grand béké*.

The fate of the indigenous Carib people of Martinique was more or less identical with their fate in other areas. After the treaty of 1660, by which the Caribs agreed to move to St Vincent and Dominica, some must have remained in Martinique. This is what is suggested by the "frequency of Carib names in eighteenth century church records of the village of Morne-Paysan" (Horowitz 1967, 10). They must have fused with the dominant populations through intermating. Some Martinicans will claim that they are able to perceive Carib phenotypical features in some of their compatriots. Often these are the same as those attributed to (East) Indian (or Chinese) ancestry (black straight hair). There is no great effort to assert any Carib focus for Martinican ethnicity, and Carib is not a concept that has competed with or is replacing black as the racial focus. It is *métisse* (mixed; cf. also Spanish *mestizo*) which fulfils this role.

Miscegenation in Martinique

In comparing Martinique with Puerto Rico and Jamaica, we first have to account for the relatively high volume of miscegenation (higher than in Jamaica, though not as high as in Puerto Rico), giving rise to a relatively high proportion of individuals between black and white, but tending towards the black pole. It is in Martinique that we find the most assertive projection of the mixed-blood (the *métisse* or the *mulâtre*) as the national ethnic/racial prototype.

This projection is to be found in the works of scholars and in the popular representations. *Métissage* and *Créolité* constitute the most current philosophical positions being proposed by Martinican intellectuals on the question of Martinican identity (see later).

We have seen that, during the period of slavery, mixed-race people were everywhere more likely to be freed than blacks. It must be recognized, however, that the records do not always make a distinction between blacks and mixed race among the free(d) people. Reference is often made to "free coloureds" (*gente de color* in Spanish, *gens de couleur* in French), but it is not always clear whether coloured includes black, and, if so, what are the proportions between blacks and mixed race. Since records were not particularly interested in racial breakdowns but more in civil status, there was a tendency to lump free mulattoes and free blacks, and even surviving indigenous people, together in the one category, free coloureds.

During the slave period, the Hispanic Caribbean had a proportionately larger free coloured population than the non-Hispanic territories. The rate of manumission in the Hispanic colonies was higher than elsewhere. In 1773, less than 1 per cent of the black and mulatto population was free in Barbados; the figure for Jamaica was 2.3 per cent, while Cuba and Puerto Rico showed 41 per cent and 82.2 per cent respectively. In 1834, on the eve of emancipation in the British colonies, it was still only twelve out of every hundred coloureds who were free in Jamaica, seven out of every hundred in Barbados. But in Cuba, in 1880, six years before abolition in that country, 60 per cent of the coloured population was free. In Puerto Rico, by the time of abolition in 1873, 90 per cent of the coloured population was already free.

For Martinique, some relevant figures are provided by Cohen (1980). In 1764, the free coloured population on that island represented 15.6 per cent of the total free population; by 1789 this figure had reached 33 per cent. Horowitz on the authority of Baude (1948), states that "the [free coloured] group remained small during the first century of colonization (in 1736 there were only 901 freedmen, 13,917 whites, and 54,742 slaves); but in 1848, the year of general emancipation, freedmen of color constituted 32 per cent of the total population of 113,357" (1960, 802).

A ledger reporting escaped slaves (SHG 1996) in the commune of Le Moule (Guadeloupe) for the years 1845 to 1848 is remarkable for the large number of runaways described as *rouge* (red) or *rougeâtre* (reddish). These are evidently two degrees of mulatto, and the two other colour descriptions given are *noir* and *cafre* (a darker-skinned mulatto). Out of a total of seventy-one runaways for whom colour descriptions are given (the vast majority), fifty-one are *noir*, nineteen are *rouge* or *rougeâtre*, and one is *cafre*.

There are two important conclusions to draw. First, the mulatto too is motivated to run away. However, this factor may have to be considered in the context of the weakening of the slave system at this time. Runaways did not all go to the bush; some went to urban centres, others found jobs in sugar factories. Second, and contrary to widespread ideas, a fairly large percentage of slaves in this location on the eve of abolition (1848) are mulatto, approximately 25 per cent.

As we said earlier, the larger proportions of free coloureds in the Hispanic Caribbean is sometimes attributed to a milder regime of slavery there. This, as we saw, can be contested by making reference to the socioeconomic conditions of the Hispanic islands, for example to the particular chronology of the development of the sugar plantation system. The same applies to the demographic rise of the specific mixed-race group. This group is formed either by forced mating of black women with white males or by consensual mating, still for the most part involving the same race/gender pairing. So that even in harsh regimes of slavery, mulattoes were being born. Indeed, as a general rule, there was more white/black miscegenation during slavery than there has been in the post-emancipation period. When and where white women were available, there would have been a reduced incidence of white-black miscegenation. There is also the psychological factor. It is reported that some white men showed a preference for black women. In some cases, this would have been a response to the stereotype of heightened sexuality attributed to black women (and subsequently extended to mulatto and Asian Indian women). This preference may have been greater among the Spaniards and the French than among the British.

The rate of intermarriage may be a measure of interracial acceptance or rejection, and may help to account for the volume of births of mulattoes. It seems that whereas interracial marriage was not encouraged anywhere, there was a higher incidence in Puerto Rico. We have seen that there were regulatory efforts in eighteenth-century Puerto Rico to prevent mixed marriages; but we suggested that this was probably not so much a prophylactic measure to prevent an unwanted social phenomenon that was threatening, as a curative measure to arrest a spreading ill.

For Martinique, in 1690, Father Labat reported that he met only two whites who had married negresses. Concubinage, on the other hand, was widespread. According to Abbé Grégoire (1826, 51), a white man living in concubinage with an African woman was not dishonoured. He was dishonoured only if he married her. The rate of intermarriage was also influenced by the rate of Christianization of Africans, as only Christianized African women were allowed to marry in any case. Roman Catholic regimes (that is, Spanish and French) had more proselytizing activity than Protestant regimes (English, Dutch); and within the Roman Catholics, the Spaniards were more busy in this area than the French.

The mulatto, the characteristic socioracial category that the Caribbean (and Brazil and the southern United States) has given to the world, epitomizes, in the view of some, the Caribbean essence of *métissage* (*mestizaje*, in Spanish), that in-between-ness, ambivalence and ambiguity, some may even say schizo-phrenia, poignantly expressed by Derek Walcott in his oft-quoted poem "A Far Cry from Africa" (1962, 18):

> I who am poisoned with the blood of both,
> Where shall I turn, divided to the vein?
> I who have cursed
> The drunken officer of British rule, how choose
> Between this Africa and the English tongue I love?
> Betray them both, or give back what they give . . .

The mulatto had a less than glorious beginning. As we saw, the naming of the category already implied a gross pejoration. Subsequently, the further gradations of mixture continued the initial derogatory valuation, with the concept of animal forming the basis of many names (see later). This took place in the context of a European philosophical current that discredited biological mixture and valued biological "purity".

In Martinique, the situation of the mulatto was at first not much different from that of the black African. There was legislation to block unions of white and black to keep the mulatto population in check. Unions of white and mulatto were also discouraged. But in both cases such unions took place. White immigration was male for some time. When white women came, it signalled the beginning of conflict between white and mulatto women.

Mulattoes fought from the beginning to escape the scourge of their black/slave ancestry. Their difficulties were expressed in the decision of the Ministry of the Navy in 1766: "All blacks were transported to the colonies as slaves. Slavery has put an indelible mark on their posterity; therefore their descendants can never enter the class of whites." Throughout slavery and right up to today, the societal assumption has been that mulattoes have black mothers rather than black fathers (cf. *¿dónde está tu abuela?* [where is your grandmother?] of Puerto Rico). Even those mulattoes phenotypically close to whites were tainted, because in a small island with a small population where everybody knows your pedigree, "passing" for white is not as easily available an option as it was and is in the United States.

Even when mulattoes were free, they experienced sociopsychological pressures and legal restrictions. In 1734, the Ministry of the Navy forbad marriage between white men and free coloured women, a move that represented a general hostility toward mulattoes. Much of the antagonism came from poor whites who competed with mulattoes in a situation of scarce resources. According to Cohen, in the French colonies, a 1788 edict stipulated that freedmen needed a licence for any trade except farming. Furthermore,

> Government ordinances prescribed special clothing, jewelry and hairdos for free persons of color so that they would not be confused with whites. To call a white person colored was the worst form of slander. . . . The fear of being classed with coloreds was so great among whites that they passed legislation establishing the principle that certain names belonged exclusively to white families. Even the titles by which people were addressed were to be restricted by race; people of color were to be addressed neither as "*sieur*" (sir) nor "*dame*". Free men of color and free blacks were not allowed to congregate in the same social gatherings as whites. (1980, 104)

In 1771, they were debarred from living in France, and in 1778 they were prevented from entering certain professions. The French Revolution abolished all these restrictions and restored the rights of mulattoes.

Cohen further reports that, while in Barbados a man of colour four generations removed from black ancestry, or in Jamaica three generations removed, was regarded as legally white, this was not the case in the French plantation colonies (but see later). Such persons would have been exempt from the discriminatory poll tax.

Victor Schoelcher, the most celebrated abolitionist in French colonial society, was extremely scathing in his evaluation of the mulatto class, which he perceived as being very hostile to the idea of abolition. For example, he speaks of them as "almost all without family, the results of concubinage and debauchery", and as possessing "reprehensible manners and a lack of dignity". He continues:

> [Mulatto] women live in concubinage and dissolution . . . whites seek their mistresses among them as in a bazaar . . . the attentions of the privileged class flatter them and they prefer to give themselves to an old white man of no value or quality than to marry someone of mixed blood . . . A mulatto man will have as many scruples about marrying a negress as a white man about marrying a mulatto. Someone said truly: A mulatto hates his father and scorns his mother . . . Coloured people would like to rise to the level of whites, but without taking the blacks up with them. They will not succeed. (Schoelcher 1976, 198–200)

The final example of the hostility of the white colonist towards the mulatto is taken from a piece published in Paris in 1810 titled "Le Cri des Colons" ("The Cry of the Colonists") and cited in Debbasch (1967, 59):

> *Le mulet est plus fort que le cheval et l'âne, mais le mulâtre réunit souvent tous les défauts de son père et de sa mère sans en avoir une seule des qualités.*

> The mule is stronger than the horse and the donkey, but the mulatto often combines all the defects of his father and mother without having a single one of their qualities.

This suggests that, paradoxically perhaps, the French regime was most harsh to the mulatto class, which in turn showed more hostility towards blacks than in the British colonies. This helps us to understand why certain historical alliances between mulattoes and blacks became more typical in the British colonies, and became an important aspect of the anticolonial struggles, whereas in the French colonies, such alliances were more difficult. The sociopsychological distance between these two groups in the French colonies shows up dramatically in Haiti where a "mulatto" republic was established in the south and a "black" republic in the north immediately after the Haitian Revolution.

All the above, however, was not able to stem the tide of the socioeconomic rise of the mulatto. In the midst of this hostility, two compelling facts emerged which were general throughout the Caribbean: mulattoes were viewed as being closer to the white phenotype than to the African, and therefore were more acceptable from the point of view of the aesthetics of the body and cultural behaviour (this provides important evidence of the role of sexuality in social relations); and, second, there was an early recognition by the colonial authorities that a social pyramid corresponding to the race/colour pyramid was the best guarantee for the preservation of social order and peace threatened by the antagonistic polarity of slave society.

A decree of 1792 finally accorded equality to free coloureds in the French colonies. Behind this was the idea of creating a buffer zone of free men, both white and coloured, to confront slave revolts which might follow the example of St Domingue (Haiti). An intermediary social role was assigned to the intermediary race/colour group. Later, this developed into an intermediary economic and political role, which placed them in strong positions to take over, or join with creole whites in taking over, social, economic and political leadership.

In the second half of the eighteenth century, an increasing number of free(d) mulattoes acquired plantations and slaves. In 1734, the minister of the navy recommended a more lenient policy of emancipation for coloured slaves, since they were the "enemies of the negroes". There was a need, felt and expressed, to enlarge the white population. It was thus recommended that a person of colour removed from his or her black ancestry by six generations should be considered white. The colonial administration faced a complex situation. It often sowed the seeds of discord between the colonists and the free coloured. The colonists in turn sometimes showed flashes of independence, frustrated as they were by France's mercantilist control of the economy, which prevented trade with the British colonies in the Caribbean and North America (Cohen 1980, 108). They then were inclined to join forces with the mulatto class which was growing in economic power. But, in the final analysis, the colonists depended on the metropole for protection, outnumbered as they were by slaves and nearly equalled in number by the free coloureds. In the view of Cohen (1980, 108), the planter class remained opposed to any amount of African ancestry.

Whites

The whites have preserved their biological purity and their socioeconomic dominance by setting up social barriers (endogamy) and economic barriers (control of resources). With a heightened sense of their economic ancestry and of their common group interests, they are the most coherent ethnic group (perhaps the only real one) in Martinique. Generally speaking, it no longer contributes its gene pool to the black population and may do so only in a minimal way to the mulatto population. It is interesting to observe that during slavery, the mulatto group was formed by intense miscegenation directed by the white male group. At the present time, however, this group hardly participates in the intense mixing that continues to take place among the other colour/ethnic groups in Martinique.

The white group has remained an integral part of the national landscape, and this has been facilitated by the departmentalization of Martinique. In other words, the group may be resented by other subsectors for its socioeconomic dominance and privileges, but it does not suffer the taint of being considered "foreign", "non-national", "disloyal" (as happens in the case of the white group in Jamaica). Their position as authentically Martinican is strengthened by the fact that they are (perceived as) the best and most consistent speakers of the creole language of Martinique, the major symbol and instrument of Martinican identity. They also resist referring to themselves, or being referred to, as *blanc* (white), preferring the local designation *béké*, which refers not so much to colour or race as to historical ethnicity and class.

If Martinique were to become independent (this continues to be an issue without much popular electoral support), the white group would either have to migrate, or break down its barriers and open up its gene pool and its control of resources. For the moment, it is another white group, the *Métros*, born in France, which occupies the space of "foreign", "non-native"; more and more they attract the resentment of the disaffected sectors of the Martinican population. Paradoxically, they are much more likely to interact with blacks and to have black sexual partners (black Martinican male with female *Métro*, or *Métro* male with black Martinican female) than are the *békés* or mulattoes.

New Migrants

Like several other Caribbean territories, Martinique suffered from a shortage of labour in the immediate post-emancipation period and had to seek indentured workers to keep the plantations supplied with manpower. Some of these workers came from France and the Madeira Islands; however, a major source was China and India (and to a lesser extent Africa: the *Nègres Congo* referred to earlier). It is estimated that 25,500 Indians and Chinese arrived in Martinique between 1853 and 1884 and between 1859 and 1860, respectively.

In 1949, an estimated 13,271 Indians remained. Of these, 5,079 worked on estates and 8,192 were free to work wherever they wished (Revert 1949, 241).

The Chinese were small in number and those numbers were not replenished by new arrivals over a long period. Their status was immediately seen as special among non-Europeans, and they were given citizenship before Indians and Africans. According to Burton, "the collective view was that the Chinese were contractual, but that the Indians were slaves" (1994, 209). The Christianization of Indians was set in motion rather late (not before the beginning of the twentieth century). In 1904, they were accorded political rights, and as late as 1923 they began to be allowed to do military service.

There is still the latent feeling among "creole" Martinicans that Indians are "outsiders", whereas the *békés* and coloured people are the "real" Martinicans. Smeralda-Amon reports the results of a survey which showed that "for the majority of persons surveyed Indians were not Martinican" (1994, 191).

By contrast, *Chine-chine* was a friendly name given to young girls with Asiatic features, and a young Chinese male was called *Ti-chine* if you did not know his name. In neither case was there any pejoration implied. Similarly, in Trinidad and Jamaica, male and female Chinese are called "Chin" and "Miss Chin", respectively, without any pejoration implied.

There was, however, some degree of hostility on the part of blacks towards the Chinese. A mixed-race person, one of whose parents was Chinese, was called a *chappé chinois* (escaped Chinese), which seems to imply that the person had escaped the taint of being Chinese. As we shall see later, the notion of "escape" is also applied to persons of half-Indian descent (*chappé couli*), and its use in relation to Chinese may be by analogy with its use to designate half-Indians (cf. also the use of *coolie rayal* and *chinee rayal* in Jamaica to refer to half-Indians and half-Chinese respectively). Burton (1994, 206) further states that, although the creole coloured population generally opposed the arrival of all indentureds, the Chinese were especially resented (but not despised or negatively stereotyped in any extreme way) as they were considered to be agents of the estate owners. They not only had straight hair but also clear skin. This allowed them to be located between whites and blacks, at the hierarchical level of mulattoes. The absence of Chinese women among the migrants prevented them from consolidating themselves as a distinct coherent ethnic group and facilitated their eventual assimilation into the largely mulatto Martinican middle class. In other areas of the Caribbean, the Chinese have remained a better established racial and ethnic group than in Martinique.

However, in these other areas, as in Martinique, they have become socially integrated into the middle classes.

The British were the first to use the term "Coolie Trade", as an alternative to "Yellow Trade". The term "Coolie Trade" to referred to the recruitment of Chinese people as indentured labourers. However, from 1860, the term is used only in relation to Indians. When the French began to use Asiatics as indentured workers in their colonies, *coolie* was restricted to the designation of Indians.

As far as Indians are concerned, the picture for Martinique was basically the same as for elsewhere. Indians replaced black field workers on plantations and later performed other menial tasks such as street sweeping, garbage collecting, gardening. Their customs, in addition, were considered strange by blacks who by this time had become totally nativized in their Caribbean surroundings, had a better knowledge than the newly arrived Indians of how to cope in these surroundings, and had even acquired (or considered themselves to have acquired) a greater familiarity with French culture. Blacks therefore placed the Indian group lower than themselves on the racial and ethnic hierarchy. Blacks finally had a group over which they could exercise some power, and this opportunity was eagerly embraced.

The same kind of negative stereotyping which was created by whites about blacks was now invented by blacks against Indians. As in the case of black stereotypes, Indian stereotypes were often antithetical and contradictory. Indians were, of course, lazy, and they were ferocious and prone to outbursts of uncontrolled violence, but they were also very gentle and obsequious. Indian women had excessive sexuality and libido, while the men were weak and lacked virility. The term *couli*, introduced by the Europeans to designate labourers from Asia and already tainted with some negative value, was given a particularly pejorative connotation, on a par with the term *nigger* for blacks.

The vast majority of Indians arriving in Martinique came from the south of India and were dark-skinned. A small minority were clear-skinned Brahmins. The Martinican Indian community was/is not highly divided or stratified by colour, nor by religion and caste, as Indian migrants to Guyana and Trinidad were/are. Their dominant pigmentation linked them to blacks, but their straight hair and "fine" features linked them to whites. It is in fact claimed by Leiris that "[Martinican] Indians, although contemptuously called 'coolies' by coloured people, consider themselves to belong to the white race, and therefore to be superior to coloured people" (1955, 139). This would certainly have been the case with the fair-skinned Brahmins among them, and this attitude may have then been generalized to all Indians. According to Smeralda-Amon (1994, 198), the *békés* of Martinique consider the Indian handsome.

While there was mutual racial contempt between blacks and Indians, a great deal of cross-racial mating took place. And unlike mating between whites and blacks, which was for the most part between white males and black females, Indians and blacks mated without any dominant race/gender pattern. It is evident that the power differentials between whites and blacks that led to white males controlling and exercising all the mating options did not exist to the same degree between Indians and blacks. It is true, however, that an Indian female was more likely to be ostracized by her ethnic group if she consorted with a black male than was the case if an Indian male consorted with a black female. This is an index of how closely knit was the Indian group and how high was its ethnicity compared with blacks. Protection of females is one of the primordial instincts of ethnic groups towards the preservation of the group and the furtherance of its interests.

However, it is interesting to note that while in the case of Trinidad and Guyana, the ostracizing of the Indian female who mates with a black man is also evident in the naming of the offspring by the term *dougla*, in the case of Martinique, the naming of such offspring does not suggest ostracizing, but redemption. *Dougla* is a Hindi word meaning "outcast"; in Trinidad and Guyana the progeny of the miscegenation was thus named by the Indian group from its own perspective. In Martinique, however, such progeny is called *chappé couli* (that is, French *échappé couli* = escaped coolie). Although it is now impossible to say which group there assumed the prerogative of naming, it is more probable that blacks did the naming from their own perspective: this progeny, in the view of blacks, had escaped some of the flaws, both moral and physical, imputed to the Indian race.

Indians object strongly to the designation *couli*, but there is no evidence that other Martinicans are about to surrender completely the use of the term. If its use is on the decline in public discourse in the presence of Indians (*indien* being preferred in this context), in private informal interactions, it is not receding. Smeralda-Amon (1994, 198) claims that the white Martinican (*béké*) does not consider *couli* to be a pejorative term. Many blacks also now claim that the term *couli* has lost its pejorative connotations and that they use it purely as a neutral term of reference. But Indians still object. As Indians rise on the socioeconomic scale, the racial stereotypes and myths weaken. It is then true that the term *couli* may still be used in reference to socially mobile Indians (teachers, university students, and the like), but only for third person reference and not as a form of address. This suggests that there is still some unease or embarrassment associated with the use of the term, which causes a decline in its use in face-to-face interaction between blacks and Indians (except when the purpose is one of abuse).

Since the referents of the term *couli* are, with increasing frequency, persons of middle-class social standing, with cultural forms of behaviour identical with those of middle-class persons of other races, the "meaning" of the term is losing somewhat its pejorative connotations and is falling back on its denotative meaning of "person of Indian extract" (cf. also the way in which the rise of African Americans from slave to middle class has removed some of the negative connotations of "black", which no longer connotes "slave" but may now connote "entertainer" or "sportsman"). Similarly, the wide range of sayings expressing pejorative stereotypes and myths about Indians is declining in use. Leiris (1955, 139) mentions several as being current in the 1950s: *couli mange chien* (coolies eat dogs); *couli pied chique* (coolies have chiggers in their feet); *faible comme un couli* (weak like a coolie); *hypocrite comme une femme couli* (hypocritical like a coolie woman). These sayings have now disappeared from usage and memory, particularly among young Martinicans.

As a powerless minority in a small space and therefore unable to isolate themselves (or to be isolated), Indians have undergone considerable cultural assimilation, while maintaining a strong consciousness of separate race and ethnicity. Social relations between Indians and the coloured population are quite fluid. Intermarriage (and intermating) is taking place. It is interesting to note that, as in Trinidad and Guyana, the dominant pattern in recent times is that black males may seek Indian females as mates rather than Indian males seeking black females. Insofar as the male is the one exercising a prerogative of choice of mate, or at least is the one initiating the quest, this pattern suggests that in the social and aesthetic pecking order, the Indian female, in spite of negative myths and stereotypes about the Indians, and their generally low social ranking, does have some positive appeal. This is undoubtedly due to the "European" features of her phenotype, particularly her straight hair, which, in the view of the black male, will improve the socio-aesthetic appeal of his mixed offspring.

The size of the Indian population, though small, has been large enough to sustain a separate identity and ethnicity. There has been, however, difficulty in sustaining objective forms of culture, not to mention transmitting them to the general Martinican population. Martinican Indians have not retained their original language(s), cuisine, religion or music, although there is evidence that less tangible forms of culture have persisted. These would be aspects of world view: aesthetic and recreational tastes, morality, child rearing.

According to Burton (1994, 208), the Tamul festival of Pongal is still celebrated. But today, apart from this event, specific overt and public aspects of the culture of southern India are not to be found. Similarly, there have been no transfers from Indian culture to the general Martinican creole culture of the order of what has taken place in Trinidad and Guyana in language, cuisine, music, festivals and folk medicine. Attempts at the revival of Indian culture in Martinique are focusing on Hindu standard culture in its musical, religious and linguistic forms.

Racial and Ethnic Awareness among the French

The French, as a people and a nation, have had the reputation of being the least racist of European peoples. On a personal level, they have had more open and comfortable relations with the different peoples of their colonial empire than the British. There is some anecdotal evidence for this, for example, in the number of cases of African American, African and Asian persons who have found psychological, spiritual and material refuge in France. In the case of African Americans, it has been an escape from a harsh and hostile racial environment created by white Anglo-Saxon Protestant culture in the United States. These were high profile cases of artists, writers, intellectuals, and actors and actresses who were eagerly accepted and even pampered by the French cultural and intellectual elite. In return, they testified as to the absence of racism among the French taken as a whole, as a people.

Revert (1949, 234) provides an interesting comment on this subject as it relates to the early period of French colonization of Martinique. He cites an anonymous writer of 1640 who reported that

> un grand succès fut réservé à son époque aux filles moresques ou nègres. Converties au catholicisme et une fois affranchies et dûment épousées, elles étaient tenues en honnête société de femmes.

at the time that he wrote, Moorish or black women were quite successful. As long as they were converted to Catholicism and were freed and were married, they were accepted in the company of decent women.

Soon, however, according to Revert, they met hostility from white women who considered them as dangerous rivals.

There is also the philosophical and political tradition of equality associated with France since the Revolution. Having combatted the Christian notion of the equality of man under God, French philosophy proclaimed equality in terms of human and civil rights. This had, and continues to have, a resonance throughout the world, and can be considered the forerunner of the great modern movements, whether it be the civil rights amendments to the US constitution, the activities of the United Nations, or the inclusion of clauses protecting human and civil rights as a routine feature of modern constitutions. The formula "regardless of race, colour or creed" sums up the modern insistence on the purging of racism and abusive ethnocentrism from the affairs of mankind, and this can be seen as one of the gifts of the French Revolution.

On the ground, matters may have been somewhat different. Today, largely as a result of the inability of France to finance its social security/welfare system and create adequate employment opportunities to meet the new demographic growth, there has been a wave of hostility in France (as well as throughout western Europe and North America) towards "foreigners". In the majority of cases these "foreigners" are people of the former empire belonging to a different race and ethnicity. Their colour, customs, religion, music, and so on, seem to have suddenly become a "problem", a "threat" to the continued well-being and even the very survival of the (former) great colonial/imperial power.

What was previously appreciated and valued by the cultural and intellectual elite of France is now seen by some politicians and ordinary Frenchmen as threatening the racial and cultural integrity of France. There is, one must admit, a social class/demographic element in this. The new migrants from the former colonies now tend to be numerous and working class or "unemploy-able", since there are no longer a sufficient number of menial and "unskilled" job opportunities to make them wanted in France. There is then an attempt to view the present hostility not so much as racism or abusive ethnocentrism as simply a socioeconomic phenomenon, a reaction to the situation of scarce resources.

It may be impossible to arrive at a definitive resolution of the nature of this contemporary phenomenon. It is at least evident that France has always been part of the general European picture of racism and ethnocentrism, even while one major intellectual/philosophical tradition abhorred racism and proclaimed equality. We have seen that the great French thinkers of the Age of Reason held some unreasonable ideas about race, and about sub-Saharan Africans in particular. Negative ideas were also held by lesser lights, and it is reasonable to assume that they filtered down to the general mass of planters, accountants, marine personnel and colonists who arrived in Martinique and the other colonies of France. Cohen, evoking French claims about the absence of racism in their ranks, finds on the contrary and "to [his] great surprise", that the historical documents which he consulted show themselves to be "impregnated with a strong racial tradition" (1981, 14).

France had begun having limited contacts with sub-Saharan Africa from the sixteenth century and, like other Europeans, Frenchmen were generally struck by the colour of the people and by their customs. These direct contacts only served to reinforce the existing prejudices inherited from the past but until then occurring only in the imagination.

We have seen that biological racism was more pronounced in French thought than elsewhere. Voltaire, one of the most important intellectual and literary figures in France in the Age of Reason, was generally most liberal in his thinking, but he was scathing in his evaluation of Africa and Africans. In one of his famous works, *Essais sur les Moeurs* (Voltaire 1963), he states:

> Their [the Africans'] round eyes, their flattened noses, their always huge lips, their woolly hair, their limited intelligence create a prodigious gap between them and other human species. And it is evident that this difference is not due to their climate since Negroes and Negresses brought to the coldest of countries always produce animals of their own kind. (1:6)

> It is probable that in hot countries monkeys have mated women . . . The race of blacks is different from ours, as different as the spaniel from the greyhound . . . one might say that if their intelligence is not of a completely different kind from ours, it is certainly quite inferior. (2:305–6)

The world ethnic hierarchy conceived by Graeco-Roman antiquity became reinforced in France, with the indigenous peoples of the New World being placed above Africans in the scale. For example, Pluchon cites a French eighteenth-century defender of the "Indian" (that is, indigenous peoples), who states that although they [the "Indians"] have some resemblance with blacks of Africa, they at least differ from these [the Africans] in not having noses so flattened, so crushed, lips so thick, so protruding; instead of that cotton-like down which covers the heads of Africans, Indians have long beautiful hair similar to that which embellishes the European head. (1984, 46)

In 1767, a declaration by the Ministry of the Navy (which held the portfolio for the colonies) drew a dividing line between Africans and "Indians". The latter, once assimilated to the French, could aspire to all the responsibilities and privileges, from which Africans were excluded. To cross this line, some mulattoes sought the grace of being considered Indians.

Slavery did not add much to these debasing views. Observations on African slaves made by French visitors to the Caribbean were of the same disparaging order. Pelleprat, a cleric, declared: "The Negroes have no intelligence and are very dull . . . smelly like scavengers and so hideous and ill-formed that they cause horrors" (1965, 85). And in 1882, in *Défense Coloniale*, a journal of Martinique (edition of 25 February 1882), Marius Hurard, the Deputy from Martinique, in a last-ditch effort to perpetuate a slave mentality, addressed blacks in the following way: "We must tell you that you are born for slavery and that your instincts are those of the slave."

There were of course persons who were opposed to these ideas and presented more balanced views of Africa and Africans. This suggests that, like today, both the racist and the egalitarian positions were well represented in France. Father Proyart (1776) is a cleric who denounced the detractors of Africa and Africans. He realized the impact of the slave trade and slavery on African society and morals. He disputed all the generalizations and stereotypes that were created by Europeans about Africans. He saw, for example, that Africans were not "lazy"; women especially were always working in spite of the intense heat. He was not shocked by African "nudity". He made an interesting comparison between the semi-nudity of women at the French Court, which was purely suggestive sexually, and African nudity, which was a rational response to the climate and in no way was indicative of moral degeneracy or lack of "modesty". Only mildly ethnocentric, he realized that the Christianization of Africans had to be a slow process, and blamed the missionaries rather than the Africans. He also saw that the prejudiced views held by Europeans about Africans were based on inadequate observation and wild speculation, and did not properly belong to a century that prided itself on reason and humanity.

Another such example was Abbé Grégoire (1826). He realized how the Bible had been manipulated by Europeans to justify slavery. He posed the following rhetorical question: Haven't they [Europeans] a hundred times applied to blacks the curse laid on Canaan? (p. 40). Grégoire then went on to show that Europeans had in turn invoked the Bible, distorted its meaning to make slavery descend from heaven, then contradicted the same Bible when they denied the unity of human nature by claiming that black is a different race on the lowest rung of the human ladder. Grégoire was also ahead of his times in recognizing cultural relativity, including phenotypical aesthetic relativity. He reported that "in the interior of Africa, black populations were found who believed that the devil was white and who, having seldom seen Europeans, considered their white pale colour as a symptom of weakness resulting from disease" (pp. 33–34).

There are finally some highlighted cases of the tolerance of the French for interracial mixing. One of the mistresses of Francois 1er was an African. And Josephine, the empress wife of Napoleon, is supposed to have been a mulatto.

Racial and Ethnic Constructions

As we said earlier, in the history of European (and Asian) social psychology, race and ethnicity became socialized through the establishment of a hierarchy of intellectual, moral and aesthetic values attributed to different races and ethnicities. The Caribbean experience of slavery added to this a finely graded racial phenotypical hierarchy in which the colour black and the other phenotypical features that co-occur with blackness underwent the final and complete degradation. They were intimately linked to the condition of "slave". The word expressing the basic most salient feature of the phenotype (the colour black) deepened its semantic degradation, already begun and recorded in the age of Graeco-Roman antiquity, by becoming synonymous with slave. In the ledger of Declarations of Runaways for a region of Guadeloupe in the eighteenth century (SHG 1996), colour is always rendered by *noir*, and the noun for slave is either *esclave* or *nègre*, in apparent free variation.

Martinique is an illustrative example of this process. The word *nègre* (like the word *negro* in the case of Puerto Rico) first of all becomes a substantive and moves to the semantic space of "slave". This phenomenon also takes place on the French plantations of the Indian Ocean (Chaudenson 1974). But there it may have been an import from the French colonies of the Caribbean. The

Indian Ocean was colonized later than the Caribbean and the Caribbean experience helped build the colonies there. *Nègre* came to mean "slave" there, in spite of the fact that slaves did not originate exclusively from sub-Saharan Africa.

Martinique saw the same devaluation of black and its associated phenotypical features as was to be found in the rest of the Caribbean. The colour is subject to attempts to escape from it: marrying a lighter colour in order to *sauver la couleur* (rescue your colour); the dark-skinned child in a family is said to be *mal sorti* (come out bad); an injurious insult is to call someone *vieux nègre* (old nigger). As far as phenotypical features are concerned, the hair perceived as typical of the *nègre* is called *cheveux jeks* (*jeks* = scouring pad), *grain poivre* (pepper grains), *boulon, tête grinnin*; and the nose is called *bombe*. All of these terms are highly pejorative.

A general distanciation from this colour and phenotype has taken place in Martinique, where there is now a general tendency (perhaps not as pronounced as in Puerto Rico) to consider black skin and African phenotypical features as not really belonging to the Martinican phenotype, or at least not to the ideal or predominant phenotype. Strong black pigmentation and the concurrent African (stereotypical) phenotypical features (flat noses, woolly hair, thick lips) are associated with "*Les Caribéens*" ("The people from the Caribbean", that is, from the English-speaking Windward and Leeward Islands; note the implication that Martinique is not part of the Caribbean but part of France). The term *nègre* is in fact widely used, but there is a complex array of meanings associated with it (see also later for a discussion of the increasing ideological definition of *nègre*). There is a redefinition away from what is considered the prototype of an African phenotype towards a more European type represented by "lighter-dark" to brown pigmentation, straighter noses, less woolly hair (which in any event, in the case of women, is generally artificially straightened).

The phenomenon of women "going natural" as to their hair is not widely known either in the past or at present in Martinique. This is unlike Jamaica, where natural hairstyles have always been worn by many people, for three main reasons: ideological/aesthetic, religious and economic (see chapter 8, Jamaica). On the other hand, some Martinican women use products to bleach the skin. The "*Miss Beauté Noire*" (Miss Black Beauty) contest is supposed to glorify a different (non-white) aesthetic of the human body; but in reality (as in the case of Jamaican non-white beauty contests), what is considered to be the prototypical African phenotype is excluded (even too black a skin colour).

This distanciation is accounted for or aided by other factors (in addition to the pejoration of *nègre*). The most important is an event that is analogous to the arrival of Dominicans (from the Dominican Republic) and Lesser Antilleans in Puerto Rico. As in many other Caribbean territories, the decline of the sugar industry in Martinique following the shortage of labour in the post-emancipation period led to the immigration of agricultural workers from several sources. According to Revert (1949, 242), in 1877, there were 6,500 Africans from the Congo in Martinique. In 1901, this number fell to 5,345; and in 1910 only 837 could be identified. They settled in the Commune of Francois, and in Morne l'Afrique in the Commune of Diamant, where the African phenotypical prototype still dominates. They are referred to as *Nègres Congo* (Congo being another pejorative designation) or *Nègres Guinée*, and, ironically, they are viewed by some Martinicans as having preserved features from the period of slavery. They provide a focus for the distancing of Martinicans from the black African phenotype; in this way they play the same role in Martinique as Dominicans and Lesser Antilleans play in Puerto Rico. They have at the present time disappeared as a group, having been absorbed into the general population. However, as we said above, if there are Martini-cans showing this prototypical phenotype, they are mistaken for *Caribéens*. The term *nègre Congo* still exists and is used injuriously, to insult.

Another factor in this distanciation may simply be that the prototypical African phenotype has ceased to be statistically dominant in Martinique because of the relatively large percentage of the population affected by some degree of white, black and Indian (from India) mixing. Whether this is in fact the case is impossible to say. Certainly a dominant Martinican ideology is that of *métissage* (mixing) and this may be affecting the perception by Martinicans of themselves. They certainly consider themselves more mixed than Guade-loupeans. This view is, however, not generally shared by Guadeloupeans.

Distanciation is a phenomenon to be observed in all stratified societies. Each stratum attempts to distance itself from the group immediately below, and to move closer to, or to become integrated with, the group immediately above. In Martinique (as in other areas of the Caribbean), this involves change not only in such things as education, occupation, speech, residence, religious affiliation, manners in general, but also change in phenotypical features such as skin colour and hair texture. For blacks in Martinique, the *Nègres Congo*, the *Caribéen* people, Haitians and to a lesser extent the *Couli* people (see later) represent the focus of distanciation, and allow the psychological movement of blacks from the lowest level of the social/racial/ethnic hierarchy. Having yielded that space to the *Nègres Congo, Caribéens* and the *Coulis,* blacks attempt to shed the values associated with that level. This is done not by raising the concept, meaning and connotations of black to another level (as is being attempted in Jamaica and the United States), but by distancing themselves from black. Black is a category formerly abandoned and now waiting to be filled, rather than a group of people striving to revalue their category.

This is not to say that some black/white racial polarization does not exist in Martinique. Polarization becomes part of the discourse, for example, when relations between *Métros* (white Frenchmen from the metropole) and locals are being debated, and to a lesser extent when the relations between Indians and blacks are discussed. Martinique has also not remained unaffected by the Caribbean and international discourse on race and ethnicity, in which the positive assertion of black is a major theme. Rastafarianism has gained, if not a foothold, at least a toe-hold in Martinican society, and more and more Martinicans are becoming open in declaring themselves *noir* or *nègre* (black male) or *négresse* (black female) in the ideological assertion of an ethnicity. But there is still for the most part no widespread ideological definition of black that, as in the case of Jamaica, extends the category beyond the mere skin colour to include even biological and phenotypical mulattoes.

For the Martinican, to recognize oneself as black is to exclude oneself from what is seen as the positive values and achievements of the world, and of France in particular, and to place oneself in the company of Haitians, Jamaicans and African Americans. On the other hand, not to recognize oneself as black but only as Martinican is an incomplete, ambiguous identification, and prevents one from benefiting from the current positive identities being forged by Jamaican reggae artistes and African American superstars. This leads to psychological uncertainties, which are more pronounced among Martinicans living in France. According to Raveau: "hospital statistics on more than 80 cases [of mental pathologies] have shown that the Martinicans' mental pathology is the most assertive on the racial theme of all the colored men living in France" (1968, 103).

Associated with this ideology of distanciation is the assimilationist policy of France and the assimilationist ideology of a large part of the Martinican population. The rejection of Africa implied in the distanciation from black may be seen as a need to make an accommodation to France, the supplier of economic and material benefits. Among the world's cultures and ethnicities,

Africa is probably the most salient symbol or pole of ethnic opposition to France. As we shall see, the *Négritude* movement has not made any significant impact on this assimilationist ideology; and the other aggressively articulated ideology, that of *Créolité*, supports the assimilationist ideology, without necessarily intending to.

As we found in the case of Puerto Rico, there is, in Martinique, the apparent paradox or contradiction of an ameliorative evolution of *nègre*. The word acquires a neutral meaning of "fellow" (male) and, to a lesser extent, *négresse* acquires the neutral meaning of "person" (female). This makes possible an expression such as *un nègre noir, un nègre clair de peau* (a black fellow, a clear-skinned fellow). In downtown Fort-de-France, an Asian restaurant calls itself *Le Nègre Jaune*, "The Yellow Fellow". In both cases, the words are also endowed with an affective connotation. Aimé Césaire, perhaps the leading Martinican public figure, internationally acclaimed author and leading politician, is referred to affectionately as "*notre petit nègre*" (our little nigger). It is both the affective usage and the neutral usage, as well as a sarcastic reference to the original pejorative usage, since Césaire is phenotypically black and African. It also suggests that the evolution of the term may have started with a hypocoristic usage, in reference to black children growing up in the Great House or in the households of white persons in general. This seems a more likely explanation than that it is an attempt to destigmatize the concept of *nègre* by universalizing it. It has to be admitted, however, that there are many such attempts at universalizing as part of a process of democratization: a reform movement in Jamaica sought to call everyone (all categories of workers, staff, and so on) at the University of the West Indies, "doctor".

Colour/Shade

Today, Martinique still bears traces of the tripartite racial division with social correlates: the *békés* are large landowners; the mulattoes and *békés gouyave* are merchants or occupy the liberal professions; darker-skinned persons are workers, small-scale farmers. Beyond this basic structure, the French Caribbean colonies, like the Hispanic ones, developed an elaborate scheme of racial/colour categories corresponding to degrees of mixture. This did not correspond to the kind of official legal system of privileges and limitations that we saw in the Hispanic world (the system of *castas*); but it may be assumed that the rich nomenclature in the French colonies indicates that the categories were recognized, and had different values in a fine hierarchy based on colour and corresponding to phenotypical features. It was important to know how many generations removed from white a particular individual was, as the stain of having black blood faded as generations went by and as one "improved" the phenotype of one's descendants by avoiding further injections of black blood.

Moreau de St Méry (1958), one of the early contemporary historians of French New World colonialism, devoted twenty pages of his work to "the detailed study of the different combinations of the mixture of whites with negroes, and of negroes with Caribs". His taxonomy calculates the thirty-second part of blood in the lineage of an individual and assigns a racial category. He identified the following scheme of racial categories in Haiti:

white with black = *mulâtre* (mulatto)
white with mulatto = *quarteron* (quadroon)
white with *quarteron* = *métisse*
white with *métisse* = *mamelouque*
white with *mamelouque* = *sang mêlé* (mixed blood)
white with *sang mêlé* = *marabout*
white with *marabout* = *quarteron*
black with mulatto = *griffe*
white with *griffone* = *quarteron*
white with *sacatra* = *quarteron*
black with *sang mêlé* = *mulâtre*
black with *quarteron* = *mulâtre*
black with *mamelouque* = *mulâtre*
black with *métisse* = *mulâtre*
black with *marabout* = *griffe*
black with *griffone* = *sacatra*
black with *sacatra* = *sacatra*

This nomenclature and the system it represented have not survived in Haiti, nor in Martinique. The terms show a double origin. One part is French in origin (*mulâtre, quarteron, métisse, sang mêlé, griffe*), and some of these terms were probably not in popular usage. The other part is probably African in origin.

The basic system which survives is a white versus non-white one, in which the mulatto still plays an intermediate and intermediary role. As a continuum of shades between mulatto (light brown) and black becomes dominant, and as the contemporary socioeconomic situation puts more dark-skinned persons in the professions and in the higher levels of the public sector, mulattoes have been moving away from a dominant desire to "whiten" themselves, socially and phenotypically, and are interacting more with persons of their own socioeconomic category, irrespective of race and colour. House parties and other types of social receptions will thus be much more mixed in terms of colour than was the case some time ago, although very private parties still tend to be colour homogeneous.

Increased social interaction includes increased mating across colour boundaries, following the basic post-emancipation pattern of darker-skinned males with lighter-skinned females. The increase in the number of successful professional dark-skinned males leads to the increase in the mating across colour boundaries. The tendency is certainly towards the breakdown in endogamy within colour groups. This trend will continue as young people free themselves from the restrictive influence of parents, extended family and traditional practice, and exercise full control and authority over choice of mate. Mates will then be chosen for other "qualities" than light skin. Or, more properly, these other qualities will reinforce skin colour or may, in some cases, even supersede skin colour in choice of mate.

The Role of Ideology

As with all other Caribbean countries, one major historical aspect of the construction of ethnicity in Martinique which has to be considered is the role of Africa. Paralleling the biological distancing from blackness, there has been in Martinique an ideological distancing from Africa. This takes on a completeness surpassing that of Puerto Rico. Whereas in Puerto Rico, there is an open recognition of the historical role of Africa (for example, the link of the musical genre *bomba* with Africa is recognized and *bomba* is considered as one of the two "national" musics), in Martinique there is no widespread recognition of an African source for either as phenotype, religion or music.

The assimilationist policy and practices of France must be seen as major contributors to this distancing. Assimilation has been played out biologically through the relatively intense miscegenation, with European colour and phenotype being the pole of attraction; politically, through departmentalization with all its socioeconomic implications; and culturally, chiefly through the French language as the most important instrument of socioeconomic mobility.

The assimilationist policies and actions of France have been more intense than those of the British and can be traced back to the seventeenth-century French philosopher, Descartes. A major philosophical current of the Age of Reason, heralded by Descartes, claimed that the differences between peoples were superficial and that there was an underlying unity of mankind based on universal reason. France embodied the principles of universal reason in her language, education and system of government; she therefore had a duty, a *mission civilisatrice* (civilizing mission) to spread these attributes to the rest of the world, that is, to bring about the administrative and cultural unification of the diverse peoples of the world. There was a concept of government and culture valid for all peoples regardless of climate, geography or cultural specificity. It is interesting to note that, in a blurb promoting the publication of the translation into "French Creole" (Martinican) of the Greek tragedy *Antigone* (and earlier of *Don Juan*, the French classical play by Molière), a leading Martinican intellectual, a staunch defender of the Martinican language and one of the founders of the ideological/cultural movement *Créolité*, defends the translation of what he calls *les oeuvres classiques de la littérature universelle* (the classical works of *universal* literature; my emphasis) and describes *Antigone* and *Don Juan* as "works of the universal repertoire".

The way in which French colonial philosophy and policy have been explicitly assimilationist, to a degree not nearly equalled by other colonial powers, and have led to the political assimilation of its Caribbean colonies, is well known. Martinique and other overseas territories became *Départements d'Outre-Mer* (Overseas Departments), and their inhabitants became entitled to the same political rights and freedoms as all citizens of France. All Martinicans are by law French. Martinicans vote in French general elections and send Deputies to the National General Assembly in metropolitan France. Proponents of this status declare: "*La Martinique, c'est la France*" ("Martinique *is* France").

The great irony of this political assimilation is that Martinique is now really politically part of Europe through France's participation in the European Union. A Martinican can now travel to the United Kingdom without passport or visa and work there, whereas a Jamaican or Barbadian cannot. And of course the Martinican economy is inextricably tied to that of France, in the sense that it depends to a large measure on transfers from the metropole. The transfers have been quite significant, and today Martinicans enjoy perhaps the highest standard of living in the Caribbean. The per capita income is higher than that of Puerto Rico and second only to that of the Netherlands Antilles (Curaçao and Aruba). The infrastructure of roads, telephone, electricity, and so on, is of the quality of the developed world.

Another feature of this complete political assimilation is a rather strange (for the Caribbean) kind of population exchange that has taken place since departmentalization. Due to the fact that the Martinican economy is not based on locally generated production and growth, there is a great deal of unemployment and frustration from unfulfilled expectations. This results in considerable emigration to the metropole. At the same time, there is considerable immigration from the metropole into Martinique, large enough to constitute a new racial/ethnic group referred to, somewhat pejoratively and cynically, as *les métros*. These are distinct from the *békés*, the local Martinican whites, and there is no question of integrating the two groups. A visitor to Martinique from the (former) British Caribbean is always shocked to see policemen, civil servants of any rank (in fact middle and lower ranks rather than upper), primary school teachers, even ditch diggers in public works, who are white. These are not local whites, but *métros*. This phenomenon is completely unknown under British colonialism, which sent only the top administrative, religious and military/police cadres to the colonies.

The departmentalization of Martinique is the logical culmination of this assimilationist policy, which regarded overseas colonies as integral parts of France and considered France to have a mission to spread its superior language, culture and administration to its colonies. Miles has this to say about this mission:

> [Under the terms of the mission], colonization should lead to the extension of the French language, civilization and economic system. This reflects the Cartesian emphasis on universal reason, according to which individual differences are subordinate to the universality of the human spirit and reason. Any existing differences reflect the essentially arbitrary circumstances of climate, geography and culture, and are amenable to the application of "correct" (that is, French) language, education, thought and religion. Thus, unlike the more hard-nosed empirical British attitude strictly separating the colonized from the colonizers ("East is East and West is West, and ne'er the twain shall meet"), we find the more generous, if patronizing, view that "French civilization can be given to those societies which have none". (1986, 201)

The assimilation picture for political administration is very clear; the picture for culture/ethnicity is extremely clouded. It is quite evident that

Martinican and metropolitan French people do not form one single ethnic group. The mere fact that they are so widely separated geographically militates against this. It is also not evident that *békés* and metropolitan French (*métros*) share one ethnicity. The more important question is whether Martinicans themselves form one ethnic group. There is evidence to suggest that in earlier centuries there was in Martinique a distinctive rural "traditional" culture built around the characteristic Caribbean components: creole language, syncretic religion combining European (Christian) and African elements, syncretic music combining European melodic structures and African rhythmic structures, a world view emphasizing collectivity rather than individuality, a kinship system based on extended consanguineal and social links.

Persons belonging to this cultural system celebrated and actualized this culture in a way that sought to sustain the group and promote its interests: oral tradition, customs and beliefs, dance, festivals, strikes, riots, endogamy and other acts stemming from the collectivity. This ethnic behaviour clashed with an historical divisiveness which dated back to the circumstances of their arrival in Martinique and which was often encouraged by the ruling classes. It clashed also with the assimilationist policies and pressures.

This traditional culture has been severely eroded in Martinique. It followed the decline in the production of local goods, resulting from the consumption of imported goods fuelled by increased public expenditure that the French government bestowed on the island. The adoption of French forms and standards of living led to a decline of cultural production and reproduction, which necessitated the creation of a special agency, the Service Municipal d'Action Culturelle, to try to prevent its irreversible demise. Interestingly, another agency, the Centre Municipal d'Action Culturelle, was also created to promote French culture in what was seen as a widening cultural vacuum in Martinique. The pursuit of a separate ethnicity eventually became, or was seen to be, counterproductive as far as the exploitation of the material benefits of assimilation was concerned.

An important instrument of assimilation was/is education. Up to recently, Martinican primary school history texts opened with: "*Nos ancêtres, les Gaulois* . . ." (Our ancestors, the Gauls . . .). Other colonial education systems in the Caribbean never reached this level of absurdity. In the British Caribbean, students were taught, like their counterparts in the French Caribbean, to feel themselves as belonging to an empire, to take pride in its achievements, to count with apples rather than with mangoes, and to believe generally in the superiority of Europe over the rest of the world. But students in the British colonial system were never encouraged or expected to believe that they were British, either by citizenship, culture or ancestry. In the British Caribbean, as early as the decade of the 1940s, an option, West Indian history, was introduced into the high school curriculum as an alternative to British/European history. It is true that West Indian history was intended for the less gifted student in lower streams, but many students in the higher streams opted for it.

In Martinique, education, especially in the twentieth century, was a consciously wielded instrument of colonial assimilationist policy. In the last two decades, there has been some change in French official policies towards cultural minorities within the French nation. For example, there is now official recognition of ethnic languages as vehicles of instruction in educational institutions. The assimilationist nature of education has been toned down somewhat, allowing more space for Martinican ethnic ideologies. However, the political context, supported by important economic and material benefits, remains as a compelling factor.

The French model presupposes the elimination of all competing cultures. Since Africa is the most contrastive cultural modality *vis-à-vis* French culture, Africa is seen as the antipode of assimilation. The assimilationist policy of France has never been aggressively resisted in Martinique. This has been, as it were, a reward to France for the economic gift of departmentalization. To receive this reward, Martinicans are required to reject Africa, seen as the cultural antithesis of France, as well as the political enemy of France, since cultural independence built on an African heritage foundation may be seen as supporting political independence. Note, however, that to the extent that today, the assimilationist ideology has little intellectual validity or popular support, particularly in the cultural sphere, Africa may become/return as a focus for the construction of identity ideologies in Martinique.

In Puerto Rico, Africa benefits from the presence of the United States as a competing pole for Puerto Rican cultural and national identity. In seeking to avoid the perceived threat of assimilation to a North American cultural identity (which is seen as the inevitable result of North American economic and political domination), Puerto Ricans may turn to emphasizing a Hispanic identity. But this is also unsatisfactory, since it links Puerto Ricans with a former colonial power. This leads some Puerto Ricans to look to the Caribbean and to Africa as source and basis, contemporary and historical respectively, for the construction of a national identity.

In the case of Martinique, the only perceived threat is France, the purveyor of material benefits and guarantor of social order. There have always been movements of cultural resistance in Martinique seeking to construct and assert a Martinican cultural identity separate from the French. One of these movements was what has come to be known as *Négritude*, a largely literary posture (see later) that contained a literary discourse about the glorification of blackness. But this did not have any appreciable echo in the population at large. And in this way, Martinique is different from Puerto Rico and Jamaica, where the issue of Africa is more than a literary trope, and is examined at academic and journalistic levels.

The cultural history of the Caribbean is often condensed (even minimized) into two dominant processes: accommodation/assimilation and resistance. The interplay between these two processes within the same society, and even within the same individual, accounts for some of the ambivalent values and structures found in Caribbean societies and individuals. It may be claimed that Martinique represents the highest degree of assimilation to the European norm in the Caribbean. It is in Martinique where primordial subordinate groups have been most thoroughly erased, both materially and in the consciousness of the people: very few phenotypical or cultural traces of the indigenous inhabitants; very few pre-Columbian onomastic influences; absence of groups of African origin still claiming African ancestry or openly recognized as having such (with the exception of the *Nègres Congo* group, which dates back just to the second half of the nineteenth century and which no longer exists as a well-defined recognizable group).

Africanisms may exist in the creole language of Martinique, as they are deemed to exist in the other creole languages of the Caribbean and even in the Spanish dialects of Puerto Rico, Cuba and the Dominican Republic. But Martinican linguists, and French linguists in general, have shown little interest in exploring the issue, and generally reject the hypothesis of an African base for the creole language(s) which emerged in the French Caribbean territories (for notable exceptions, see Sylvain 1936, and Cérol 1992).

Martinique has no syncretic religion. There is nothing paralleling Vaudoun of Haiti or Pukumina, Revival and Rastafarianism of Jamaica, or Santería of Cuba and Puerto Rico. Roman Catholicism remains dominant (with an increasing presence of Protestant churches, however). Martinique has no festival that has an African origin and serves a black ethnicity. Carnival is the major festival, but it is linked historically to Roman Catholicism and the mulatto middle class, although today it is a completely national celebration, perhaps more associated with the working class.

With the exception of Aimé Césaire, who is quite enigmatic as a leader, there have been no "black" leaders in Martinique championing "black" ethnic causes (or causes perceived as such); certainly none equalling the importance of Nanny, Paul Bogle, Sam Sharpe, Marcus Garvey, Alexander Bedward, among others, of Jamaica. As we said above, Aimé Césaire is affectionately (but also cynically and patronizingly) dubbed by Martinicans as "*notre petit nègre*". And the semantic complexity of this characterization reflects the enigmatic, ambiguous and multifaceted nature of the man and of his significance. Garvey of Jamaica had no such ambiguity. Césaire is the co-founder of the *Négritude* movement, but the movement remained largely a literary, philosophical stance and never developed a social praxis as the Garvey movement did. *Négritude* did challenge the concept and policy of cultural assimilation and the acceptance of European forms as universal canons. It affirmed black identity and solidarity among all black peoples, and espoused pan-Africanism. All of these are also basic tenets of Garveyism.

Césaire did recognize the role of Africa in the formation of Martinican society and culture, but he was not positively assertive about it, and neither he (nor any one else in Martinique) ever pushed this recognition to the point of advocating a return to Africa. Césaire assessed the situation in the following way:

> One may speak of a great family of African cultures that merits the name of Negro African civilization and that binds together the separate cultures of each of the African nations. Furthermore, one realizes that, because of the vicissitudes of history, the range and extent of this civilization have far outspread Africa, and thus it may be said that in Brazil and in the West Indies, and not only in Haiti and the French Antilles, and even in the United States, there are, if not centres, at least fringes of this Negro African civilization. (1956, 191)

Initially a communist, Césaire broke with the French Communist Party precisely because, like other communist parties of the immediate postwar period, it proclaimed the commonality of working peoples' interests all over the globe. Communist ideology rejected the notion of separate cultural and racial identities, believing that such identities were an inhibiting factor in the achievement of working-class solidarity.

Césaire rejected the French Communist Party for ignoring Martinique's cultural originality and specificity and, in a sense, its racial originality. In

Césaire's view, this originality produced a social order which was quite different from that of France. But while supporting cultural/ethnic individuality, Césaire opposed political separateness and promoted the idea of political assimilation leading to departmentalization in 1946. Martinique has been struggling ever since to resolve this dilemma (or contradiction), that is, to preserve and reinforce a separate cultural/ethnic identity while at the same time accepting political and administrative assimilation, seen as vital (or indispensable) for the preservation and reinforcement of economic and material benefits. Puerto Rico is facing the same dilemma. Jamaica's dilemma is the opposite: Jamaica is struggling with the problem of how to maintain and enhance cultural/ethnic separateness and political independence and still achieve economic prosperity.

Today, *assimilation* and *assimilé* (asssimilated) are virtually pejorative expressions among a growing number of Martinicans, referring as they do to a rejection of Martinican cultural and ethnic identity, and an espousal of French values and French cultural behaviours and tastes.

There are two main areas where these cultural/ethnic issues are being played out: language and music. The creole language of Martinique is being proposed as the symbol and the instrument of the challenge to French metropolitan hegemony. It is the foundation of *Créolité*, the latest literary and philosophical movement to sweep across Martinican history. The basic premise is that the creole language, called simply *le créole*, but also increasingly *le martiniquais*, expresses much better than French the racial and ethnic particularity of Martinique. This racial and ethnic particularity is, according to this movement, *le métissage*, the rejection of polarities and primordial essences, and the embrace of new hybrid structures.

Some Martinican writers, like many other writers elsewhere in the former colonial world, are grappling with the problem of the authentic voice, the search for a medium of expression that resolves a major contradiction of Martinican "national" literature. This is a literature which metaphorically, symbolically, implicitly, and often explicitly, strikes out against French metropolitan dominance and speaks of the problems of alienation, anomie, physical and psychological displacement, and so on, but does all this through the vehicle of French, as if the writer is an outsider looking in at Martinican society.

In resolving this dilemma, some writers go all the way, employing the creole language as the language of dialogue (except where the diglossic structure of the interaction calls for non-creole dialogue) as well as the language of narration. Other writers attempt to reconcile two mutually exclusive imperatives: the use of the creole language as the authentic voice and the search for a wider audience for economic reasons. They use (and often contrive) a level of expression that is both defiant of French and comprehensible to metropolitan Frenchmen, Franco-Canadians and others in the wider francophone world.

In virtually all the other areas of the Caribbean, the local creole language is not seen as representing an ethnicity founded on *métissage*, but as one of the most important historical links with Africa. Nationalist separatist ideologies in Jamaica, Haiti, Suriname and Guyana, seeking to counter ideologies of Euro-dependence, reject the traditional interpretations of creole languages as simplifications, corruptions or pathological social variants of European languages in the context of slavery, poverty, lack of education, and so on. The recognition of African language origins puts the creole language within an evolutionary tradition outside of European hegemony, thus countering the argument that creole languages are pathological manifestations of European languages, and helping creolophone speakers to develop more associative attitudes towards their languages.

This is the case of the creole language of Jamaica where ethnic ideologies based on Africa are strong. It is not the case of the creole language of Martinique, where historicity in the area of language has not been a matter of great concern for scholars and intellectuals. They have been content to postulate the novel nature of the language, corresponding to the novel nature of Martinican society. In Martinique, where Africa-based ideologies are weak and mixed-race or non-race ideologies are strong, the creole language is not seen as having any particular historical links that should be asserted, but is seen as supporting or reflecting a similar ahistorical, or non-historical, character of the population and society.

It is true to say that, compared with other Caribbean territories such as Jamaica, Haiti, Suriname and Cuba, the African content in Martinican culture is very weak at the present time. In the area of language, where African continuities have been most thoroughly debated, Martinican creole lacks several of the structural features of African origin found in other creole languages of the Caribbean. If, for example, Martinican creole has the "give" serial verb in sentences such as "he send the book give his brother" (*li voyé liv-la ba frè-li*), it does not have the "take" serial verb, as in Jamaican *im tek naif kot di bred* (he cut the bread with a knife). Martinican creole has the predicate cleft sentence: *se voyé li voyé liv-la*; cf. Jamaican *a sen im sen di buk* (he did in fact send the book). But it does not express plurality by placing the third person plural pronoun after the noun as in Jamaican *di buk dem* or Haitian *liv-la-yo* (the books). Nor does it have the associative plural *Jan dem* (Jamaican) or *Jan-yo* (Haitian), meaning "John and his pals".

Even in Puerto Rico, where African continuities in language are relatively weak (and weaker than in Martinican creole), there has been study and documentation of African elements in the language and culture, including the monumental work of Alvarez (1961). There is no work for Martinique paralleling Alvarez's for Puerto Rico or Alleyne's (1980, 1988) for Jamaica.

As far as music is concerned, the picture is much less controversial. There have been in the history of Martinique a number of music and dance genres that have approached the status of national musics. The current one is *zouk* which has achieved a great deal of international recognition and is an important symbol of Martinican identity. Earlier forms such as *bel air* and *biguine* have virtually disappeared from active production but remain as folkloric spectacles.

Current Ideological Currents

As a general rule, since the decline of *Négritude,* and with political assimilation no longer seriously contested, the only competing ideologies are *Antillanité* and *Créolité.* Martinique has inherited what may be a French penchant for the construction of philosophical-ideological "movements" and "schools". These are often linked to fictional literature, and the borders between philosophy and literature then become rather blurred. These movements are to a large extent hypotheses or theories of Martinican society, and seek to interpret the essence of Martinican-ness. They therefore deal with questions of Martinican identity: racial, cultural, ethnic and national. They may or may not lead to social and political movements.

They are also rather idealistic and mainstream in their approach to society. They do not fully recognize or deal adequately with a number of issues that are part of the Caribbean reality. These include: the marginalization of minorities (even, in some respects, of majorities), ambivalence and ambiguity, double identity, within the same individual, which stems from the co-existence of two "worlds", one real which is rejected although internalized, the other virtual, which is sought after but never attained; a world in which the majority are confronted with a double network of contradictory symbols and values. Some try to escape this by becoming absorbed in the pursuit of material goals; others battle to restore former polarities of Europe and Africa.

These movements also generally fail to recognize the social barriers to *métissage,* barriers which are racially founded and racially linked. Social, cultural, racial and phenotypical hierarchies still exist. We shall see that, by contrast, Jamaican movements generally do not seek simply to offer theories of Jamaican society, but, unlike the Martinican movements, are firmly fixed in social praxis and seek to transform society, not only the social order but also its values and symbols.

The issue of *Négritude* dominated Martinican thinking about identity from the decade of the 1930s up to the 1960s, when it lost steam and stalled in the face of the assimilation movement and the general widespread notion of *métissage. Négritude* was at first essentialist in its interpretation of Martinique, and totalitarian in its failure to recognize the ethnic diversity of the island. Burton (1994) is of the view that there were attempts, at least by the political wing of the movement, to accommodate the Indian presence within the context of proletariat solidarity with the oppressed Indian. The Trinidad Black Power movement also attempted this type of accommodation, with equal lack of success. As we said in the introduction, this shows how race and ethnicity may be a more powerful force than social class and socioeconomic circumstances in the mobilization of people.

Burton further observes that *Négritude* (or what he calls neo-*Négritude*) sought finally to recognize ethnic diversity by proposing the formula *"La Martinique, plurielle mais une"* (Martinique, plural but one). This was to be later echoed in the Jamaican national motto, "Out of Many, One People". In both cases, there is a reluctance to recognize the dominant race/ethnicity and a desire to promote the idea of national unity. In the case of Jamaica, the oneness proposed is at the level of nation. In the case of Martinique, unity or oneness is linked to the biological notion of *métissage,* and to the cultural notion of melting pot. In Jamaica, the idea proposed is that of a society made up of different ethnicities who are being encouraged and invited to suppress their separateness in favour of a common national goal. But it leaves each ethnic group to pursue its own cultural forms, especially its symbolic ones. In Martinique, biological *métissage* finds a cultural analogue in *Créolité,* the current movement that dominates the Martinican discourse on ethnicity.

Creolization is the process recognized by the *Créolité* movement as the dominant dynamic in the formation of Martinican society. It is closely related to the concepts of *métissage* and hybridity that are currently in vogue to interpret global society. These concepts are all part of current postmodern thinking.

These concepts are seen as opposed to the essentialist notion of races. They begin as interpretations of biological phenomena, but they subsequently have been extended to all the phenomena of mixing or fusion that affect society and culture. In the metaphorical extensions, they again reject the essentialist notions of homogenous societies and cultures, or of plural societies composed of groups defined as to their distinctiveness and diversity. In reality, however, they are based implicitly on the notion of race, that is, on the idea of some earlier stage characterized by fixed racial types. Similarly, they imply an earlier homogeneity of cultures and societies which then come together to mix or fuse. Fundamentally, as we know, this was not the case; creolization and hybridity have been ongoing processes throughout human history.

Globalization is also contributing to the elimination of cultural frontiers, and it is claimed that creolization is a global process, or at least a prefiguration of future world society. We know, however, that there are also contradictory currents in the strong contemporary assertion of separate ethnicity being witnessed all over the globe.

Créolité is defined very broadly, and elaborated in a rather diffuse way. In the main work that sets out its tenets (Bernabé, Chamoiseau and Confiant 1989), *Créolité* is, at one point, "not a synthesis, not simply *métissage*, but a kaleidoscopic totality" (p. 28). Elsewhere, it is syncretism (p. 31), or "the interactional or transactional aggregate of Carib, European, African, Asian and Middle Eastern cultural elements" (p. 26).

The work is more than just a treatise. It is replete with very imaginative literary assertions, many of them metaphorically based, about what *Créolité* is (and is not). It begins with a forceful assertion: "Neither European, African, nor Asian, we declare ourselves Creole" (p. 13). It then goes on to reject external (European) definitions and advocates an "interior vision" (*vision intérieure*) and a "self-acceptance" (*acceptance de soi*).

Créolité recognizes *Négritude* as a precursor, but it proposes to go beyond the essentialist approach of its precursor and even beyond the notion of racial categories towards a recognition of creole. But it does admit the multiracial character of Martinique, even as it urges Martinicans to abandon the habitual race-based distinctions and adopt the habit of designating themselves, whatever their complexion, by the only appropriate word: Creole (p. 29). In this sense, the work is often more wishful and idealistic than objective and analytic, as it proclaims that "*les relations socio-ethniques au sein de notre société devront désormais s'opérer sous le sceau d'une commune créolité*" (socio-ethnic relations should now henceforth operate under the seal of a common *créolité*) (p. 29).

The issue of language is central to the *Créolité* movement. In fact, its leading protagonists are linguists and novelists. *Créolité* in its linguistic praxis proclaimed *déviance maximale* (maximum deviation) as the basic principle for the construction of the Martinican language. According to this principle, forms of language which belong to a zone of interaction between the creole language and French were to be rejected, even if they were part of actual everyday usage among the populace. Forms which showed no compromise with French were to be favoured. In other spheres, however, the principle stops short of maximum deviation, certainly in phenotype, where it supports the idea of phenotypical levelling, some mid-point between the two phenotypical poles of white and black, which is the result of *métissage*. Nor is it clear what the position of *Créolité* is in other cultural spheres such as aesthetics, music, world view, where it seems to admit complexity and diversity.

The System of Representation

The Martinican terminology of race and ethnicity is richer than that of Jamaica, but perhaps not as rich as that of Puerto Rico. Martinique and Puerto Rico show a much more nuanced and differentiated representation of race and ethnicity than Jamaica which has preserved more faithfully than anywhere else in the Caribbean the post-Columbian primordial tripartite division into white, brown and black. The Martinican system of representation, as do those elsewhere in the Caribbean, has three major dimensions or meaning categories: (i) phenotype/colour, (ii) race/ethnicity and (iii) social class. (Ideology may constitute a fourth, particularly in Jamaica.) But, of course, there is no one-to-one correspondence between a term and a meaning category. A term may belong to two or three meaning categories, although one meaning may dominate over the other(s). For example, *béké* belongs to both the race/ethnicity and social class categories; *blanc* is phenotype/colour, race, and only marginally social class; *indien* is strictly race/ethnicity, whereas *couli* is both race and social class; *cafre* is strictly phenotype.

Blanc (white), as an adjective, refers to colour; it is also used as an adjective or noun to designate a race and ethnic group. It has no particular social class reference, except that there is an underlying notion that this race dominates the rest of the world socioeconomically. However, since in Martinique there is a relatively high incidence of members of this race holding non-dominant socioeconomic positions, there is less of an assumption of socioeconomic superiority than is assigned to the parallel white group in Jamaica. Jamaicans (and other people in the [former] British Caribbean) would be shocked to see white people in work gangs digging ditches or even as primary school teachers, as happens in the French Caribbean. The assumption that white people do not do manual labour is so strong that for many West Indians (persons of the [former] British Caribbean) arriving for the first time in England, the first thing that produces culture shock is the sight of white people performing menial jobs that were thought to be the natural preserve of blacks and Indians (from India).

Béké, on the other hand, is always a noun and refers to a member of a race/ethnicity occupying a dominant socioeconomic position. A phenotype (white skin colour, straight hair, thin lips, and so on) may be implied secondarily, but not necessarily. The (former) British Caribbean has, too, a separation of colour from social class in the terms *white* and *bakra*, paralleling Martinican *blanc* and *béké*. As we shall see, the term *bakra* has virtually become obsolete in Jamaica, matching the decline of whites as a local ethnic group. But *béké* is still very strong in current usage in Martinique, referring first of all to an ethnic group mainly of white planters and, more recently, of big businessmen. This group is known to be very closed, practising rather strict endogamy, and even identified by the geographical location of their residence. Because of the close association between the *béké* group and socioeconomic power, the meaning of *béké* has come to be (or, to be true, has remained) "manager", "boss", or someone behaving like, or perceived as, such. This gives rise to the possibility of adding any skin colour adjective to *béké*. Thus *béké blanc* ("white boss"), *béké noir* ("dark-skinned boss"), *béké brun* ("brown-skinned boss"), and so on.

As we have seen, *nègre* and *noir* are analogous to *béké* and *blanc*. *Nègre* refers to race/ethnicity, while *noir* is basically a colour term. But the separation is not as rigid as that between *béké* and *blanc*. *Nègre* and *noir* are in some ways synonymous denotatively, with *nègre* connoting lower socioeconomic value. *Nègre* can (exceptionally) be an adjective designating colour (*un béké nègre* sometimes being used for "a manager who is black in colour", but more usually, *un béké noir*). *We have seen that nègre* has become de-racialized and de-ethnicized. It can also be used without social class content. Thus *un nègre noir*, and so on (a dark-skinned fellow, and so on), but not *un noir nègre*, or *un nègre nègre*, or *un noir noir*.

As both *blanc* and *nègre* are stripped of social class value, *vieux* (old) has to be added to both in order to form an injurious term: *vieux blanc, vieux nègre* are both pejorative. In Jamaica, and other parts of the (former) British Americas, *nigger*, unqualified, is used injuriously, although in the Caribbean "old" added to "nigger" achieves a higher degree of injury. This may be both a case of the general pejorative use of "old", as in *vieux con* (old fool), and a reference to the habits and customs of an earlier time held to be unflattering.

Nègre may sometimes be used for strong affirmation of ethnicity and race, especially when there is a need to make a contrast with *béké*. In this case, the people take a pejorative term, particularly as used by outsiders, and throw it back defiantly. *Nigger* has been used in this way. Indians in the Caribbean also use *coolie* similarly. Thus, also, Bernabé (1997, 117) contrasts *une créolité béké* with *une créolité nègre* in discussing how the notion of "creole" has shifted from a white definition to a non-white, Martinican (but not black) one.

CHAPTER EIGHT

Jamaica

Overview

*J*amaica represents the anglophone Caribbean in this study. Although the island was under Spanish rule for a little more than 150 years, it is the British influence which dominates Jamaican history and provides the European input into the race and ethnicity picture. Generally speaking, the British attitude to other races was no different from that of the other European colonial powers. For example, a perhaps extremist, though generally typical, assessment of Africans was recorded by the historian Long:

> We cannot pronounce them [African slaves] unsusceptible of civilization since apes have been taught to eat, drink, repose and dress like men. But of all the human species hitherto discovered their natural baseness of mind seems to afford the least hope of their being (except by miraculous interposition of Divine Providence) so refined as to think as well as act like men. I do not think that an Orang Outang would be any dishonour to a Hottentot female. (1774, 23)

However, English literature suggests that some British intellectuals were wrestling and trying to come to terms with the new problem of racial and ethnic differences which increasing European contact with Africa and the arrival of Europeans in the Western Hemisphere had presented. Shakespeare's *The Tempest* presented a confrontation between Europe and the "uncivilized" world symbolized respectively by the characters Prospero and Caliban. They have become a major trope in Caribbean intellectual discourse.

The other major analysis of the issue of race and ethnicity is Shakespeare's *Othello, the Moor*. Moors were featured in British, French and Spanish theatre of the sixteenth and seventeenth centuries. Generally speaking, the characters were built on the prevailing prejudices, stereotypes and symbolism of black. Shakespeare had earlier, in the play *Titus Andronicus*, created Aaron, a Moor, as a person fearsome, cruel and lustful. Against this Elizabethan stereotype of a Moor or black man as ugly, cruel, evil, pagan, sexually bestial, Shakespeare then created a very complex Othello, apparently the opposite of the stereotype.

Shakespeare's depiction of Othello may indicate a diversity of opinions existing at the time. As we said in the introduction, it is wrong to make generalizations about the attitudes of a people or of an age. There must have been individuals in the Elizabethan period who had more balanced, unprejudiced, non-stereotypical views about Africa and black people. But it is more likely that rather than, or at least in addition to, wanting to represent a contrasting view of the time, Shakespeare created a complex contradictory Othello, noble and civilized, but with a lingering paganism and savagery, in order to heighten the dramatic impact of a hero overcome by tragedy.

Jamaica and Haiti lie on the African/black pole of the Caribbean race/ethnicity continuum. White is receding and is virtually non-existent as a local category. It remains a conceptual element of bipolarity and a symbol of historical and contemporary power, oppression and domination. But this is as much within the global context of the antagonism between black and white symbolizing two racial, cultural and ethnic poles in the world hierarchy, as within the local context. In Jamaica, "brown", signifying the "highest" shade of mulatto, has become the more active pole of opposition and antithesis to black.

There is in Jamaica nothing equalling the degree of denial of blackness and Africa that exists in Martinique and Puerto Rico. That is not to say that there is not some ambivalence about these categories. But anyone who wishes to propose the theory or ideology of the irrelevance of blackness and Africa in the construction of Jamaican identity has the onus and responsibility to argue his or her case. The "default" assumption is that they are quite relevant and fundamental to Jamaican identity. The debate is over whether they constitute assets or obstacles to Jamaican social and economic development in the context of globalization. The case for the irrelevance of blackness and Africa would have been openly argued say thirty or forty years ago, but if there are any supporters of this ideology today, they now remain quite silent.

It can be said that Jamaica follows the dominant Caribbean pattern of a basic tripartite racial division with socioeconomic correlates. These are simply represented in Jamaica as "white" (receding), "brown" and "black". They continue the primordial divisions which were established in post-Columbian Caribbean societies, and which corresponded to master, his (freed) offspring of mixed blood, and his slave, respectively. These divisions later developed into the socioeconomic categories of upper class, middle class and work-ing/peasant class.

It could be argued that this basic tripartite racial division, with its socioeconomic correlates, still exists in Jamaica. There has been some movement of blacks to share positions in the middle and to a much lesser extent upper, strata with whites and browns. But this is very slow or insufficient to change the general perception of the socioeconomic correlates of the "racial" divisions. Jamaica is in a perceptual/psychological transition period. There is some notion that race is not a dominant factor in socioeconomic mobility; that black persons with the necessary education and skills can achieve economic prosperity. On the other hand, there is also the persistent perception that, regardless of the economic status of a black person, he or she does not belong, or cannot rightfully aspire to, the highest echelons of the social order which are, to a large extent, still the preserve of whites and browns.

More significantly, there persists, although in a much diminished form, the notion that blackness is not simply a correlate of poverty but the cause of it. "We poor because we black" still reflects the understanding by black people of the way in which, historically, their race and colour have been the object of exploitation and degradation. Needless to say, this "victim" syndrome extends beyond poverty, and blackness is still widely perceived as the cause of unfair treatment in public services. "It is because we are black that we are treated so!"

This perception and reaction are most evident in areas where tourists are most present (the north coast of Jamaica). It is there that black/white polarity is most stark. In the general local community, "brown" people may be seen as the point of comparison in assessing the treatment that one receives. It should be again noted that the black people who react in this way (the victim syndrome) belong to all socioeconomic strata. This suggests that colour/race remains a strong motive force in social attitudes and relations. While it is evident that gains have been made in changing the racial basis of the socioeconomic structure, the historical symbolizations of colour/race are still very powerful, and come to the surface especially in situations of crisis.

As in all other Caribbean territories, racial mixing in Jamaica has continued such as to produce a range of nuances in a colour and phenotype continuum. But in Jamaica this continuum is not the dominant aspect of the picture; the large number of blacks at one pole (phenotypical and socioeconomic) is the dominant one. There is, correspondingly, no rich vocabulary to represent colour/phenotypical nuances. We shall see later that whereas Jamaica also exemplifies the dominant Caribbean pattern of greater social value corresponding to the movement from black to white through the colour (and phenotypical) continuum, there is also a countervailing strong affirmation of black skin pigmentation and natural hairstyles.

If it may be said that the dominant ideology of race and ethnicity in Puerto Rico and Martinique is *mestizaje, metissage,* that of Jamaica would be "marronage" and "blackness". Other competing ideologies in Jamaica are being eroded by the dominant one, but they still exist, and this leads to a situation of considerable racial/ethnic ideological complexity. The result is contradiction, ambivalence and ambiguity, as Jamaica wrestles with the problem of enhancing and asserting its black ideology and identity, in the context of a world and a Caribbean where there is growing hybridity and where "white" values dominate and are still rampant. Jamaica's official ideology as expressed in the motto "Out of Many, One People" may seem to be proposing an ideology of ethnic assimilation and unity, but this is largely considered to be an ideal yet to be concretely realized. It also represents some degree of denial of, and distancing from, the concrete reality of the dominance of black in the ethnic composition of Jamaica.

Although, as we have said, Jamaica follows the dominant Caribbean pattern, the differences between Jamaica and Puerto Rico and Martinique are quite evident, and are to be explained by the particular social and economic history of Jamaica.

Sociohistorical Background

Jamaica was under Spanish rule from 1494 to 1655, during which time the indigenous population was virtually wiped out. According to Cundall and Fietersz (1919, 34–55), in 1611 there were only seventy-four left. Jamaica is on a par with Martinique in that racial and ethnic identities have no "Indian" (that is, Carib/Arawakan) component. There are also no claims of Arawakan traits in any Jamaican phenotype. There is, however, a belief (quite unsubstantiated) that some Maroons of Jamaica have black straight hair and other facial features that are derived from an Arawakan (Taino) ancestry. The historical basis for this claim is supposedly that either during the Spanish colonization or at the capture of the island by the British in 1655, Africans fled to the hills and joined with Tainos already there to form Maroon bands and communities.

The indigenous peoples of the Caribbean passed on certain aspects of their culture to the post-Columbian societies, and a number of words to all languages of the colonizers. To the emerging Jamaican society and culture, the Tainos passed on the particular technique of smoking and preserving meats, known today as "jerk" and now an integral part of the national cuisine contributing enormously to the national identity of Jamaica. The Tainos also bequeathed the technique of removing the toxic element from cassava in order to make it edible in the form of *bami*, of similar importance to "jerk" in the construction of Jamaican national identity.

It is in the demographics of the proportionate rise in the black and white populations, and in the general sociology of the two groups, that the major differences between Jamaica and Puerto Rico and Martinique lie.

The white population of Jamaica was relatively small from the inception of European colonization and remained small during the entire period of slavery. A census of 1662 counted approximately 3,600 whites on the island. In 1673, the figure was 7,768, with just a slighter higher number of slaves, 9,504. This initial growth of the white population did not persist, a number of unfavourable conditions, including the disastrous earthquake of 1692, contributing to a decrease in the white population. So that in 1695 it was estimated that there were 2,440 white inhabitants; and in 1696, the figure had fallen further to 1,390 (Patterson 1967, 18–19).

In 1730, the white population was calculated at 7,148; in 1737, it was 8,000 (Patterson 1967, 47). There was some significant growth during the hey-day

of the sugar industry. According to Brathwaite (1971, 105), the white population in 1764 was 9,640 persons. In 1768, it was estimated at approximately
17,000. It increased from 18,000 in 1786 to 30,000 in 1807. At its highest, in
1824, the group of whites numbered only 34,152 (Eisner 1961, 127). By
contrast, in 1817, there were 346,150 slaves (of whom 126,903 were born in
Africa and 219,247 in Jamaica). At the end of the nineteenth century, whites
accounted for only 2 per cent of the total population of Jamaica. The 1960
census found 12,428 whites; by 1991, the census of that year turned up only
5,200.

An important aspect of the sociology of the white presence in Jamaica is
that, by contrast with Martinique and particularly with Puerto Rico, small
settlers were discouraged, as large owners attempted to monopolize available
land. Patterson states that

> less than two decades after the occupation of the island [by the British] we begin
> to detect tendencies toward monopolization which later were to prove disastrous
> in terms of making the island a "*colonie de peoplement*" [colony of settlers]. . . .
> By the opening of the eighteenth century, Jamaica had entered an entirely new
> phase of development, that of a large-scale, largely mono-crop agricultural
> system. (1967, 23)

The other dominant aspect of the demographics of British settlement of
Jamaica was the absenteeism widely practised by plantation owners. These
persons, who would normally represent the social, economic and cultural elite
in a plantation colony, were absent from Jamaica in relatively large numbers.
According to Patterson (1967, 37), citing Long (1774, 1: ch. 2), "in 1774,
one-sixth of the Jamaican proprietors were absentees. The full import of this
figure is not appreciated until it is understood that this one-sixth owned most
of the properties and slaves."

This had several important consequences, as have been noted by Patterson. Of interest to this study is the fact that the resident white group was
relatively homogeneous, as far as social status and level of "culture" were
concerned. There was no super-elite segment of viable size in their ranks
(as occurred in Martinique and Puerto Rico), and generally speaking they
did not command the respect of English visitors to the island nor of the
slaves themselves. Patterson rejects "the common view that the leading
members of early Jamaican white society came from the gentry and
upper middle class sectors of English society". He concludes that the white

population of 1678 was "lower class or at the most petty bourgeoisie in origin" (1967, 44).

Later, some stratification obviously began to emerge within the white population, based on status (indentured servant versus the rest), on regional origin (English versus Welsh, Scottish, Irish), occupation (attorneys, overseers, administrators, military, and so on). But the significant fact is that there were relatively few wealthy resident planters. They generally preferred to go back to England to enjoy their wealth in more appealing and congenial surroundings, and also had their children schooled there. There is consequently today in Jamaica no high visibility white ethnic group comparable to the *békés* of Martinique, nor a group of "poor whites" comparable to the Redlegs of Barbados or the *Blancs Matignons* of Guadeloupe. A minor exception is a small group of country folk of German extract residing basically in one single village, Seaford Town, in the parish of Westmoreland (see later). This historical white presence has not been sufficient to sustain a high visibility white ethnicity in Jamaica.

It is appropriate to mention at this point the introduction of Jews to Jamaica from the mid-seventeenth century, because, although they were not included at first in the racial/ethnic category of "white", they have so become as a result of their perceived racial/phenotypical identity with whites and their position at the highest level of the socioeconomic structure. Portuguese-speaking Sephardic Jews began to arrive in the Caribbean in 1654, following the reconquest of Brazil by the Portuguese. Some Spanish-speaking Sephardics may have already been in Jamaica as part of the Spanish occupation of the island. The Sephardics were joined by Ashkenazi Jews from north-west Europe in 1700. At the end of the seventeenth century, there were about eighty Jewish families in Jamaica, and by 1736 the Jewish community had grown to about 750 persons.

These Jews represented a commercial and technocratic elite, having brought with them the knowledge of sugar cane cultivation and sugar processing, and having dominated commerce, money lending and foreign currency dealing. There are important ways in which Sephardics and Ashkenazi represent significant sub-ethnic differences within global Jewish ethnicity. In Jamaica, these differences manifested themselves in separate synagogues until 1921, when the different factions amalgamated. Today, there is no separate sub-ethnic behaviour or identity observable between the descendants of these two groups.

At first the victims of restrictive laws, the Jews saw all their civil disabilities removed in 1831 and today they are perhaps the strongest subcomponent of the racial/socioeconomic category called white, such as it exists as a group. Their Jewish ethnicity is low keyed and they behave simply as upper-class Jamaicans. The Sephardics seem to have contributed their gene pool to the general population, since Portuguese surnames (such as DeSouza, daCosta, daSilva, Soltau, Henriques) are to be found across the colour continuum of Jamaica. By contrast, north-east European Jewish Ashkenazi names (Ashenheim, Lyons, Levy) are not broadly distributed. The disposition of Sephardics to mix sexually with other populations perhaps comes from their Latin/Mediterranean background.

There are several aspects of the historical demographics of the African presence in Jamaica that have important implications for the ethnic character of contemporary Jamaica, especially when compared with Puerto Rico and Martinique. The first is the high proportion of Africans relative to whites, which was achieved very early in the establishment of the plantation society. Jamaica was a huge market for slaves, both to supply local demand and for re-export. It is estimated that between 1655 and 1807, 747,500 slaves were imported into Jamaica. "Long before the end of the 17th century, slaves had replaced white servants as the mainstay of the island's labour force" (Patterson 1967, 24). According to Heuman (1981, 3), in 1673 there were 9,504 slaves in Jamaica. This figure rose to 86,546 in 1734, and then doubled in the next thirty years. By 1820, the number of slaves had risen to 339,000. Eisner reports that

> at the time of emancipation, except for the slave population, no official returns of numbers are available. The most widely accepted estimate, however, puts the total population [of Jamaica] in 1834 at 371,070, of whom fifteen thousand were whites, forty-five thousand were free coloureds and blacks, while the remaining 311,070 were slaves. (1961, 127)

According to Patterson,

> there were, on average, during the 17th and 18th centuries, over ten slaves to every white person in the island; and in the 19th century over thirteen slaves to every white. In Barbados, on the other hand, the average ratio during the entire period of slavery was very close to four slaves to one white . . . Thus, of all the British slave societies, Jamaica had by far the highest ratio of slaves to whites. (1967, 274)

Second, Jamaica is one of those places in Afro-America where a dominant African "focus", a concept first suggested by Herskovits (1941), can be plausibly established. If the Ewe-Fon modality dominates in Haiti, and the Yoruba in Cuba, it can be said that the Akan modality (in the specific Twi-Asante variety) dominates in Jamaica. This concept of an identifiable African focus has to be considered in the context of the well-recorded ethnic diversity of Africans brought to the Americas.

The Role of Africa in Jamaican Ethnicity

A major factor in the evolution of Afro-American culture and in the historical construction of "black" ethnicity in the Caribbean is the role of Africa. The issue concerns the continuity of African cultural forms and the persistence of the consciousness of Africa as the "motherland". It is often claimed that the conditions under which Africans came to the Americas precluded any such significant role. It is the ethnic diversity of Africans brought to the Americas as slaves which is of interest and relevance here. African diversity is said to have been so marked that it led to the early demise of African culture, and to a loss of consciousness of, and psychological allegiance to, Africa as motherland.

At its extreme, this argument alleges that slaves were deliberately distributed on plantations in such a way that those of similar ethnic origin would not find themselves on the same sites. This was supposed to minimize the possibility of conspiracy and revolt. The claim that such a policy (if it existed as policy) was ever implemented has not been substantiated. Whether it could be effectively implemented remains a question of considerable doubt. In any case, whether as a consciously formulated and implemented policy or as a function of the vicissitudes of the slave trade, it is true that at any moment in time, plantations in Jamaica and elsewhere were characterized by ethnic diversity, not only in the African population but in the white population as well.

However, there were also the countervailing preferences expressed by different European colonial establishments for Africans of particular ethnicities, based on stereotypes that had developed about them. According to Patterson,

> various writers referred to this great "predilection" on the part of the [Jamaican] planters for slaves from the Gold Coast . . . On the other hand, the Jamaican planters had an aversion to Nigerian Negroes, especially the Ibos who were

considered to be "the lowest and most wretched of all the nations of Africa", possessing a relatively marked tendency to suicide. (1967, 138)

Ethnic diversity has to be interpreted for its significance in each case. Its effect would have to be considered in the light of a total set of circumstances. For example, in the case of the Berbice province of what is now Guyana, African ethnic diversity is more a feature of the latter period of slavery. In the initial period, it seems that there was fundamentally one African group, the Ijo, from what is now eastern Nigeria. Thus the virtually extinct creole language, known in the literature as Berbice Dutch (lexically based on Dutch), has one clearly identifiable African base, the Ijo language. This is said to be unlike other creole languages, where a precise African base is not easily identifiable (in the maze of different African languages present); and this is said to call into question the validity of postulating an African base at all.

If, therefore, African ethnic diversity was everywhere a reality in the Americas, its inhibiting effect on the development of an African-based ethnic identity in Jamaica may have been minimized by the existence of a particular dominant African group. Alleyne (1988) proposes an Akan-Twi dominance for Jamaica. This is based, first, on their numerical importance (if not their majority) in the formative period. In the first part of this formative period (1655 to 1680),

> perhaps as much as a third of all slaves imported into the island came from the eastern Caribbean, particularly Barbados . . . The Barbadian planters tended to buy almost all their slaves from the Royal African Company, which, in turn, meant that the greatest single source of their slaves was the Gold Coast. (Patterson 1967, 134–35)

Another factor may be the ethnic personality of the Akan people. A consideration of this runs the risk of taking us into the area of stereotypes. It is certainly the case that the Akan people were portrayed by Europeans as aggressive, recalcitrant and prone to revolt. According to Patterson, these slaves "were rejected by most of the planters of the Eastern Caribbean (there was even a law in Barbados forbidding their entry into the island; hence perhaps the reason why they were sent to Jamaica)" (1967, 138). However, they were preferred by the Jamaican planters. If, as it seems, they were also the leaders of revolts in Jamaica, it is not clear whether this personality trait was a causal factor in their assuming leadership of the revolts or whether the fact of their leadership led to the stereotyping. Rather than speculating on whether the Akan were in fact dominant at any point in the period of slavery, or on their ethnic personality, it would be more useful to make inferences from the empirical data on Jamaican culture and reconstruct the historical ethnic situation.

There is evidence in the historical record, and in the history of Jamaican language and culture, that the Akan-Twi language was learned by other Africans. The religion of the Twi, in its modified Jamaican form, and with inputs from other African religions, was generally adopted by Africans in Jamaica, and evolved into Myalism, Pukumina and Revival (Alleyne 1988). The vast majority of lexical items of African origin in the Jamaican language come specifically from Twi. This suggests that the language, or at least its lexicon, was accepted by Africans of other linguistic groups interacting in Jamaica.

Other aspects of Jamaican culture allow us to reconstruct a Twi dominance. Anansi, the folk hero of Jamaican folk tales, is of Akan origin, and so is his principal accomplice, Takuma (cf. Twi *Ntikuma* meaning "son of Anansi"). Indeed, it has been claimed or proposed that Anansi now epitomizes the Jamaican national psyche. Similarly, another important figure, not imaginative but real, the obeah-man, is also of Twi origin.

The obeah-man and obeah exemplify the ambivalence and contradiction in the role of Africa in the construction and representation of Jamaican ethnicity. They had a positive value during slavery. They became depreciated in the cultural evolution of Jamaica, at least in urban and westernizing/modernizing sectors of the population (where they are associated with malevolent, supernatural practices), while they maintain their positive values and meaning in traditional (rural) sectors (where they are associated principally with spiritual/herbal healing).

The strongest evidence for an Akan-Twi dominance in Jamaica comes from the Maroon societies. The three existing Maroon communities of Jamaica all recognize and assert a "Coromanti" (that is, a Twi-Asante) ancestry. Dallas (1803, 33) reports that slaves from other ethnic groups had joined the Maroon bands but that the Coromanti language triumphed over all the others and succeeded in imposing itself on general usage. The Maroons have retained a knowledge of Twi, and some can still use the language in special contexts. Bilby (1981) adds that several other tribes are cited by the Maroons of today as having contributed to Maroon society, and that all these individual tribes are regrouped under the most powerful of all, the Coromanti tribe. Gardner (1873, 84), dealing with the general history of Jamaica, states, in reference to the religion practised in Jamaica, that the influence of the Coromanti seemed to have modified, if not completely effaced, all that had been introduced by other tribes.

In considering the demographics and sociology of the African group in Jamaica, it is important to take into account white owner absenteeism, which led to neglect of the slaves, and to harsher treatment than was the case where the owner was resident. The first major effect of this, as far as this study is concerned, is that the excessive brutality of the attorneys and overseers representing the absentee owners may have contributed to the development of a rebellious nature in the Jamaican slave, leading to many acts of resistance and flight from plantations. Patterson states that "several Governors of the island attributed the frequent slave revolts to the ill-use resulting from absenteeism" (1967, 44). We shall see that there was a symbiotic relationship between ethnicity, preservation of African culture, and resistance, one manifestation of which was the desire to maintain a physical distance from the white population. An important difference between Jamaica and Barbados, partly responsible for differences in culture and ethnicity in the two countries, is that after emancipation in Jamaica there was a massive exodus by the former slaves from plantations to remote hillside communities, while in Barbados the former slaves generally remained on plantations.

Whereas there were a host of other factors at play (summarized simplistically in the literature as a choice between "push" and "pull" factors), the harsher slave regime in Jamaica would have been one of the causes of this flight. Whereas a slave plantation anywhere was a very inappropriate context in which to learn and assimilate a dominant culture, it was a much more favourable context than the remote hillside communities that were set up in Jamaica, which became repositories for the preservation of a separate, black, African-based culture and ethnicity.

The second effect of this brutality and neglect was the high mortality rates among Jamaican slaves. Patterson cites, among others, a witness to the Select Committee on the Slave Trade (1790–91) who testified that

> It was more the object of the overseers to work the slaves out, and trust for supplies from Africa; because I have heard many of the overseers say, "I have made my employer 20, 30 or 40 more hogsheads per year than any of my

predecessors ever did; and though I have killed 30 or 40 Negroes per year more, yet the produce had been more than adequate to that loss." (1967, 44)

Apart from high infant mortality rates (and high mortality rates in the general adult slave population), the harshness of the regime seems also to have led to low levels of fertility in female slaves. In addition, one instrument of the resistance that was the hallmark of the response to slavery in Jamaica was the high rate of abortions, as female slaves were unwilling to produce children who would suffer the same terrible and ignoble fate as themselves. In other words, Jamaican planters either preferred, or were obliged, to resupply their manpower needs more by new imports than by the birth of "creole" slaves. The continuous replenishment of the slave group by imports from Africa meant a reinforcement of African elements both in phenotype and in culture.

There was a continuous flow of imports from Africa, such that African-born slaves (*bozales*) outnumbered Jamaican-born slaves (creoles) until 1780. According to Craton (1982, 139), it was only after 1780 that creole slaves outnumbered Africans. Indeed, ten years after the abolition of the slave trade, persons born in Africa still made up as much as 36 per cent of the slave population of Jamaica.

We may also note that, in contrast with Jamaica, the larger proportion of resident plantation owners in Barbados correlated with a less harsh slave regime there, lower slave mortality rates, replenishment of manpower by births more than by new purchases of Africans, and consequently less reliance than Jamaica on Africa as a historical basis for the construction of ethnicity and identity.

Miscegenation in Jamaica

In general outline, Jamaica followed the Caribbean pattern of the emergence of a mulatto group. The forced subjection of black females to the sexual desires of white males was the general pattern, although, in the case of Jamaica, this form of mating was much more dominant over consensual mating than in the case of Martinique and Puerto Rico. At least, the historical literature abounds with records of the sexual exploitation of black females practised by the white population in Jamaica during the period of slavery (see, for example, Hall 1995). As in every other New World society, this pattern of mating was an expression of the absolute power enjoyed by white males, as well as a consequence of the scarcity of white females.

The Jamaican coloured group grew steadily throughout the history of slavery, though not as much as similar groups in Puerto Rico and Martinique. Heuman (1981, 7) estimates that the number tripled during the three decades after 1790 and that it surpassed the white population during the 1820s. The first census after emancipation, taken in 1844, estimated that there were 68,529 coloured inhabitants representing approximately 19 per cent of the total population (with whites accounting for approximately 4 per cent).

Initially, the attitude of whites towards the new mulatto group was mixed. Mulattoes were likened to mules, and a number of stereotypes and myths emerged about them. It was thought that, like mules, they could not bear children, a myth that was very quickly exploded as sexual activity involving mulattoes proved otherwise. Ironically, the myth about their feebleness and incapacity for field work helped to ensure better treatment for them, and guaranteed that they were preferred over blacks as house servants.

Mulattoes first inherited the slave status of their slave mothers. But because in many cases they were either the children or the mistresses of slave owners (since it seems that they were considered more sexually desirable than black women), they were more likely to be freed. Heuman states that, "according to one contemporary estimate [in an unspecified year during the period 1792–1865], 80 per cent of freedmen were colored and 20 per cent black" (1981, 4).

At first, the important index of social status was not colour, but civil status, that is, free, freed and slave. Restrictions were placed on brown and black freed persons alike, and when new rights were secured for the freed population, these rights applied to both brown and black. Appeals could be made for exemption from the provisions of restrictive legislation by both brown and black persons. Heuman (1981, 6) cites some such cases, among them those of two black men who were allowed by the 1707–8 legislative session the right of trial by jury. In 1748, the Jamaica Assembly finally "granted black and brown the same rights in court as those who had been born free" (p. 5).

However, at the same time, and very early, some legal provisions began to distinguish between coloureds and blacks. In 1733, a privilege bill "accorded a brown man and his family all the rights of Englishmen born of white ancestors". While this was a considerable concession, the acts that followed it usually required the privileged freedmen to marry whites if their children were to inherit the same immunities. According to a later report, some freedwomen complied with this stipulation by marrying white husbands. Certainly those who applied for privileges after 1733 were mulatto or quadroon women and their children.

In 1780, an act was passed by the House of Assembly which decreed that no one should be deemed a mulatto after the third generation, and that such persons should enjoy all the privileges and immunities of His Majesty's white subjects of the island, provided they were brought up in the Christian religion. This is testimony to the establishment of the shade/phenotype system whereby shades closer to white were ascribed higher social and moral value (and for a time more legal privileges), and correlated with higher social status. It also shows the beginning of the blurring of the racial/ethnic frontier between whites and "high" browns in the Jamaican situation. As we noted above, this has developed today into a dominance of the brown category and the weakening of white as a local racial/ethnic group.

Colour, shade and phenotype became the significant variables, as browns began to distance themselves from blacks and to seek a closer identification with whites. The white establishment, while maintaining a great deal of hostility to browns, began to see them as logical allies against the threat of the black masses. On the one hand, browns were not generally admitted to the society of whites. Heuman reports that, "often accepted as whites in Britain, these coloreds [those who were educated abroad] were dismayed by their reception in Jamaica when they returned home" (1981, 11). On the other hand, some fluidity in the social system began to appear, as wealth was already able to secure some brown men an entry into Jamaican high society. Heuman (p. 13) mentions some cases in the early nineteenth century which show that white Jamaica had begun to take account of economic power as well as colour in considerations of status and social acceptability.

Needless to say, browns distanced themselves from blacks regardless of civil status as the colour system became more entrenched and the value of approximations to white became more recognized. Indeed, it is ironical to observe that the bleaching of the skin, now being practised by Caribbean and North American persons nearer the black end of the colour continuum, is first reported for "lighter complexioned coloreds" in pre-emancipation Jamaica. According to Heuman, Governor Manchester noted in a dispatch to the Colonial Office in 1823 that

> the dark coloureds and blacks were indignant at the superiority which those of fairer complexions claim over them . . . A decade later, a letter writer to the *Herald and Literary Journal* directed his anger at the offending browns:

"You boast of personal attractions, but even after you have added to your loveliness by the application of patent washes for the improvement of your skins, I can discover nothing in you but your ignorance and conceit." (1981, 15)

The use of terms such as "loveliness" and "improvement" in that writer's strictures does not seem to be sarcastic, but points to a general social consensus about the higher value of approximations to white, at least among persons who were removed from the black pole of the colour continuum.

The Post-Emancipation Period

The post-emancipation period saw progressive changes in racial and ethnic relations in Jamaica. Economic and political considerations played an increasing part in the structure of these relations as groups sought alliances to further their own interests. The coloureds came to challenge the whites for political and economic power, and allied themselves with the Jews.

Jamaica experienced the general shortage of manpower on plantations in the post-emancipation period. The solutions that were chosen to remedy this situation had important consequences for the race and ethnicity picture. The first solution agreed on by planters and the colonial establishment was also attempted in other areas of the Caribbean, and particularly in Puerto Rico. This solution had as its goal the massive "whitening" of Jamaica. Of interest to us here are the implications of this option for the stereotypical racial and ethnic representations of the time.

One of the justifications for the enslavement of Africans for work on the plantations of the New World had been that they were suited to tropical labour while Europeans (and even the indigenous peoples of the region) were not. However, this was cast aside when the need was perceived for an increase in the white population to improve the security of the colony of Jamaica against the threat of the black majority. Another myth in circulation at the time, which was also used to justify the enslavement of Africans, was their alleged "barbarism" compared with the "civilized" character of Europeans. The rationalization was that work on the plantations would be an improvement on the type of life experienced in Africa. The whitening of Jamaica was supposed to provide a "model" of industriousness, thrift, honesty and sobriety which, it was hoped, the recently liberated slaves would follow for their own uplift, lest they relapsed into barbarism. There was of course little evidence that the reality of peasant life in Europe at the time conformed to this "civilized" stereotype which European mythification created. As it turned out, the European workers did not display these qualities in any abundance; and in these particular respects they were indistinguishable from the ex-slaves.

Numbers of European indentured workers were brought to Jamaica between 1834 and 1843. They were intended to occupy the interior hillsides and so deny ex-slaves the opportunity to acquire land or find work outside the estates, which they had been abandoning in large numbers. These European immigrants were in the majority English, Scots and Irish, and were distributed around the countryside but mostly in the western region. There is no trace of them as a group today among the peasant class. They evidently contributed their gene pool to the general miscegenation taking place. There is the occasional individual to be seen showing pure European phenotype, but with the social appurtenances (including rough skin and ruddy complexion) of peasant origin.

A major non-British group arrived from Germany. According to Senior (n.d., 6), 1,038 Germans arrived between 1834 and 1836; of these, 249 were sent to found the township of Seaford Town in Westmoreland. Their numbers increased steadily, but their demographic rise has taken a downturn in recent decades as a result of out-migration to urban centres in Jamaica and abroad and of social mobility to the professional and business classes. They have practised endogamy to a large degree and are still viewed by the general Jamaican population as being "clannish". Their endogamy is seen negatively by the rest of the Jamaican population: the initial small size of the population has led to "in-breeding" and this is considered to have produced a number of perceived or imagined flaws in the physical, intellectual and moral make-up of the Seaford Town population.

On the other hand, some miscegenation has also taken place both from exogamy with mulattoes and from casual mating with black members of neighbouring villages. There are a number of obvious German surnames in the general Jamaican population (Rhyman, Haase, Stockhausen, Eldemire, among others). Persons carrying these names may run the full range of the colour/shade continuum.

There is also a very generally held perception and construction of a certain social/phenotypical category referred to as "St Elizabeth" (the name of the parish in which it is believed the German population is located). This is a person of perceived working-class/peasant origin who goes against the expected colour/phenotype correspondence by showing white/ruddy complexion and corresponding eye and hair colour. Other phenotypical features are non-white (hair texture, anatomy, nose, lips). This category is not considered to be particularly attractive. Indeed, one important effect of the presence of this German category in Jamaica is that it contributed to the general depreciation of "white" as a racial, social and aesthetic category in Jamaica.

By 1841, the policy of whitening was seen as a failure (Senior, n.d., 15). This led to the further diversification of the racial and ethnic composition of the island by the arrival of groups of indentured workers from Africa and Asia (China and India) and the Middle East (Syria and Lebanon).

Africa

We have seen how, in the post-emancipation period, the introduction of Africans in Martinique and of *Dominicanos* and Leeward Islanders in Puerto Rico led to their occupying the black/African polarity, contributing to the weakening and denial of this category as a national category. In Jamaica, a similar event had the opposite effect. Approximately ten thousand Africans came to Jamaica between 1841 and 1867 (Schuler 1980; Roberts 1954). The major contingent was liberated Africans of different ethnic origins who had been assembled in Sierra Leone and the Kru Coast. Another group was liberated Africans from slave ships intercepted by the British navy after England abolished the slave trade.

They were distributed across the island, principally in St Mary, St Thomas and Westmoreland. However, as in the case with the Germans in Seaford Town, one community of these Africans has preserved some measure of ethnic and cultural distinctiveness and has come to represent, together with the Maroon communities, the African pole of the cultural continuum of Jamaica. Seaforth Town in the parish of St Thomas has preserved a "Congo" identity. Some remnants of the Kikongo language have been maintained. But it is the Bantu-based Kumina religion which most distinguishes the community ethnically (see Alleyne 1988). A Yoruba-based community is to be found in the Waterworks/Abeokuta area in the parish of Westmoreland. It preserves a distinctive tradition of music (drumming) and dance called Etu. Some Yoruba words and expressions are still remembered, but, in general, this community has a much lower ethnic profile than Seaforth Town.

Unlike the case of Martinique and Puerto Rico, the arrival of these Africans did not add a new (or a newly perceived) racial, ethnic or phenotypical category. They were able quite easily to fuse with the surrounding population. One of the features which distinguish the Jamaican Maroons from their Suriname counterparts is that in Jamaica, and especially in the eastern region, Maroons carried on a great deal of intercourse, both social and commercial, with the surrounding population. In fact, the eastern part of Jamaica, where Seaforth Town is located, is also the location of two Akan-based religions: Convince (a geographical modality of Myalism) and Maroon religion. There have been ongoing mutual influences among these three (Kumina, Convince and Maroon). According to Alleyne,

> these people [the newly arrived Bantu indentured workers in St Thomas] re-Africanized Myalism by introducing Kongo religious elements and Kikongo language into it. As a result, they gave it an undoubtedly Kikongo name that has come down to us as *Kumina*, and as *Pukumina*. They also prevented the further movement of Myalism away from its African origins, giving rise to Convince as a religious form close to the African pole of the religious continuum. (1988, 95)

These eastern parishes (St Thomas, St Mary and Portland) now occupy a special place within the general spirituality of Jamaica. Myalism and obeah, particular aspects of this spirituality inherited from Africa and concerned with communication with the spirits and with herbal/spiritual healing, have become significant features of Jamaican ethnicity. There have even been proposals that the laws banning the practice of obeah (which were first passed during the period of slavery, when the practice of obeah was greatly feared by the planter class) should be repealed.

The effect of the arrival of Africans in the post-emancipation period was therefore to reinforce African-derived cultural forms, especially in the expressive areas of religion, dance and music, and to strengthen the perception of an African source of Jamaican culture. Kumina music and dance have become accepted forms of the Jamaican national culture. Kumina drumming and the Kumina "shuffle" dance movement performed to it have become standard elements of the Jamaican dance theatre, and the Seaforth Town performers themselves are invited to perform at national celebrations. In this sense there has been a theatrification of Kumina culture which so far has not led to a dissolution of its integrity in its local setting, but which, on the contrary, seems to be contributing to a growing acceptance of Kumina as part of the national identity.

India

The situation of Indians in Jamaica is more like that of their counterparts in Martinique than like that of their counterparts in Trinidad, Guyana and Suriname. In these latter countries, the numerical importance of the Indian population has been perhaps the main factor in their current socioeconomic and political advancement. This advancement has been nurtured by the high degree of ethnicity, based not only on racial distinctiveness but also on cultural forms which their numbers have allowed them to preserve and assert. On the other hand, Indians in Jamaica (and in Martinique) were and have remained a small minority which, as a group, has not emerged from its original socioeconomic situation as agricultural workers and small farmers. They have been forced to view their progress in terms of cultural and, to a lesser extent, racial integration into the mainstream black community rather than in terms of a continued separate, vigorous ethnicity based on a distinctive culture. Their ethnicity is mild, and is based on a still strongly perceived racial (rather than cultural) distinctiveness. It is also mild because of their small numbers and their geographical dispersion over the island.

Their high degree of acculturation is manifested in the absence or weak presence of the larger cultural forms (religion, language, music, dance, social organization, and so on), as well as in the micro-forms of cultural behaviour. For example, Indians in Jamaica are no longer distinguished (as they are in Trinidad) from Afro-Jamaicans by their method of setting out vegetable market gardens or by their working stance. In Trinidad, Indians keep different vegetables separated in different beds, and work in the fields from a squatting posture. Afro-Trinidadians mix vegetables within the same bed, and work from a stooping stance. Shepherd (1994) provides a comprehensive study of the factors affecting the sociocultural position of Indians in Jamaica.

Between 1845 and 1916, 37,000 Indians came to Jamaica as indentured workers. Some (38 per cent) were repatriated on the expiry of their indenture. Various factors led to a relatively low birth rate, including the small number of women. So that, by 1930, when organized repatriation was terminated, the Indian population in Jamaica totalled 17,599 persons (Shepherd 1994, 104). The population census of 1943 recorded 21,278 Indians (that is, about 3 per cent of the total population). In the 1960 census, there were 27,912. The number increased only slightly to 29,218 in the 1991 census.

As in the case of Africans (and to a lesser extent Europeans) coming to Jamaica, Indians may have been perceived as racially homogeneous, but they were by no means ethnically homogeneous. As was the case with the African and European groups, the Asian Indians quickly lost their cultural and ethnic heterogeneity. If intra-African acculturation and assimilation remains one of the biggest gaps in African diaspora studies, so intra-Indian assimilation has hardly been treated in Indian migration studies. The Indians who came to Jamaica (and elsewhere in the Caribbean) originated from different linguistic and cultural zones (Shepherd 1994, 46). The only clear cultural distinction that remains is the religious one between Muslims (the minority) and Hindus (the majority). Whereas this distinction is the basis for ethnic separation in Trinidad, where Muslims and Hindus maintain separate political, economic and cultural institutions and have different voting behaviour in national elections, this distinction is very weak in Jamaica, where there have been large scale conversions to Christianity. Where this distinction still exists, it hardly translates into any significant ethnic separation. In Jamaica, it is the perceived *racial* homogeneity and distinctiveness of Indians as a group which forms the basis of their ethnicity.

Shepherd concludes that the Indian immigrants to Jamaica "constituted a fair reflection of the North Indian population . . . with the majority being Hindus of the middle and lower social positions" (1994, 47). Though proprietors in Jamaica specifically requested agricultural labourers and were adamant that higher castes should not be dispatched, inevitably non-agricultural/high caste Hindus arrived in the island. The levelling conditions and circumstances of their lives in Jamaica resulted in these immigrants becoming generally undifferentiated as to social class or caste.

Some, however, came from the Madras region, and there were reports of conflict between Madrasis and North Indians in cases where they found themselves on the same estates (Shepherd 1994, 50). Madrasis are generally (or are so perceived in the West Indies) of darker pigmentation than North Indians. The term "Madras Indian" remains in use to refer to any dark-skinned contemporary Indian in Trinidad and Jamaica. Although the caste system could not be maintained in the Caribbean, and initially the common occupation and conditions of life placed all Indians on the lowest rung of the socioeconomic ladder, colour/shade persisted as a significant factor in societal relations. As we noted earlier, Indian migrants brought with them from their homeland a colour/shade hierarchy which valued lighter shades more highly than darker shades. This fitted in perfectly with the same hierarchy which had developed on Jamaican and Caribbean plantations and in the societies at large.

Perhaps they would also have brought with them some idea of the global cultural hierarchy that European imperialism and their own cultural self-consciousness had imposed on themselves, whereby Africa and Africans represented the pole of lowest value. There developed between Indians and Africans in Jamaica (and in Trinidad) a curious interplay of racial and ethnic hostility on the one hand, and racial tolerance and interaction on the other. Indians and blacks each felt superior to the other, and created a number of ethnic/racial pejorative myths and stereotypes of each other. This also occurred in Trinidad and Guyana, where the residential segregation between Indians and Africans that was instituted on the plantations during indentureship continued in the form of Indian villages in the post-indenture period.

In Jamaica, the initial segregation on estates gave way to considerable cultural assimilation under common residence in the same villages. Other circumstances, such as the scarcity of Indian females, made exogamy more necessary there than in Trinidad or Guyana.

Indians today continue to rate themselves higher than blacks in the racial phenotypical hierarchy. According to Erlich,

> most Indians are prepared to dig into the colonial bag of arguments of racial superiority. In discussions about race, Indians merely point to their Caucasoid physical features as proof of their superiority to Negroes. However, equal emphasis is not given to such features as "thin lips", "narrow nose", "light skin" or "straight hair". Rather, it is the last feature, that of "straight" or "good" hair, which is most continuously singled out by the Indians . . . A type of cultural "fixation" upon "hair" seems to exist among Indians in the village . . . Intermarriage, it was feared, would bring "bad hair" to the Indian's family line. (1976, 21)

This would again suggest the primacy of race in the context of competition for scarce benefits as a motive force in social psychological organization, overriding the common social and economic status and circumstances of Indians and Africans.

Contrary to the stereotype of the "docile, cringing, obsequious coolie" whose only passion is for domestic crime, "the Indians in Jamaica, as in other receiving colonies, employed a variety of strategies both to resist and to register their disaffection with repressive aspects of the [estate] system" (Shepherd

1994, 66). However, there is no report that they conspired and collaborated with the blacks who were similarly exploited. As we noted earlier, they kept well apart from the 1938 riots and other forms of agricultural labour unrest in Jamaica. According to Shepherd, "they [the Indians] were beaten as strike breakers and subjected to a hostile reception by the rank and file members when some evinced a desire to join trade unions afterwards. Only a minority showed such interest" (p. 144).

The effect of the Indian presence was to strengthen the perception of the black Afro-Jamaican population that they were the "inheritors" of Jamaica, and that they represented the "national" essence. Indians, on the other hand, were represented as aliens, not "true" Jamaicans. This perception was validated, in the view of the blacks, when it was alleged that Indians in Jamaica cheered for the visiting Pakistani cricket team in 1986 in their games against Jamaica and the West Indies. This was also reported for Trinidadian Indians. To the extent that this was true, the fact that it happened both in Trinidad and Jamaica, where Indians have different socioeconomic, cultural and ethnic experiences, and the fact that the Pakistanis are Muslims whereas Jamaican and Trinidadian Indians were/are, in the vast majority, Hindus, suggests that it was perceived "racial" identity and loyalty which superseded any national or cultural affiliation.

There is no doubt that "Indian" or *coolie* remains a recognized "racial" category in Jamaica. This suggests that some degree of endogamy is sill being practised, and maintains the "pure" Indian phenotype in Jamaica. On the other hand, there are not many distinctive cultural attributes associated with it. There have been a number of Indian organizations that have attempted to promote or revive Indian cultural forms. There was also an Indian newspaper, *The Indian*, published in the 1930s, as well as a few Indian schools in the same decade. A radio programme, *Indian Talent on Parade*, appears intermittently, providing Indian music and information on the Indian community.

This distinctive racial identity, and the fact of being marginalized by the dominant black majority and by the white and brown establishment, have been sufficient to nurture a separate ethnic consciousness. This ethnicity, however, has little opportunity to express or assert itself and does so more by omission, that is, by refusal to participate in black ethnic activities and by viewing themselves as competitors rather than as collaborators with the black working and peasant class.

China

Four hundred and seventy-two Chinese arrived in Jamaica in 1854, a little less than half of this number coming from Panama, where they had gone to work on the Panama Railway. But the high death rate and repatriation so reduced their numbers that the 1881 census reported only 99 Chinese on the island (Lind 1958, 149). In 1884, thirty years after the first group arrived, 696 Chinese arrived from Hong Kong, and were distributed mainly on plantations in St Mary and St Thomas. However, the census of 1891 counted only 481 Chinese. The next wave of arrivals, between 1891 and 1911, was of commercial immigrants, and they not only increased the population of Chinese to 2,111, but also signalled the change in occupation from agricultural worker in certain parishes to retail grocer all over the island. There were 9,234 Chinese counted in the 1943 census. From 10,267 recorded in the 1960 census, the number fell to a mere 5,372 in the 1991 survey, owing to a large extent to emigration to the United States and Canada.

The Chinese came chiefly from the Kwang Dung area of southern China and were mostly Hakka people. The Hakka were nomads, moving whenever conditions were not to their liking. They migrated to many areas of the Americas and Europe. In Jamaica, as elsewhere, they were a tightly knit racial/ethnic group. Unlike the Indians, they developed and financed their own institutions: a benevolent society, a public school where Hakka was taught, a newspaper, a sanitarium, a cemetery, social clubs. In the mid-twentieth century, when national sentiment in Jamaica became very strong, the Chinese abandoned many aspects of their ethnic identity and participated more in the national forms of life and culture (for example, popular music, football). Since the decade of the 1970s, emigration has reduced the size of the Chinese group, leading to a further weakening of Chinese separateness.

As with other immigrant groups, the shortage of Chinese women led to miscegenation. Chinese men seem to have been more active in this area than the males of other ethnic immigrants, so that the census of 1943 showed almost as many mixed Chinese persons as pure Chinese.

As a group, the Chinese did not remain for a very long time in agricultural work. They progressed through the retail grocery trade to the banks and the professions. In so doing they rid themselves of the stigma of rural agricultural labour. In addition, their phenotypical features of straight hair and light skin allowed them to cash in on the resulting social benefits. Thus, when banks had to expand their employment pool beyond whites and "high" browns, the Chinese became the first group to be employed, long before blacks or Indians of similar or superior education. There is no doubt that these phenotypical features made them more acceptable to the white bank owners and managers. However, there was the additional factor of the ethnic myths/stereotypes associated with the Chinese: that they were quiet, stable, not talkative or boisterous like blacks and Indians, and especially that their tradition in the retail grocery business meant that they could count and handle money.

Syrians

These are, properly speaking, Middle Easterners, originally from Lebanon, Syria and Palestine; but in the popular representation they are all "Syrians" (earlier, they were also "Syrian-Jews"). They began arriving in the last two decades of the nineteenth century and have become prominent in commerce. The 1943 census recorded 857 "Syrians". The number increased by childbirth within the group to 1,354 in the census of 1960. But by 1991, the Syrian population had decreased by emigration to the United States and Canada to such an extent that they could not be listed as a separate category in the census of that year; they were listed as "others". As a group, they are now firmly placed in the middle and upper classes.

Syrians are losing their character as a separate ethnicity, and are being seen as simply part of the phenotypical socioeconomic category represented as brown or white. However, there are latent evaluations based on a memory of their background. A put-down similar to that used by Puerto Ricans to uppity mulattoes (*Y tú, dónde está tu abuela?* meaning "As for you, where is your grandmother?") is used by blacks to uppity Syrians. Syrians are reminded of the time when they went around on foot peddling cloth or were reputed, by stereotype, to be ragged, unkempt and disorderly. In Trinidad, *rab* (from "Arab") is still used to mean "a disorderly person"; and the *Dictionary of Jamaican English* (Cassidy and Le Page 1967) cites *raba,* presumably of the same root, in the meaning "shabby, ill-kept person".

Racial/Ethnic Constructions

One of the outstanding features of Jamaica is the apparent contradiction between a strong "black" ethnicity on the one hand and the persistence of aspects of the pejoration of black on the other. Jamaica has always been in the forefront of struggles for the reclaiming and reappropriating of black dignity. At the same time, all the pathological expressions of marginalization persist. But even here, and somewhat reminiscent of similar patterns among African Americans of the United States, some of these expressions become a part of a neo-black popular aesthetics and world view, and do not have all the elements of mimicking of whiteness typical of other expressions of marginalization.

If in the United States "black" is defined in terms of a socially constructed genetic factor of "one drop of blood", in Jamaica "black" is being increasingly defined in ethnic ideological terms. There is a vibrant black consciousness on the one hand, but on the other hand a quite understandable victim syndrome that pits black against white (and to a lesser extent against Chinese and "Syrians"), but not against Indians, who are not seen as "oppressors". There is no chauvinistic belief in the superiority of blackness. There is defence against marginalization, a strong desire to rehabilitate black people and to reappropriate their history. The black ideology is therefore an experiential social phenomenon, and not racist per se. Indeed, the boundaries of black are open to those other "races" who qualify by showing themselves not to be oppressors.

A further aspect of the racial/ethnic complexity is that, politically, at the national level, Jamaican blacks have accepted, and still do, the leadership of non-blacks. There has been, at the level of national politics, the absence of strong political movements that have succeeded on the basis of race. Indeed, in *the* outstanding case, the People's Progressive Party, which claimed to be a revival of the party of Marcus Garvey and campaigned openly on the basis of race in the Independence elections of 1962, suffered an ignominious defeat at the polls. All its candidates failed to receive the minimum number of votes that would have qualified them for a refund of their deposits. There is apparently a recognition that a black ideology can serve the purposes of ethnicity, but that it is insufficient to serve national needs. It was considered that national needs required skills (including language skills), resources, and other capacities that were thought to reside exclusively in whites and mulattoes.

This picture has changed in recent times. There is now a claim that Jamaica, in 1993, elected its first black prime minister. There have since been somewhat veiled appeals to race in consolidating the tenure of that prime minister and in campaigning for his re-election in 1997. One of the dominant themes in the 1997 campaign was: "Is blackman time now"; the incumbent prime minister sought to win support from the crowds at public meetings by reminding them that if he were to leave the platform and walk among them, they would not recognize him as being in any way different from them. This was a highly contextualized appeal to race, as the other main contender for the office of prime minister was someone of European/Middle Eastern extract who was generally considered "white" in the complex representational system of Jamaica (see later). Many persons (particularly young voters) proclaimed that they could not vote for a white man to run the government of Jamaica.

There have been movements, throughout Jamaica's history, which have fought for black emancipation – political, spiritual, mental and cultural. These movements are all subsumed under the rubric "marronage". Rastafarianism is only the most recent one in a long tradition that began with the first Maroon rebellions. It is not that such movements were absent from other parts of the Caribbean. But they have had a particular character in the case of Jamaica, and have culminated in a certain personality profile of the Jamaican, and in a national image, which has come to be expressed in recent times in the sociological literature by the term "marronage".

This character has been canonized by the elevation to the status of national hero of prominent actors in this struggle for black emancipation: Nanny was a Maroon leader; Sam Sharpe led the last slave revolt which signalled the death knell of slavery; Paul Bogle led the Morant Bay Rebellion, which heralded the new, modern period of black ethnicity; and Marcus Garvey internationalized this spirit and ideology. And there are several others who have not been accorded official national recognition but remain icons in the popular consciousness: Kojo, another outstanding Maroon leader; Alexander Bedward, a religious leader who challenged the white establishment; Bob Marley, who articulated the aspirations of black and oppressed people worldwide.

Walter Rodney is another recent protagonist. In the decade of the 1960s, he articulated an ideological position that found resonance among a large section of the Jamaican population. This position was fundamentally a recognition that Jamaica was a black country with firm historical ties to Africa, and that this ethnic, racial, historical fact should be fully recognized in the official and public life of Jamaica. This was a direct challenge to the official motto, "Out of Many, One People". Subsequently, perhaps in no small measure, consequently, the concept of a black Jamaica became more openly and forcefully asserted, with organs such as the newspaper *Abeng* publicly defending it.

Jamaican history is replete with the struggles of the black population to assert its ethnicity in the context of resistance to slavery. Whereas slave revolts and uprisings were typical of all slave regimes throughout the Caribbean and the New World, Jamaica had more than a full share; and it was not simply a matter of uprisings or acts of rebellion and resistance, but rather of organized revolts. These had as their goals, not merely an escape by individuals from the harshness of slavery, but the desire to create a way of life based on a cultural and spiritual allegiance to Africa.

Maroons

The Maroon communities of Jamaica (and those of Suriname) are the only extant cases of well-established, culturally viable free communities dating back to the period of slavery. In these communities, there developed a symbiotic relationship between ethnicity and freedom. For the Maroons, Africa is not merely an ideological construct, but is a living consciousness and focus of historical allegiance. The preservation of an African-based ethnicity was not simply the result of isolation from the dominant plantation culture, but also an actively exploited instrument, an asset in the struggles against the slave regime and in the continued existence of the communities.

The resources that played a pivotal role in ensuring Maroon freedom and in securing a way of life which Maroons wanted for themselves were derived from their African heritage. Maroon religion is a derivative of Akan religion. The pantheon and general belief system have been well preserved (see Alleyne 1988, 76–105). Maroons recognize Yanking (or Nyame) as the supreme deity. They still invoke the divinity known to the Akan as *Asaase* (Earth Goddess) in the greeting *Yankipong adu Asaase*. Below the Supreme Deity are the spirits of the ancestors ("duppies", cf. Twi *adope*, meaning "spirit"). These spirits are arranged in a hierarchy: the older ancestors are the most powerful, but they are rarely invoked because of their remoteness in time. More recent ancestors are closely linked to the living and exert great influence on their daily lives. Bilby (1981) and Schafer (1974) provide copious records of the links between Maroon religious ritual and Akan traditions.

It is well known and well documented that religion is of considerable importance in the construction of ethnicity and has been especially exploited in times of conflict and struggle against external enemies. In the case of Maroon and slave religion, certain aspects of the belief system were vital in the resistance effort and in coping with the generally adverse conditions. Slaves and Maroons believed that upon death, their spirits would return to Africa to dwell with the ancestors. They believed that a religious oath administered by a priest-like figure (obeah-man or myal-man) would render them immune to the weapons of the British colonial establishment. Most dramatic of all was the supernatural ability of Nanny, the female Maroon ruler, to catch the bullets of the enemy and hurl them back. Nanny has been elevated to the status of national heroine of Jamaica.

As we said earlier, it is possible to reconstruct a Twi-Asante dominance among the African languages of the slave population of Jamaica in the early period, giving rise to a preponderance of Twi-Asante traits in the creole language of Jamaica. Maroons learned the creole language of the plantations, but, unlike the plantation population, they have preserved Twi-Asante (which they call Coromanti) up to today. The role of Twi-Asante was a political and military one. It was tactically important in the wars against the British as it offered a secret code to which the enemy was not privy. Its political and military role declined at the end of the wars, but even today the language is still used in conversation among Maroons when non-Maroon strangers visit the communities. The purpose is not so much to shut out those strangers, as to express the African identity of the Maroons and to preserve the African tradition, of which Maroons are very proud. The abeng, a horn made of cow horn or conch shell, and talking drums were used in the military struggles to transmit messages. These two means of communication (abeng, drums) are both related to the Twi-Asante (Coromanti) language, as they transmit meanings by reproducing the distinctive tones of that language. The abeng is still blown at rituals and ceremonies, and may still be heard when strangers approach a Maroon community.

Rastafari

The Rastafarians have developed a religion, a world view, an art, an ethnicity and a language that set them off from the rest of the Jamaican population. It is well known that philosophical, political and intellectual movements shape languages. The lexicon of French, for example, changed greatly at the time of the French Revolution. Special interest groups in a society often "create" a new "language", chiefly in the lexical field. Languages of such groups are strongly influenced by the need for secrecy and for an esoteric form of communication. But Rastafari language has no such motivation or intent, for Rastafarianism is universalistic. Rastafari language flows directly from Rastafari philosophy and expresses a fundamental relationship of humans to nature and the universe. The Rastafari goal is not to restrict communication but to widen it, by removing internal inconsistencies in the semantic structure of the language, reducing incompatibilities between language form and function, and reducing the arbitrariness of the linguistic sign (for examples of this language, see Alleyne 1988 and Pollard 1994).

These aims are related to a philosophical view of language and of the word, as well as to an aesthetic view of language that leads to the cultivation of various forms of verbal art. Rastas believe in the "evocative power of the word", that is, the power of the word to evoke and, in a sense, to be the thing meant.

There is little in the historical record to show a continuous link between the word philosophy of Africans and of modern Rastafarianism. But it has been claimed that the word is productive and imperative in traditional African society. Jahn explains that

> the central significance of the word in African culture is not a phenomenon of one particular time . . . If there were no word, all forces would be frozen, there would be no procreation, no change, no life . . . Naming is an incantation, a creative act . . . for the word holds the course of things in train and changes and transforms them. And since the word has this power, every word is an effective word, every word is binding. (1961, 21)

Thus, in traditional African society, all religion, music, medicine and dance are produced by vocal expression, inasmuch as creativity is called into existence by man speaking.

This language created by Rastafarians is perhaps the strongest cultural focus of Jamaica at this time, and its influence has spread to metropolitan centres of Europe and North America. It is, especially when coupled with Rastafarian music, the most compelling symbol and instrument of Rastafarian identity, and by extension of "black African" Jamaican identity. It is now even offering itself as a symbol of Jamaican national identity, one of the strongest challenges to the Eurocentric world view and value system which have dominated Caribbean life and experience throughout the post-Columbian history of the region.

Jamaica, therefore, has been constantly challenging the European canons, seeking to replace them with local ones, not only in popular representations but also in the construction of the national identity (*pace* postmodernism). The Rastafarians have boldly constructed a black God; Pukumina and Revival have created a pantheon which includes both African and Christian saints and deities. Black messiahs and prophets have dotted Jamaica's history, with Marcus Garvey and Alexander Bedward being the best known. The National Dance Theatre Company has developed a Jamaican dance idiom based on the Afro-Jamaican anatomical structure and restoring the symbolic and aesthetic values of movements such as pelvic thrusts, and others centred on the hips and the buttocks, many of them taken directly from folk dance.

On the other hand, as we said earlier, all the above is contradicted by the persistence of the virtually universal pejoration of "black". As far as Africa is concerned, we have seen that the Maroons preserve a strong consciousness of that continent, and specifically of the ethnic group Twi-Asante as their forebears and as the basis of their ethnicity. The Rastafarians have reconstructed and re-formed an African-based ethnicity, in this case focusing geographically, but perhaps also symbolically, on Ethiopia, the domain of Jah. In the general population, however, this consciousness of a Twi ancestry is lost, and the allegiance to Ethiopia has not spread beyond Rastafarian ethnicity. It is a general African ancestry concept that is adhered to by those persons who have either maintained a continuous conscious tradition of Africa as their original place of origin, and as the source of their cultural identity, or have now, intellectually, developed an ideology which has recreated this consciousness.

In general, there are only vague notions in the population of the "African" origin of aspects of Jamaican culture. In cases where certain words or the artifacts to which they refer are known to be part of the African legacy (for example, *bankra,* meaning "basket", *dukunu,* meaning "type of pastry"), the words are used with a considerable amount of ethnic consciousness and pride to express an African-based ethnic identity. However, the historical complexity and ambivalence of Jamaica are well illustrated in the fact that many African words now carry negative connotations when compared with their English synonyms. Thus, for example, *nyam* is still used, especially in some parts of the rural sector, in the neutral denotation "eat". However, in other sectors, it has developed the negative connotation, "eat in a gluttonous, inelegant manner".

Twi day-names continued to be regularly used for naming children in Maroon communities, at least up to the first decade of the twentieth century. The historian Edward Long, in his work published in 1774, noted this naming tradition among plantation Africans as well. However, it underwent severe pejoration in the general non-Maroon population. Thus *Quashi,* the name of a male born on Sunday, came to be used to mean "peasant, country bumpkin, stupid person who refuses improvement". The female counterpart, *Quasheba,* underwent the same semantic degradation. Other examples of this evolution of meaning involving day-names are: *Quaco,* "male born on Wednesday" to "unsophisticated, uncultivated person"; *Kuba* "female born on Wednesday" to "a casual woman servant", "a womanish man"; *Quao* "male born on Thursday" to "stupid, ugly person"; *Kofi* "male born on Friday" to "backward or stupid person, unable to speak clearly"; *Quamin* "male born on Saturday" to "stupid person" (see Cassidy and Le Page 1967).

Further evidence of African pejoration is in the low values attached to names of African ethnic groups and African places of origin. *Bongo* and *Congo* are listed in Cassidy and Le Page (1967) as meaning, respectively, "suggestive of blackness, stupidity, backwardness" and "very black, African, ugly, stupid, country bumpkin". Again we find that there exists a countervailing value, as in some contexts *Bongo* expresses value. Among the Rastafarians, it is used as a title of honour and respect bestowed on the leadership. In the general rural population, it is a title given to, or self-conferred by, obeah-men, themselves figures of considerable ambiguity and ambivalence in Jamaican society and culture. In the case of *Congo,* it underwent a slight phonetic change to become *gungo* when it had to be applied to a pea ("pigeon pea") that is a special favourite with Jamaicans.

In summary, as we have suggested, Jamaica has witnessed throughout its post-Columbian history, a counterpoint: on the one hand, rejection of blackness and Africa in the construction and representation of personal and ethnic identity, and on the other, an assertion of them. These two ideologies may separate groups; they may separate individuals, siblings, twins within the same family. And finally, the same individual may exhibit both identities, organized in terms of public versus private behaviour, surface versus deep structure, and even moral versus immoral (as in the case of code-shifting between "eat" and "nyam"). A parent may show off an offspring with a European-leaning phenotype (brown complexion, straight nose, "good" hair, for example), but feel stronger affective bonds with the offspring of African phenotype (something akin to the "ugly duckling" syndrome). Many Jamaicans periodically return, if only for short periods, to the traditional life of their grandmothers in the country, to refresh their spirits with the food, song, stories, language, dress and religious observances that are seen, not merely as from "the old-time days", but as belonging to a non-European cultural tradition. Women are both proud of their full bottoms (they deride flat ones) and ashamed or embarrassed by them. Code-switching is a phenomenon that goes beyond language behaviour where it has been most widely studied. It is to be observed in other aspects of behaviour as Jamaicans endeavour to operate two (idealized) cultural and value systems (see Alleyne 1984).

The effect of the "creolization" and nativization of Africans in the Americas was to cause the rejection of Africa, its norms and its values, in favour of European norms and values. In the most general terms, this reordering of values and norms may be said to be the consequence of extremes of inequality in the distribution of power in New World slave societies. Creole slaves were at the same time affectively attached to their African mothers and grandmothers, and distancing themselves from, and depreciating, Africa. According to Long, "the creole slaves held the Africans in the utmost contempt styling them salt-water Negroes and Guinea birds" (1774, 2:410). In this, they were aided by the white population who, if Long was a representative example, considered that creoles slaves differed from Africa-born slaves "not only in manners, but in beauty of shape, feature and complexion" (2:410). And according to Edwards, a friend of his found that creoles "exceed the Africans in intellect, strength and comeliness" (1794, 185). We see here the early beginnings of the formula by which worth was measured in terms of degrees of approximation to European norms. This formula applied both to cultural behaviour and phenotype.

As we saw in our discussion of philosophical and ideological currents in Martinique, there is an attempt to glorify "creolization" as a positive process in the creation/emergence of a new Caribbean personality, culture and identity, one which does not depend on a link with essentialist components of the past. There is no doubt that Caribbean peoples are engaged in the reconstruction of identities which were severely devastated in the colonial period. But one aspect of this creolization process is the devaluation of "black" and "Africa", which has as its mirror image the glorification of "white" and "Europe". Jamaica has not been immune from these pathologies, and it is not clear how creolization will overcome them without a revaluation of these essential historical components, "black" and "Africa", of Caribbean ethnic identities.

At the contemporary period, Jamaica manifests a series of beliefs, attitudes, values and behaviours which continue the pathologies of the period of slavery. There is abundant anecdotal evidence to illustrate and support this. By way of example, in Nativity-type plays, Mary and the angel will most likely be played by light-skinned children. Photographs which represent a person as "too black" are regularly discarded. In the area of phenotype, the hair is "straightened", nose bridges of children are pinched in an effort to raise them, and lips are tucked in to make them appear thinner. Perhaps most significantly (if significance is to be measured by what is most discussed in private and in the public media), there is a current obsessive focus on mitigating the blackness of the skin tone by bleaching. The goal is to achieve a less black and a more brown tone.

Up to, say, forty to fifty years ago, Jamaican women routinely used white cosmetic powder on their faces in quite liberal quantities when going out. This practice has been discontinued or at least has considerably declined. (Whether as a cause or as a coincidence, "white" has simultaneously declined as a high profile ethnic category and "black" has extended and expanded its value.) New cosmetic technology as well as folk science have produced a variety of bleaching agents which are reputed to achieve the new desired result, that is, not of whitening but of browning.

"Brownings", as females of brown skin shade are termed in the popular argot of Jamaica, are highly favoured over black-skinned females, and are much sought after by males as partners. This is one aspect of what, as we have seen, is a very generalized Caribbean syndrome, whereby an individual (alone or egged on by his or her family) seeks a mate of lighter complexion than himself or herself in order to "improve" the quality of the progeny (in terms of the phenotypical features of colour and hair). The progeny then is considered to have a much better total set of chances in the social order. In the case of the "browning", the appeal is basically aesthetic and erotic, and exemplifies the general triumphing of brown over white in this particular area (the aesthetics of the human body).

This female figure was highly praised in a popular song hit which went: "Mi love mi car, mi bike, mi money and ting / But most of all, mi love mi browning." The song caused great offence to the black ideologues, and several performers retorted by composing songs extolling black women and chiding those who bleach their skin. One such song went thus:

Mi no stop cry fi all blackwoman
nuff tings a gwaan fi unu complexion
Dem a bleach up dem skin
To look like browning
Gyal mi honour you
Ka you no bleach out you skin
You no use chemical to look like browning

Bleaching of the skin is said to be a huge commercial business in Jamaica, and has been the subject of newspaper articles looking at the phenomenon from several angles: social, psychological, health, economics (individual and national). There is nothing to suggest that the practice is abating.

Hair is the other major area of contestation. This feature of African phenotype suffers as much pejoration as black skin colour. Indeed, whereas references to black skin as "bad complexion" and to light skin as "nice complexion" are diminishing in frequency, "negroid" hair (unmodified) is still routinely referred to as "bad hair" and departures from it towards the European (or Indian or Chinese) model are referred to as "good hair". Negroid hair may be referred to derogatively as "pepper grain" (in males) and "picky-picky" (in females). Since hair is more amenable to modification than any other phenotypical feature, including the skin, it has been modified in the direction of the European norm on a much greater scale than in the case of skin. Skin modification is still severely contested; hair modification is much more accepted, although some contestation still takes place.

There are three basic responses to hair. First, there is the "straightening" of it. This initially stemmed from a clear desire to modify the African texture and bring it closer to the European norm of straightness, or even of curls. Later, black women rationalized that imitation was not the motive for straightening, but rather it was ease of care and management. Straight hair was simply easier to comb. This practice has achieved a high degree of acceptance, and is much more engaged in, and considerably much less contested, than bleaching of the skin.

There may be a reason for this. Hair is a feature of salience, and of equal value to skin colour, in constructions of social value. We have seen that, for Puerto Rico (but also valid elsewhere), straight hair can "compensate" for black skin and reward the person with placement in a "higher" category (*indio* in Puerto Rico, *capresse* in Martinique, for example). And we have seen that Jamaican (East) Indians focus on hair as their most positive racial asset, an asset which, in their view, places them on higher level than blacks in the racial hierarchy. By contrast, in Jamaica and elsewhere, fair skin combined with African-type hair places the person in a very low category (*chabin* in Martinique, *red Ibo* in Jamaica, for example; see later). On the other hand, hair is external to the body when compared with skin and therefore is amenable to modification with less sensitiveness, reluctance and fear of health contraindications.

The second response is natural hair. This may be of two types: the first lacks affectation – is non-fashionable, no-frills. This kind of natural hair is a quiet assertion of black ethnicity, a rejection of the mimicry of whiteness implied in straightening. There may also be a religious, moral factor underlying the practice of natural hair, since straightening may be associated with worldliness, whereas natural hair may symbolize godliness and piety, especially among members of the lower-class denominations and religions, almost exclusively racially black.

The determination of the moment to begin the straightening of hair may be a major issue in child rearing, and may divide father, mother and children. Parents may postpone it as long as possible, so as not to appear to be too loose or not strict enough – even not moral enough. In Jamaica, the timing of straightening was mostly associated with the onset of puberty or with the act of confirmation in the case of Anglicans. Today, however, the age at which straightening begins, as also the age of the onset of puberty, is trending downwards.

The second type of natural response is the fashion Afro. Today, in Jamaica, as elsewhere, this type has a lower profile than in its heyday, the decades of the 1960s and 1970s. The bouffant Afro is now virtually obsolete. It had expressed in its very form a loud, revolutionary challenge to the white establishment, and was a major symbol and icon of Black Power. Now, its lower profile seems to symbolize the mitigation of the force of Black Power, and a new era in the kind of "message" which blacks wish to project by their body language. Other natural hair modes are the "corn row" (or "cane row") and "chinee bumps" (also called "Nubian knots" in middle-class speech), which are preferred for children, although some adult females may wear them in order to make black ethnic statements.

Rastafarian dreadlocks would have to be classified as the ultimate expression of natural hair. In its pure form, the hair is not combed nor brushed and is allowed to grow and configure itself naturally, without artificial interventions. This does not mean that for the Rastafarian hair has no significance or that Rastafarians are negligent in grooming. On the contrary, hair is of fundamental importance in the Rastafarian world view. It is part of the concept of purity, and of harmony with nature. Biblical authority is often cited by Rastafarians for the embargo on razors, scissors and combs. When accompanied by a copious beard, dreadlocks give an impression of venerableness, a link with an ancient royal and religious heritage. Dreadlocks are also used as a weapon of challenge and defiance, as one major gesture of the militant Rastafarian is to "flash his locks". In addition, Rastafarians have expressed their psychological triumph over the attempts at pejoration of the black phenotype by taking one of the pejorative references to African-type hair – "knotty" – and accepting it as a positive reference to themselves. Thus Rastafarians frequently represent themselves as "Natty Dread". Dreadlocks is the hair "style" that Jamaica has given to the world. Both the artefact and the word have now been diffused beyond Jamaica, and, like reggae music, they give a boost to Jamaican ethnic/national identity as their local and international acceptance increases.

The third response is a syncretic creation which produces a variety of styles. Straightening is mixed with black aesthetics to create styles based on dreadlocks, "corn row" and "chinee bumps". Twists may be done on hair that is chemically treated. Braids may be listed here, as they achieve the length of European hair but may range from European-type texture to textures approaching dreadlocks. Wigs are now widely used in "Dance

Hall" fashions. They combine European straightness with black African colour aesthetics (in the manner of Dennis Rodman, the US basketball player).

It is interesting to consider whether the fashion of colouring the hair and other attention paid to hair by blacks represent a continuous unbroken link with African aesthetics or a modern revival of a lost tradition, analogous to the use by contemporary "traditional" (also called "primitive" or "intuitive") artists of techniques and representations that are also to be found in African traditional art. Hutton (1996, 12) cites two nineteenth-century reports which show the link between African hairstyles and black Jamaican hairstyles. The first is from John Speke (1906) who noted, in reference to Africans, that "as the hair of the negro will not grow long, a barber might be dispensed with, were it not that they delight in odd fashions, and are therefore continually either shaving it off altogether, or else fashioning it after the most whimsical designs". The other report is from the nineteenth-century explorer John Burton (1966) who noted that

> the prettiest of the hair-dresses was a short crop, like lambswool, sometimes stained blue, as with indigo. The plainest was a melon stripe, where the short hair was plaited in lines, exposing the scalp between. The most grotesque was the semblance of pepper grains, or of cloves stuck in a ham, formed by twisting up single wool spirals.

Jamaica has inherited the value symbolizations of black and white. The pejoration of black has been extended and generalized and is expressed in the direct aphorisms: "black no good", "nothing black no good", "black as sin". The negative symbolization even achieved official national recognition in the colour composition of the national flag. The colours black, gold and green are officially declared to mean, "Hardships there are, but the sun shineth and the grass is green." The way in which "black" is treated here is an instructive example of the pervasiveness of the ambivalence concerning that colour. Instinctively, at a deep level, there is a consciousness that the racial and ethnic reality of the country should be represented in the flag, or rather, one might say that if other colours were chosen, it would be an affront to the majority of the population. There was evidently the hope that the black majority population would recognize this act of deference to them. However, the public official position could not privilege the blackness of the population, since there is the other deep-seated attitude, especially among conservative middle-class persons, of denial of black. In addition, official recognition of the black majority would encourage radical "racist" elements in the society in their confrontation with browns and whites (and other ethnic groups). Racially inspired behaviour by blacks in the diaspora has often been seen as "confrontational", and detrimental to social order and progress. The colour black in the flag was therefore officially interpreted as "hardships" to be faced.

However the second half of the decade of the 1990s saw a change in the official public position. The 1997 national election campaign of the incumbent party accepted (or did nothing to suppress) the slogan: "Is blackman time now!", which emerged from within the ranks of its supporters. Every inadvertent use of the word black by the other contending leader (of white/Syrian descent) was seen in its pejorative meaning and was interpreted as his "dissing" (that is, not liking or respecting) black people. The government itself had at the same time restored Emancipation Day as a national holiday and had given it prominence over Independence Day celebrations. Emancipation Day was used to highlight the struggles of "our black forefathers against white oppression".

The System of Representation

"White", in relation to persons, is strictly a racial and ethnic term. It is not used as an adjective to refer to the skin colour of persons (as "brown", "red" and "black" are; see later). As a descriptor of skin colour, "light-skin", "fair-skin", "white-skin" are preferred. "White" is also not used to denote a socioeconomic category (upper class). Nor is it used as a noun ("a white" is not possible). Its use is in the compounds "white-man", "white-woman", "white-people". It is the stress and the pitch pattern of the form which indicate that these are compounds, rather than adjective plus noun (even though the standard convention is to write the form as two words, rather than as one hyphenated word).

A socioeconomic connotation of the term does exist, but it is only infrequently utilized. A rich upper-class black man is never today called a "white man" or a "black white man". Cassidy and Le Page (1967, 51), however, cites *black white* as often used epithetically in the meaning "a black person with plenty of money; a rich negro". There is a lingering relic of this association in the expressions (more and more infrequently used): "you think you white", "you playing white", meaning "you are behaving like an upper-class owner/boss". There is also an increasing use of a pejorative derivative, "whitey", which may be a borrowing from North America. The only local pejorative form cited for Jamaica by Cassidy and LePage (1967) is "white-*jeg*", which they (perhaps erroneously) relate to *jege-jege* (of various meanings, all derogatory). *Jeg* is more likely the Jamaican form of English "dregs".

At an earlier period, the term *bakra* denoted "boss", "owner". It is derived from Efik or Ibo *mbakara* , "he who governs or surrounds". In this case, it needed an adjective to specify race, colour or ethnicity if such specification was required. Thus "white bakra", "brown bakra", "red bakra" and exception-ally "black bakra". Because of the close association both in Africa and in the Americas between "white" and "boss", given the virtual absence of white men who were not bosses, *mbakara* and *bakra* came to mean "white person", or collectively "white people". This is an interesting case of a term which begins with a socioeconomic meaning and later acquires a racial/ethnic meaning. Another example of this type is *dougla*, which originally means "outcast", but which in Trinidad now simply means "of mixed Indian/African extract", without any socioeconomic connotations. The perhaps more usual case is for a racial/ethnic term (such as "white", "black", "brown", "negro", "arab", "coolie", "slave") to become socialized. The meaning "white-man", "white-people" is the core denotation which the term *bakra* carries into the twentieth century in Jamaica. From the 1960s, the term becomes moribund, with the decline of "white" as a high profile racial/ethnic category, and it is now virtually obsolete. It was not transferred to the new "brown" ruling class.

"White" and "bakra" are used in a number of compounds which have ameliorative connotations in addition to denoting the colour white. Thus *white cassada* refers to the non-poisonous variety. *Bakra* is the preferred component in the compounds *bakra calalu; bakra pine; bakra yam; bakra cabbage* – all referring to a "refined" variety of the product. The connotation "refined", associated here with "white", may have been influenced by the distinction made since the period of slavery between white, "refined" sugar, and brown, "coarse" sugar.

Negro is not a term of the popular vernacular. The vernacular word is pronounced variously /nyega/, /neega/ (written "nayga" in anglicized spelling), and is a continuation of the Old English form *neger*. The raising of the initial vowel, which produced the North American form *nigger*, is unknown in Jamaica, except as a borrowing. It seems, however, to exist in the Jamaican derivative *niggrish* , meaning "backward", "unenlightened".

"Black", *niega,* "negro" are not synonymous, and the features which make up the meaning of each are quite complex. "Negro" seems to have been transmitted through usage in the white establishment, while *niega* came through the popular channel. This would explain the fact that in the popular vernacular, "negro" is never used to refer to a person, but is only found in compounds such as "negro-yam", "Negro-Town".

Cassidy and Le Page (1967) cite a number of other compounds which go back to the period of slavery, when a number of things related to the life and habits of slaves were named by the white establishment "negro-——". Examples such as "negro-breakfast", "negro-day", "negro-driver", "negro-ground", "negro-itch", "negro-house", "negro-worm", "negro-pot" attest to this.

When these compounds occur in the popular vernacular, "negro" cannot be replaced by *niega.* Thus the particular yam species is always "negro-yam", never *niega-yam.* In some cases, these "negro-——" compounds are contrasted with the "white-——" and "*bakra*-——" compounds (cited above), with pejorative and ameliorative connotations respectively. Thus "negro-yam" is said to be a "coarser" variety of yam, while "white-yam" is more "refined"; and "negro-pine" is a "pineapple of poor quality", while "*bakra*-pine" is "a fine variety of pine". It is probable that these "coarser" varieties were reserved for slaves and were thus named "negro-——", while the "refined" varieties were reserved for the master class and were thus named "white-——". This is evidence of the way in which language reflects and records social systems, allowing us to reconstruct such systems from an earlier period. An analogous example is the division in English between "pig", "cow", "ox", "lamb", "deer" on the one hand, all words of Anglo-Saxon origin designating the animal tended by the Anglo-Saxon serf, and on the other hand "pork", "beef", "mutton", "venison", all words of French origin designating the meat of the animal served on the table of the Norman lord.

The term *niega* is losing currency, as the rise of black ethnicity makes the negative connotations of *niega* unacceptable. It is often used in an insulting way by blacks in reference to other blacks thought to be backward in "culture" or reprehensible in behaviour. A black man is free to use the term either in direct address to a second person or in third-person reference. This pejorative usage is more a feature of urban blacks than of rural blacks. These latter use it with a less derogatory intent. Among elderly rural people, it may simply refer denotatively to "black person" or "black people".

Brown or white persons may hesitate to use *niega* in direct second person address. It could then be interpreted as crass "racism" (cf. the same phenomenon occurring in North America with respect to the use of the term *nigger*). However, (East) Indians and rural Chinese of the lower classes (for example, running small rural retail groceries) will not hesitate to use the term in arguments and conflicts where insults are being traded. If a black man uses *coolie* or *chinee* in addressing Indians or Chinese respectively, the latter two may retort using niega. In all cases, the degree of pejoration may be increased by adding "old" or "black" to *niega* (cf. also vieux nègre, literally "old negro" in Martinique, and "old nigger" in Trinidad and Barbados).

Cassidy and Le Page (1967, 49–50) cite *black niega* with the meaning "a negro", suggesting that *niega* may have a neutral meaning akin to *negro* in Puerto Rico and *nègre* in Martinique. However, Cassidy and Le Page go on to say that "the 'black' [in *black niega*] is not altogether redundant as it refers to the darker, more purely African negroes. The term is used by negroes about negroes and is not necessarily insulting." The examples of usage provided by Cassidy and Le Page do perhaps suggest a neutral meaning for *black niega*: "How you sell what no worth three pence self to black naygur for a bob?" ("How could you sell a guy something that's not worth even three pence for a shilling?") However, there may be sarcastic self-deprecation in this remark.

"Black" expresses a complex category or categories ranging from colour to ethnicity to ideology. Its connotations range similarly from the most pejorative to the most positive. Attitudes toward "black" range from totally dissociative to hyper-associative. We have seen that the negative connotations of "black" are epigrammatically expressed in "black no good", "nothing black no good".

On the other hand, "black" has been strengthening in value throughout the history of Jamaica. It is not simply a spill-over of the North American revaluation, but a process which has its own dynamics due to the particular sociohistorical experience of Jamaica.

Because of the socialized dimension of race in Jamaica (unlike the United States, where race is ascribed immutably at birth), there is considerable volatility in the definition of the category "black" in Jamaica. In the United States, people have no choice in or prerogative of racial self-classification (although some individuals may attempt to circumvent a classification "black" by "passing" for white). Their only choice is the label for self-characterization;

and this has changed through time from "negro", to "coloured", to "black", to "Afro-American" to "African American", as the search for appropriate dignified and dignifying symbols continues.

In Jamaica, a person has some element of choice. That choice includes, first of all, rejection of racial/ethnic labels. Some individuals will say that they are simply "Jamaican". (The 1991 census recorded 11,317 persons who refused to declare their race.) This may either be a case of denial of, or distanciation from, black/African, similar to what was observed in the case of Martinique and Puerto Rico, or a case of the individual's recognition of his or her mixed racial origin. This particular case is therefore to be found more with those persons who do not have (or perceive themselves as not having) the stereotypical black/African phenotypical features and therefore assume (without necessarily knowing for sure) that there is some non-black/African mixture in their lineage.

In earlier times, it would have been usual for such persons to claim "Scottish" ancestry. But this is no longer seen as an asset and is therefore no longer available as a refuge for those persons not wishing to be classified as black/African. Since the independence of Jamaica in 1962, the category "Jamaican" has become more available and meaningful. It is seen as logical and appealing and avoids racial/ethnic classifications which are difficult or embarrassing. The national motto, "Out of Many, One People", also supports this representational option.

"Black" is first of all a colour term. "A black (or black-skin) *bredda* (brother)" is simply someone visually perceived as of "black" colour. However, in an extension of meaning, "black" goes beyond this physical colour and indeed can represent a wide range of skin colour zones (and other associated phenotypical characteristics). The range may even reach skin tones very close to white. But the basis of such extended categorization is not the biological factor of "one drop of black blood", as it is in the United States. It is rather ideological and open, and can be bestowed on virtually any person of any racial type who fits the ideological requirements. In this sense, it is similar to the "honorary white" classification of apartheid South Africa that was bestowed for political reasons. The case cited above of (East) Indians (in Trinidad and Jamaica) being invited to enter the category "black" in times of crisis and confrontation with the ruling elite is an example of this. Although the invitation was not accepted at the level of the group, Indian individuals have entered the category and some have also become Rastafarians.

The precise ideological profile of "black" is Jamaican nationalism, socialist or radical political orientation, identification with Jamaican popular culture, opposition to Europe and the United States. A most illustrative case is that of the late Michael Manley, former prime minister. Racially, he was the son of a white British mother and a father who was at least three-quarter white. Michael Manley himself was phenotypically white/light brown, socioeconomically upper middle class, and culturally, in language, aesthetics, behaviour, tastes in food, music, and so on, very European. In spite of all of this, he was, at least at one stage of his political career, considered "black". His opponent, Edward Seaga, son of an Arabic father and a white American mother, lived and did sociological fieldwork among inner-city residents, was one of the pioneers of the commercialization of Jamaican popular music, and now represents an inner-city constituency with a virtual 100 per cent black population; but he was never considered "black". In fact, his party lost the 1997 general elections in some measure because he was seen as white and anti-black. Later in Michael Manley's political life, when he shifted his ideological position, made his peace with the United States and espoused free market policies, he lost his "black" status.

The Jamaican language exploits the resource of pitch to distinguish between the two meanings of "black", that is, the colour meaning and the ethnic/ideological meaning. "A black man", with high pitch on both "black" and "man", means "a man of black complexion". (To refer to colour only and to avoid the pejoration of "black", it is possible for "dark" or "dark skin" to be used instead of "black".) By contrast, "a blackman", with low pitch on "black" and high pitch on "man", means "a person belonging to the ethnic/ideological category "black", and who need not be black in skin colour.

This semantic system was lucidly expressed by a young person in a letter to the editor (*Daily Gleaner*, 12 March 1998, B15). She wrote: "I think all black people should see it [the movie *Amistad*]. And I don't mean just dark people – I mean brownings as well." The category "black" has therefore increased considerably in number, as more and more persons overcome the sensitivity to the historical pejoration of the colour and as fewer and fewer persons continue to represent themselves and other black Jamaicans as "*niega*" or "negro" or "coloured". This is dramatically illustrated in a comparison between the 1960 and 1991 censuses. All categories except black/African have fallen considerably in number. Black/African rose from 1,236,706 in 1960 to 2,080,323 in 1991. On the other hand (apart from the decreases mentioned above for whites, Chinese and Syrians), "mixed" fell from 271,520 to 166,991, and "others" from 49,627 to 1,252. This decrease can only partially be explained by emigration. Put together with the increase in "black/African", it suggests also a greater readiness on the part of "mixed" and "others" to declare themselves "black".

The same mode of distinction exists for "brown". "A brown (skin) *bredda* (brother)", with two high pitches, is a male of brown complexion; similarly "a brown (skin) sister" is the female counterpart, now more popularly called "a browning". There is no socioeconomic nor ideological implication here. By contrast, "a brownman" or "a brownwoman", with low pitch on "brown", is, in addition to being someone of brown complexion, a member of the middle or upper socioeconomic class. The socioeconomic elite is often referred to as "brown people" (also with low pitch on "brown").

"Red" is a colour/phenotype term, with a slight connotation of unattractiveness. It is used preferably in the case of persons of "light or yellowish skin" (Cassidy and Le Page 1967, 376), but with phenotypical features which are less European than those recognized in "brown" persons. If these features are manifestly African, particularly in hair texture, the terms *red niega* or *red Ibo* apply (*Ibo* being the name of the ethnic group of eastern Nigeria). In these cases, the connotation is clearly negative. They are the Jamaican counterpart of the Martinican *chabin*. In the oral forms of several African languages, the colour spectrum is coded in ways different from the coding in standardized forms of European languages. One word may express a range of spectrum colours which includes English "red", "orange", "yellow". There is evidence that this African interpretation of the physical world was transmitted to the Americas. For example, many biological species are called "red ——" in Jamaica or "—— *rouge*" in Martinique. These may correspond to what are described in English as "yellow", or "orange", or "red" (cf. for example "red wasp", "red cane").

In the case of two minority racial/ethnic groups, there are double terminological representations that contain different connotations. In the case of (East) Indians, there is a wide difference between *coolie* and "Indian", the former being highly derogatory. There is little indication that Jamaican blacks are about to renounce the use of *coolie*, as their racial counterparts in Trinidad and Guyana are legally obliged to in pubic discourse. This indicates the relative socioeconomic and political powerlessness of the Indian group in Jamaica. Groups which are powerless are obliged to tolerate the negative terms used to represent them. Their rise in power is accompanied by demands for more positive representation. Indians in Jamaica retaliate by hurling the term *niega* back at blacks. It may be that since blacks use the term *niega* themselves in reference to other blacks, there is less offence taken at the use of the label by Indians. Thus, there is no evidence of any transaction going on to remove both terms (*niega* and *coolie*) from public usage.

The word *coolie* is originally the name of an ethnic group of Gujarat, India. When these people became frequently employed to perform menial jobs, their name came to mean "unskilled native labourer", applied to any person in east Asia in this type of employment and activity. This is similar to what took place in Trinidad where the ethnic name "Arab" acquired the meaning "person who behaves in a disorderly way". Cassidy and Le Page (1967, 372) also cite *raba* in the same meaning for Jamaica. In the case of *coolie*, a purely ethnic meaning became socialized, virtually losing its particularistic ethnic dimension, and then later reacquired an ethnic meaning (person of a particular race/ethnicity – East Indian – in the Caribbean) with an implied low social value.

As in other parts of the anglophone Caribbean, *chinee* is used in Jamaica to refer to the ethnic group of Chinese. The difference between *chinee* and "Chinese" is purely sociolinguistic: the former belongs to the vernacular variety (Jamaican "Creole") and the latter to the standard variety. Thus "a *chinee*" or "a Chinese", "a *chinee* man/woman" or "a Chinese man/woman", "a China man/woman". Where the two terms are known by an individual, they are distributed in use according to the formality/informality of the speech context. There is neither pejoration nor amelioration implied in the choice of any of these, and this is very instructive of the social position occupied by this group from the early period of their arrival in Jamaica. They very early removed themselves from competition with blacks or Indians as they went into the retail grocery business and later into laundering. Nor did they seek any social intercourse. The *chinee* shop in a village was seen as a convenience, even as an asset.

It was only in periods of great social unrest, as in the decade of the 1930s, that there was open hostility shown by blacks to Chinese. There may have been a slight resentment for their separateness, but it was never seen as aloofness or snobbery. They never became the objects of pejoration. Indeed, a typical case was that the name of a Chinese person was neither known nor asked for. He or she was simply referred to as "Chin" or "Chin-Chin", "Miss

Chin", "John", even after living and working (as retail grocer) for many years in a small community.

The most evident connotation associated with *chinee* in Jamaica is "small in size". Thus it is used to designate a number of fruits smaller than other varieties: *chinee* banana, *chinee* okra, *chinee* yam. There is also some slight negative stereotyping targeting the sexual organs of both male and female Chinese.

As we said earlier, the position of the Chinese reveals an interesting dimension to the race/phenotype picture in the Caribbean and the world. There is evidence to suggest that the Chinese features of hair texture and skin colour were interpreted as closer to those of the dominant group. Whereas the Chinese did not openly assert this or use it as an index of superiority over blacks (as Indians did in relation to their hair texture and length), nevertheless the dominant group ranked the Chinese in an intermediate social position together with mulattoes.

Mixtures of Indian and black and Chinese and black are called *coolie rayal* and *chinee rayal* respectively. In both cases, the resulting phenotype in a female is well appreciated aesthetically and sexually, but the parallel male enjoys no particular value in these regards. The origin of *rayal* is doubtful. Cassidy and Le Page (1967, 381) treat it under a headword *rial*, and suggest a (rather improbable) derivation from the name of the Spanish coin of low value. *Rayal* is also used to designate the result of cross-breeding in other species: "mule *rayal*" is a cross between a she-donkey and a horse; "turkey *rayal*" is a fowl with no neck feathers which is assumed to be a cross with a turkey. Popular etymology in Jamaica associates the term with English "royal".

Conclusion

The socioeconomic and political rise of blacks in Jamaica, perhaps unsurpassed anywhere else in the Caribbean, questions the validity of a racial/ethnic interpretation of Jamaican society. It suggests that the former neat correspondence between race/colour and socioeconomic position has broken down, and that class stratification, ignoring racial differences, is the dominant order. The many blacks and the growing number of Indians in the professional and business elite have more in common with their white, brown or Jewish colleagues than they have with their racial brothers in the lower classes. They go to the same clubs, the same restaurants, the same cocktail parties – in other words, they have the same social networks and interaction. There are no longer in Jamaica any all-white or all-brown clubs. Even private parties are no longer uniformly white or brown (as they still may be in Puerto Rico, Martinique, Barbados). Blacks in the upper classes may then refer to blacks in the lower classes by the distancing "they". For example, the street children of Jamaica find no more support from black motorists who speed past in expensive cars than they do from motorists of other racial groups.

However, as far as cultural tastes and cultural behaviour in general are concerned, the picture may be less clear. Since many of these socially successful blacks have ascended from humble beginnings, they may carry with them into their newly acquired socioeconomic status a number of old tastes and behaviours. They also carry their racial stereotype. For example, many banks and other financial institutions collapsed in 1997. These were locally owned and managed, in contrast with the foreign-owned banks which did not suffer the same misfortune. Some of the failing institutions were managed by blacks. There was a general recognition that it was the locally owned institutions that were failing. But it was often further suggested in private discourse that these failures were due to black managers who, in accordance with the racial stereotype, were unable to manage. This was usually suggested in jest, but it pointed to a persistent underlying racial stereotyping of black people, regardless of their socioeconomic status.

One of the most persistent cries is the one that such blacks who have "made it" forget their origins and do not help those left behind. The greatest praise given to successful blacks (especially sportsmen and entertainers) is that they remain loyal to the humble communities from which they sprang. This has to do not only with the provision of material help but also, and often more importantly, with cultural attitudes. Whereas in the case of other such situations (that is, people anywhere returning to the "old country"), the problem is one of not providing the material support and not maintaining the old cultural values and behaviours, in Jamaica there is a racial and ethnic dimension to it. Persons are viewed as "letting down the race" and continue to be described as "playing white".

In 1993, Jamaicans were very conscious of, for the first time, voting in a black prime minister (as against the previous brown, white, Middle Eastern leaders). There was great expectation that finally the condition of the black masses, especially in the inner-city communities, would be improved. Such improvement has not (yet) come, and there is already some regret that a black prime minister is doing nothing to alleviate the conditions. There is therefore a lingering association of blackness with poverty, and a hope for and expectation of black racial/ethnic solidarity on the part of those black persons who have been elevated to positions of power.

Class continues to become more salient as a basis of social organization. Identities are being constructed on the basis of class in addition to ethnicity. However, this is played out chiefly in the form of blacks who move into the upper classes losing or surrendering part of their black ethnicity, rather than of lower-class blacks losing ethnic consciousness in favour of exclusive class consciousness. Attempts to reinforce this incipient class consciousness by introducing Marxist concepts and praxis of class struggle, especially in the 1970s, did not succeed. Today, with the demise of Marxism, it is national identity which is challenging racial and ethnic identity as the prime motive force. The national motto "Out of Many, One People" seeks to ensure the triumph of national identity. However, what seems to be happening on the ground is that, rather than being suppressed, black racial and ethnic identity is being extended to a national scope. National identity is being constructed on the basis of reggae, the Reggae Boyz soccer team, and a number of other features, all of which presuppose "black".

"Blackman time now" in the Morant Bay Rebellion of 1865 referred not only to the revendications of the dispossessed peasant class for relief but was also an appeal to race and ethnicity. It is the same today more than 130 years later. "Blackman Time Now", the (unofficial) campaign slogan of the successful political party in the national elections of 1997, was an appeal primarily to racial and ethnic solidarity, in addition to a cry for relief for the dispossessed classes.

In summary, the system of racial and ethnic organization in Jamaica may be seen as having three dimensions: colour and phenotype, race, and ethnicity. Colour and phenotype constitute a finely shaded continuum based on visual perception. It is not open to wide subjective interpretation, but there is some subjectivity nonetheless. There may be, first of all, slight differences or disagreements in visual perception, in determining "who is lighter than who", or "who is darker than who". This takes place quite often in the context of sibling rivalry. Second, the subjectivity may be in terms of whether an individual is able to "see" these colour and phenotypical differences. Many people say that they do not "see" them. Individuals may also differ in the labels to be attached to different shades, particularly in the case of "red" and "brown". The colour descriptors include white (-skin), red (-skin), fair (-skin), clear (-skin), brown (-skin), light brown, dark brown, cool black, jet black, black black.

The movement along the colour continuum from black through brown to white corresponds to an increase in social value. However, the values are changing, though how rapidly or fundamentally is a matter of debate. White is losing its high value, especially in the domain of aesthetics and sexuality. The associated phenotypical features of straight hair and thin, straight nose retain their prestige, but other features of the torso do not – indeed, they may never have prestige. Black colour and hair are increasing in value, assisted no doubt by successful super-stars like Michael Jordan and fashion models like Naomi Campbell who are "cool black". At the same time, as in Puerto Rico and Martinique, and perhaps the rest of the world, "brown", that is, a shade some distance from the polarities of white and black, may be emerging as the preferred colour.

The race dimension distinguishes a number of basic or "pure" categories: black/*niega,* white, *chinee*/Chinese, *coolie*/Indian, Syrian. Then there are the mixtures which are recognized and coded: *malata, coolie rayal, chinee rayal.* In addition, the formula "half——", or "quarter——", or "three-quarter——" is widely used. The formula can be used with any basic category ("half-*chinee*", and the like) with the notable exception of "black". There are thus no "half-*niega*" or "half-black". Black is the assumed, but unspoken, other portion in these mixtures.

The ethnicity dimension corresponds largely with race, but has a great deal of volatility in the area of the category "black". Here it is greatly affected by the ideology factor. It can cut across the other dimensions, so that virtually any colour or race category can be ethnically "black", although obviously persons who are black in colour and race are stronger candidates for this category. Other ethnic categories are closed and neatly circumscribed by race. However, some black persons (black by race/colour) may be assigned to a special subcategory of ethnic whites called "roast-breadfruit", that is, black on the outside, but white on the inside. There is also the concept of "playing white", which is more culturally (rather than ethnically) related – in other words, it refers to cultural behaviour in terms of tastes, preferences, personal conduct. Hutton (1996) relates that in the 1960s he was told that he was behaving like a white man because of his love for books. The implications are, however, ethnic, insofar as such persons who are "playing white" are seen as not acting in the interest of the ethnic black group. The concept is also a manifestation of the lingering black/white polarity, since no one is accused of "playing brown".

CHAPTER NINE

Conclusion

*R*ace and ethnicity constitute a major focus for identification among Caribbean peoples. Basic structures going back to the period
of slavery and even beyond remain tenacious throughout the Caribbean, even
though a number of changes can be observed. The plantation economy
persists, with the descendants of the former master class ("white" and
"brown") still in control of the major portion of economic resources, and
employing the descendants of former African slaves and Indian indentured
workers. These latter still populate the working and peasant classes. The
economies are still fundamentally based on the production of commodities for
export, with consumer goods being imported. Tourism, which has become
almost everywhere the major economic activity, has not changed the basic
race and ethnicity picture; rather, it has reinforced it.

The economic and social situation has, however, not been static. Emancipation, and, later, adult suffrage within a democratic framework, responsible
and responsive government (which has become the biggest employer of
persons), and above all the expansion of educational opportunities have led
to social mobility for blacks and Indians. First of all, already during the period
of slavery, the mulatto group had taken advantage of educational opportunities

to move into the professional and business areas. Later, in the post-emancipation period, blacks began to see education as the main or only means of socioeconomic mobility, and themselves began to seek the professions. In very recent times, changes in the mode of capitalization and in the ownership and management structure of companies have resulted in technocrats becoming managers, chief executive officers and presidents of corporations. An increasing number of technocrats are black.

All this has modified, and continues to modify the basic pattern. The basic pattern inherited from slavery is that as you descend the socioeconomic scale, you go through a corresponding colour continuum. Whites occupied, and still do, the higher echelons of the socioeconomic scale. But today they are no longer alone there. Blacks (and Indians) occupied, and still do, the lowest echelons; and today they remain the sole occupiers in Jamaica and Martinique. There is still the lingering notion that whites have a natural power to lead. This notion began to break down first of all in the trade unions, then in local government. The domains of public service and national politics followed. The last bastion of white dominance is leadership in the corporate world, where blacks and browns (and Indians in Trinidad and Guyana) have entered but do not seem to command the same confidence as (foreign) whites.

It is customary to consider that in the Caribbean, racial categories have become socialized, that class has replaced race as the organizing principle. However, it still is the case that race and the derived phenotypical categories that have emerged (colour/shade, hair) remain important organizing bases of Caribbean societies. It is possible to trace the broad outlines of the historical development of these racial and phenotypical categories and their values. The colour black and the "race" that became represented by it had come in for severe pejoration by white European and Asian peoples. However, the social status of slave in antiquity and in medieval Europe had no particular racial exclusiveness.

The racialization of this low social status of slave began to develop slowly, and by the end of the medieval period, before the beginning of the European arrival in the Americas, slavery in Europe had begun to take on a racial character. New World slavery confirmed this and completed the racialization of socioeconomic status. "Black" and "slave" became synonymous; as did "white" and "master". The new current direction is towards a return to the non-racial character of social status. But at this point, and as far into the future as one can see, there is no change in the racial character of *low* social status.

Race as a coherent, discrete set of physiognomic features dividing the populations into clear-cut, unambiguous divisions has become a more complex phenomenon as new categories, the result of new migrations and racial mixing, have had to be fitted into the racial and social structures. A colour/shade hierarchy has been grafted on to the racial/ethnic hierarchy, and together with other phenotypical features (of which hair texture is the most important), a finely woven continuum of colour/phenotype differentiation emerges. This continuum is, broadly speaking, also a continuum of social values. The poles are still occupied by members of two (or three) "pure" races, or at least by persons who maximize the colour and phenotype associated with the black (and Indian) and white races.

In this new complex structure, ethnicity can no longer be squarely and simply based on race, except in the case of Indians and Chinese. Severe problems of ethnic identity arise for those engaged in the original black to white continuum, including the new racial mixtures (involving Indians and Chinese) which have entered the continuum. "Black" has been redefined and is no longer a simple racial/colour category, but has a strong ideological component. The search for identity continues.

Academic interest in race and ethnicity has followed the vicissitudes of these themes as practical issues. To summarize, and perhaps also to simplify, in the immediate post–World War II era, many people saw race and ethnicity as a tired old organizing principle, its worst manifestation, Nazism, having plunged the world into a terrible catastrophe from which it had only just emerged. Marxism began to assert itself as a theory of society and as an organizing principle that interpreted social dynamics in terms of class conflicts, and defined social progress partly as the suppression of unproductive ethnicities and the uniting of the oppressed classes of the world. It interpreted racism as a capitalist device to divide the working class into hostile segments for easier control. And there was, even outside Marxism, the notion of the melting pot, a concept which the Americas was giving to the world as the final solution to ethnic/nationalistic conflict among humans and nations.

Of course, the world has proved to be more complex than the assimilationist ideologies or world communism were or are able to accommodate. It is true that current free market globalization, without always explicitly formulating a theory of ethnicity, implies the spread of technology and capital that seeks to overcome any national or ethnic barriers put in their way.

But at the same time that technology and capital have been moving across national and cultural borders, leading to some degree of cultural levelling among the business classes and scientists of the world, the peoples of the world have also been moving, creating ethnic diversity within national borders to a degree unparalleled in the history of human society. This movement of peoples creates pockets of separate minority ethnicities within larger dominant national entities. This may lead to further levelling, but may also create further ethnic assertion and conflict. In the case of blacks, migratory movements and contact through the electronic media increase the awareness of a wider ethnicity that takes in the Caribbean, the Americas (including especially Brazil, most visibly through its soccer team), and the world.

At present a number of competing ideologies exist, offering different views of, and approaches to, ethnicity and ethnic diversity. The earlier assimilationist and Marxist approaches persist with weakening support (cf. the new conflicts over language threatening the "melting pot" ideology in the United States). The former comes in two basic forms, best identified as liberal egalitarianism and conservative egalitarianism, both of which espouse the notion of the melting pot. In the case of the conservative version, the mainstream into which all ethnicities are expected to melt is unambiguously white Anglo-Saxon Protestant English-speaking.

There is currently a great deal of interest in hybridity; in 1996 there was a conference at the University of Texas devoted to this theme. In some ways it restates elements of some versions of creolization, a theory of Caribbean culture that is both so ill defined and so variable within each social and intellectual modality of the Caribbean as to be unuseable. Hybridity rejects, as monolithic and essentialized, the multicultural multi-ethnic discourse that counterposes whiteness and blackness, Europe and Africa.

Its relationship with globalization is rather complex. Globalization, as discussed earlier, may be seen as leading to the blurring of ethnic and national boundaries. There is no overt, explicit regard for departures from the basic North Atlantic cultural pattern. In so far as globalization is led by the North American and west European economies, it is the North Atlantic cultural system, chiefly the North American modality, which is erasing boundaries all over the globe. There are, of course, inevitably some influences in the other direction. North American and west European elites now are quite at home eating Japanese sushi or listening to Jamaican ska. These influences do not in any way threaten the dominance – some will say the hegemony – enjoyed by the North Atlantic economic and cultural systems.

Hybridity is implicitly opposed to any notion of cultural hegemony or dominance, seen as another essentialism. In this view, transnational exiles seek new identities, and are led to the remaking of self in a process that looks less to the past and more to the future. There is a movement away from history and causality, the need to explain everything by origins.

There is no simple monolithic theory that can capture the contradictory currents in race and ethnicity. The United States is one illustrative example of this complexity. At one time southern Italians and eastern Europeans were separate ethnic groups, but they have now become totally absorbed into the mainstream. And soon Hispanics and Asians may be. In other parts of (former) colonial empires, Asians have entered multiracial societies and have become positioned in the middle levels between whites and the black or native population. In South Africa, they were assigned to the category "coloured". In Fiji, Indians entered the middle levels. In Malaya, the Chinese were placed between the white European colonial establishment and the native Malays; in nineteenth-century Cuba, they were considered "white".

In the United States, it is evident that Asians are on the way to being classified as white. It is interesting to note that "Asian" here includes Chinese, Japanese, Koreans and Vietnamese, but not (southern) Indians. Nevertheless, this case presents the classic way in which race and racial stereotypes can be overcome by socioeconomic position and social behaviour. These Asians have begun to demonstrate social behavioural features (and to a lesser extent cultural behaviours) that are being seen as not incompatible with whiteness.

Racial categories thus can be reconstructed and redefined on the basis of social and cultural factors, as well as ideological factors (as we saw in the case of attempts at the reconstruction and redefinition of "black" in Jamaica and Trinidad). However, racial phenotypical features cannot be erased, and continue to be one of the factors that form the basis of social structure and social interaction. On the one hand, the skin colour and hair texture of Asians will facilitate their movement into the category "white"; on the other hand, the only thing that may prevent them from becoming totally "white" (as southern Italians have become) is the other phenotypical features (especially eye shape) which still identify them, and which still form the basis of a lingering pejorative stereotyping.

It is very unlikely that African Americans, as a group or as individuals, will be, or can be, assimilated into the category "white", regardless of the socio-economic position and cultural behaviour of the individual. The "most" they can become is "oreo". This again shows the strength of racial categories in social organization – or at least it shows that the black/white opposition will remain with us for some time.

On the other hand, there may be a considerable amount of racial mixing taking place at the present time in the United States (and elsewhere). This is not only between black and white, but now involves Hispanics, Asians and other recent migrant groups. This will certainly lead to changes in racial and ethnic constructions. The case of Tiger Woods, the golf superstar who rejects classification as "black" and asserts his mixed ancestry, is putting the matter of racial categories and their meaning fully into the public discourse. This will certainly lead to a weakening of the system based on "one drop of black blood", and to the strengthening of the other system based on gradations of colour and phenotypical features with corresponding social values. The most likely development is the complete demise of the "one-drop-of-black-blood" di-chotomous hypodescent system, and the full installation of a Caribbean-type colour/phenotypical continuum, with white and black (colour and phenotype) still occupying the poles.

The Caribbean is another illustrative example. Race and ethnicity are still strong organizing principles, although there are clear signs that class is becoming increasingly important and that the assimilationist narratives of national unity are beginning to impose themselves. The region has been relatively free of ethnic strife, which suggests that it may be useful to examine the Caribbean to get a better understanding of what conditions may attenuate ethnic conflict in a world where such conflict seems generally to be on the rise.

Caribbean scholars and citizens hold different views and defend different models of race and ethnicity. They differ in their assessment of the relative significance of race, colour, ethnicity and class. The complex, ambiguous character and structure of Caribbean societies have generated a variety of analytic models, ranging from the strictly racial to the almost purely economic, including various intermediate alternatives. My own perspective is that people construct their own systems, and at different historical moments, given the particular circumstances of the times, the systems show the relative primacy of race, ethnicity, culture and class as alternative bases of individual and collective identity.

It is futile to try to embrace all the differing sociohistorical systems within one theory, and these systems are undergoing such change that any theory may appear to be invalidated by contradictory data that can be found or by different angles from which the data can be presented. Even a simple classification may prove to be inconclusive. Is Jamaica linguistically bilingual, monolingual or a continuum? Is Barbados a creole-speaking society?

Caribbean societies were once interpreted as caste societies. There may be wider agreement that they once were (in fact, non-white groups in the early post-Columbian period were referred to as *castas* in Latin America), but much less agreement that they still are. The question to be asked is whether certain occupations are (still) now reserved for members of certain ethnic groups; whether a black doctor with upper level wealth partly inherited is still excluded from the upper classes. In all Caribbean societies, one would have to say that caste, as exemplified by examples of the type presented above, is a thing of the past. But the fact that the social status of the black or Indian doctor may not be viewed as the same as that of the white doctor shows that we have not evolved clearly to a state where occupation and wealth are unambiguous and sufficient indices of social class.

It is evident that the Caribbean in general, in the course of its post-Columbian history, has been moving from a caste-like system, through one of rigid social differentiation to one of social stratification, with an uninterrupted continuum of status positions, and with increasing opportunities for social mobility available to more and more people. On the one hand, there is some degree of overdetermination, as both race and colour coincide with the economic/occupation factor to account for the stratification. But some will argue that the economic/occupation factor is the determinant, since there are people of all shades and races in the upper classes, and blacks who gain high socioeconomic status may cease to view themselves or to be viewed by others as ethnically black (except where ideology intervenes to preserve black ethnicity). The terms "roast breadfruit", and more recently "oreo", are used to depict such persons.

Others may argue, however, that the bottom rung of the ladder is populated exclusively by a certain race or colour, and the very highest rung, the thin uppermost crust, is similarly populated by one race and colour, in many cases in spite of declining wealth and non-prestigious occupation. So that the economic/occupation factor cannot by itself account for social stratification. I myself think that the situation has become quite dynamic and will continue to be so, particularly in the anglophone Caribbean where white is a minority and fading. Indeed, the whole notion of stratification and classes may become increasingly invalid, and we will have to construct models that describe and account for social mobility, in other words, models which identify the factors and that promote or inhibit movement and determine their relative weighting.

It still is the case, however, that the Caribbean has shown and hopefully will continue to show the world that racial and ethnic divisions do not necessarily lead to severe social disharmony, dislocation and conflict. There have, of course, been periods of tension, and cases of "racial rioting". (We are not here including the frequent slave rebellions and the post-emancipation worker uprisings, which were first and foremost attacks on an unjust and oppressive overall system.) But these have not been prolonged or widespread, or excessively destructive, although the conditions for such seem to be present: small spaces to accommodate burgeoning populations and scarce benefits, especially employment and housing. To explain this, one would have to refer to such factors as the foreign character of all the existing racial/ethnic groups in the Caribbean, without any sacred ancestral territory to defend; and the role of colonialism which allowed no scope for fighting over economic power and political control.

The case of St James, a basically upper-working-class suburb of Port of Spain, is very illustrative. All the races came from outside and met and lived there, and continue to do so, in a very small space: blacks, whites, Indians, Chinese, Portuguese, Syrians. Each had a stereotype of the others; there were slight differences in status; there was occupational differentiation: the Chinese ran retail grocery shops, which no one else wished to do; Indians swept streets and kept dairy animals and vegetable gardens; blacks were bartenders, teachers and policemen; Syrians peddled cloth or ran haberdasheries. But there were mixed schools, mixed clubs, intermating and intermarriage, with a high regard for *dougla* and other mixed-race types. In this small space, groups could not isolate themselves. An individual had to deal with the Chinese shopkeeper, the Indian fresh produce vendor, the Syrian cloth merchant, the black teacher or policeman.

The Caribbean was the location in the world which saw the birth of the modern period of human socioeconomic history. It may be claimed that the area saw the first seeds of globalization planted. It also heralded one of the most important non-economic spin-offs of globalization. In addition to the movement of capital to wherever profit could be maximized, people were also moved in order to maximize profit, or moved themselves to maximize their life chances. Caribbean societies have become in some ways microcosms of a macrocosmic pattern of world society now emerging, in which racial and ethnic divisions will either exist harmoniously or will be suppressed in favour of some mainstream (itself culturally complex and ill defined/non-definable), or will breakdown biologically through miscegenation in such a way that the hybrid will become the dominant category, biologically and culturally. This does not speak to the question of whether globalization is a good thing economically, or whether ethnic assimilation and hybridity are good things. There is still considerable resistance to globalization and assimilation, which suggests that not everyone and not every society are "buying into" that model.

McDonald sums it up in this way:

> The test is whether or not the fundamental allegiances, be it race, religion, or heritage of whatever variety, can be absorbed but not lost in a wider allegiance. I believe in the West Indies we have proved over time that fundamental allegiances can be, and have been, so absorbed. That is not to say that all is sweetness and harmony. Far from it. There have been, there are, there will be resentments and suspicions. Tensions will rise and grow, certainly, but they will pass again. We have learnt enough about each other, we have grown used to making the essential basic accommodations, so that tensions will never tear us apart as they have torn apart Lebanon, Yugoslavia, Sri Lanka and may yet tear apart more than one African state . . . . (1997, 2)

However, he makes the precise error that many advocates of racial/ethnic harmony make, and which is at the root of the sociopsychological problems of the Caribbean. He accepts the fact of "East [sic] Indian" allegiances to their heritage and considers this a positive factor, but he seems to have some problem with analogous allegiances to an African heritage. He berates the captain of a former West Indian cricket team for having referred to the team as "African" in their racial/ethnic heritage. The team indeed had some East Indian and mixed-race members. But the captain was merely referring to what he saw as the dominant component, both of the team and of the West Indies in general, and was asserting that he was not one of those who denied or was uncertain or embarrassed about the African heritage.

The important thing is that in spite of the obvious evidence that class is becoming increasingly significant vis-à-vis colour and race in social organization, there is the persistent problem with black and white. Blacks consider the few who have made it to the top as exceptions, "face-cards", "sell-outs", in addition to "roast breadfruit". Blacks still view their colour and phenotype as a problem, and therefore have low self-image and racial confidence.

This question of low racial confidence among blacks remains the most burning sociopsychological problem in the Caribbean, North America and other parts of the world where blacks suffered the colonial domination of Europe. Perhaps the most dramatic expression of this is, paradoxically, the need by persons who claim to have overcome this problem to be constantly asserting "black pride" and "black achievements". For a too-large part of the black population, there is still the persistence of a victim syndrome, the perception of still being exploited, disadvantaged and discriminated against, of being at the lowest level of the world's racial and ethnic hierarchy. This perception is not altogether imagined. It is based on a lingering historical consciousness and on a lingering socioeconomic system that is unable to lift the large mass of the population in the Caribbean out of poverty and general social degradation. This large mass is black and, to a lesser extent, Indian. It would seem, therefore, that, in the final analysis, it is economic development which will change the racial ethnic picture. Even if blacks (and Indians) remain at the lowest rung of the socioeconomic ladder, economic development could so lift the quality of life at this lowest level that the victim syndrome could be erased, and the correlation between race/colour and depressed living and non-standard behaviours could be destroyed.

On the other hand, even with the end of severe economic deprivation and the rise of blacks into the upper classes, the question remains as to whether this does/would affect or erode the social values ascribed to blackness as a colour and phenotype. In Puerto Rico, where whites, browns and blacks populate the peasantry and the urban dispossessed classes, and in Martinique where *métissage/créolité* is being proposed as a national ideology and where "black"/"African" has been eliminated by new social constructions, the different values attached to colour and phenotype remain.

Race and ethnicity have two sides: positive and negative. They are positive where racial/ethnic solidarity leads to improvement in the lives of members without also leading to the suppression of other groups (unless one believes that the rise of one group, whether class or race, is always at the expense of another group). The rise of the Chinese in Jamaica may be such a case, where a group without excessive inherited privileges simply seized the few opportunities available to them, and increased and extended their human and material capital from one generation to the next, through heightened racial/ethnic solidarity.

On the other hand, economic deprivation will continue to nourish ra-
cial/ethnic assertion and polarization. In the context of scarce resources,
persons and groups may fall back on ethnicity and ethnic rivalry to protect
themselves. Ethnicity may be a latent resource that remains submerged or mild
in "normal" circumstances and is used for the upliftment of the group.
Periodically, problems may arise that are interpreted within the mould of race,
and may set negative ethnic activity in motion. In Jamaica, periodically, when
black craft vendors in the tourist belt feel marginalized, the cry during the
demonstrations is that "the Indians [duty-free shop owners competing for the
same tourist dollar] are against us". Thus, they may attribute their situation
to hostility from other groups, heightening ethnic/racial tensions. In the case
of the West Indies, there is a lingering consciousness of hegemony and
dominance by one group and victimization of another. In Jamaica, in particular, this consciousness is very strong, and many social, economic and political
problems are interpreted in terms of race and ethnicity. When one political
party in Jamaica wished to enhance its election chances (especially in the
context of not having any achievements on which to campaign), it pointed to
the white/Syrian ancestry of the leader of the opposing party.

Economic deprivation will continue to nourish racial/ethnic assertion and
polarization. The dilemma of the Caribbean and the world is that economic
development (if and when it comes in the context of globalization) may
remove racial and ethnic tensions; but it may also weaken ties with cultural
backgrounds and heritages identified with race. Will this mean increasing
anomie and continuing white bias? Will cultural and biological hybridity
undermine the cultural and phenotypical hegemony/dominance of the North
Atlantic and undermine the very existence of cultural and phenotypical
polarities? The answer to these questions may require a crystal ball.

References

Abbad y Lasierra, Fray Inigo. N.d. *Historia, geografía, civil y natural de esta isla, San Juan Bautista de Puerto Rico.*

Abdalla, I.H. 1990. "Neither Friend Nor Foe: The *Malam* Practitioner–*Yan Bori* Relationship in Hausaland". In *Women's Medicine: The Zar-Bori Cult in Africa and Beyond,* edited by I.M. Lewis, A. Al-Safi and S. Hurreiz, 39–48. Edinburgh: Edinburgh University Press (for International African Institute).

Aboud, F. 1988. *Children and Prejudice.* New York: Blackwell.

Abraham, R.C. 1962. *Dictionary of the Hausa Language.* London: University of London Press.

Adams, F.M., and C.E. Osgood. 1973. "A Cross-Cultural Study of the Affective Meanings of Color". *Journal of Cross Cultural Psychology* 4:135–56.

Adelaide-Merlande, J. 1994. *Histoire générale des Antilles et des Guyanes.* Paris: Harmattan.

Affergan, F. 1983. *Anthropologie à la Martinique.* Paris: Presse de la Fondation Nationale des Sciences Politiques.

Allahar, A. 1993. "When Black First Became Worth Less". *International Journal of Comparative Sociology* 34:39–55.

Alleyne, M.C. 1980. *Comparative Afro-American.* Ann Arbor: Karoma.

———. 1984. "The World View of Jamaicans". *Jamaica Journal* 17:2–8.

———. 1985. "A Linguistic Perspective on the Caribbean". In *Caribbean Contours,* edited by S. Mintz and S. Price, 155–79. Baltimore: Johns Hopkins University Press.

———. 1988. *Roots of Jamaican Culture.* London: Pluto.

Allport, G.W. 1954. *The Nature of Prejudice.* Reading, Mass.: Addison-Wesley.

Alvarez Nazario, M. 1961. *Elemento Afronegroide en el Español de Puerto Rico.* San Juan: Instituto de Cultura Puertorriqueña.

Aristotle. 1946. *The Politics of Aristotle,* translated by Ernest Barker. Oxford: Clarendon Press.

Atkinson, G. 1935. *Les nouveaux horizons de la renaissance française.* Paris: Droz.

Babin, M.T. 1958. *Panorama de la cultura Puertorriqueña.* New York: Las Americas.
———. 1973. *La cultura de Puerto Rico.* San Juan: Instituto de Cultura Puertorriqueña.

Baldry, H. 1965. *The Unity of Mankind in Greek Thought.* Cambridge: Cambridge University Press.

Banks, W.C., G. McQuater, and J. Ross. 1976. "On the Importance of White Preference and the Comparative Difference of Blacks and Others: A Reply to Williams and Morland". *Psychological Bulletin* 86:33–36.

Banton, M. 1983. *Racial and Ethnic Competition.* Cambridge: Cambridge University Press.

Basham, A. 1971. *The Wonder That Was India.* Calcutta: Fontana.

Bastide, R. 1968. "Color, Racism and Christianity". In *Colour and Race,* edited by J.H. Franklin, 34–49. Boston: Houghton Mifflin.

Baude, P. 1948. *L'Affranchissement des esclaves aux Antilles Françaises, principalement à la Martinique, du début de la colonisation à 1848.* Fort-de-France, Martinique: Imprimerie Officielle.

Benoist, J. 1963. "Les martiniquais: Anthropologie d'une population métisse". *Bulletin de la Société d'Anthropologie de Paris* 11:241–432.

Bernabé, J. 1997. "Brèves remarques sur la créolité et ses perspectives". In *L'Identité Guyanaise en question: Les dynamiques interculturelles en Guyane française,* edited by S. Mam-Lam-Fouck, 115–20. Cayenne: Ibis Rouge Editions, PUC/GEREC.

Bernabé, J., P. Chamoiseau, and R. Confiant. 1989. *Eloge de la créolité.* Paris: Gallimard/Presses Universitaires Créoles.

Bernal, M. 1985. "Black Athena: The African and Levantine Roots of Greece. African Presence in Early Europe". *Journal of African Civilisations* 7, no. 2:66–82.
———. 1987. *Black Athena: The AfroAsiatic Roots of Classical Civilisation,* 2 vols. London: Free Association Books.

Beteille, A. 1968. "Race and Descent As Social Categories in India". In *Colour and Race,* edited by J.H. Franklin, 166–85. Boston: Houghton Mifflin.

Bilby, K. 1981. "The Kromanti Dance of the Windward Maroons of Jamaica". *Nieuwe West Indische Gids* 55:52–101.

Blanco, T. 1985. *El prejucio racial en Puerto Rico.* Rio Piedras: Huracán.

Braithwaite, F. 1976. "Race and Class Differentials in Career (Value) Orientation". *Plural Societies* 7:17–31.

Brathwaite, E. 1971. *The Development of Creole Society in Jamaica, 1770–1820.* Oxford: Clarendon.

Brau, Salvador. 1956a. *Historia de Puerto Rico.* San Juan: Boriquen.

Brau, Salvador. 1956b. "Las clases jornaleras de Puerto Rico". In *Disquisiciones sociológicas.* Universidad de Puerto Rico: Ed. Instituto de Literatura.

Bryan, P. 1996. "The Creolization of the Chinese Community in Jamaica". In *Ethnic Minorities in Caribbean Society,* edited by R. Reddock, 173–201. St

Augustine, Trinidad: Institute of Social and Economic Research, University of the West Indies.

Buriel, R. 1987. "Ethnic Labeling and Identity Among Mexican Americans". In *Children's Ethnic Socialization: Pluralism and Development,* edited by J.S. Phinney and M.J. Rotheram, 134–52. Newbury Park: Sage.

Burton, R. 1966. *A Mission to Gelele, King of Dahomey.* London: C.W. Newbury (edition Routledge and Kegan Paul).

Burton, R. 1994. "Penser l'Indianité". In *Présence de L'Inde dans le monde,* edited by G. L'Etang, 205–16. Paris: Harmattan.

———. 1997. *Afro-Creole: Power, Oposition and Play in the Caribbean.* Ithaca: Cornell University Press.

Butler, R.O. 1976. "Black Children's Racial Preference". *Journal of Afro-American Issues* 4:168–71.

Cassidy, F., and R. Le Page. 1967. *Dictionary of Jamaican English.* Cambridge: Cambridge University Press.

Cérol, Marie-José. 1992. "What History Tells Us About the Development of Creole in Guadeloupe". *Nieuwe West-Indische Gids* 66:61–76.

Césaire, Aimé. 1956. "Culture et colonisation". *Présence Africaine* (June–November): 190–205.

Chaudenson, R. 1974. "Le noir et le blanc: La classification raciale dans les parlers créoles de l'Océan Indien". *Revue de Linguistique Romane* 38:75–94.

Clark, K.B., and M.P. Clark. 1939. "The Development of Consciousness of Self and the Emergence of Racial Identification in Negro Pre-School Children". *Journal of Social Psychology* 10:591–99.

Cohen, R. 1968. *The Color of Man.* New York: Random House.

Cohen, W. 1980. *The French Encounter with Africans: White Response to Blacks, 1530–1880.* Bloomington: Indiana University Press.

———. 1981. *Français et Africains: Les noirs dans le regard des blancs, 1530–1880.* [Translation of Cohen 1980.] Paris: Gallimard.

Craton, M. 1982. *Testing the Chains: Resistance to Slavery in the British West Indies.* Ithaca: Cornell University Press.

Cundall, F., and J. Fietersz. 1919. *Jamaica Under the Spaniards.* Kingston: Institute of Jamaica.

Dallas, R. 1803. *The History of the Maroons.* 2 vols. London: Cass.

Davidson, B. 1971. "Slaves or Captives: Some Notes on Fantasy and Fact". In *Key Issues in the AfroAmerican Experience,* edited by N. Huggins, M. Kilson, and D. Fox, 54–73. New York: Harcourt Brace Jovanovich.

Davis, David Brion. 1988. *The Problem of Slavery in Western Culture.* Oxford: Oxford University Press.

Debbasch, Y. 1967. *Couleur et liberté: Le jeu du critère ethnique dans un ordre juridique esclavagiste.* Paris: Dalloz.

de Gobineau, A. 1967 [1853–1855]. *Essai sur l'Inegalité des races humaines.* Paris: Belfond.

Délumeau, J. 1973. *La civilisation de la Renaissance.* Paris: Arthaud.

De Pass Scott, R. 1979. "Spanish and Portuguese Jews of Jamaica: Mid-16th–Mid-17th Century". *Jamaica Journal* 43:90–100.

Désanges, J. 1875. "L'Afrique noire et le monde mediterranéen dans l'Antiquité". *Revue Française d'Histoire d'Outre-mer,* 62:391–414.

de Saintonge, Alphonse. 1904. *Cosmographie,* edited by G. Musset. Paris.

Devisse, J. 1959. *L'Image du noir dans l'art Occidental.* Lausanne: Fondation de la Menil.

Diaz Soler, L. 1953. *Historia de la esclavitud negra en Puerto Rico (1493–1890).* Madrid: Revista de Occidente.

Diller, A. 1971. *Race Mixture Among the Greeks Before Alexander.* Westport, Conn.: Greenwood.

Doke, C., D. Malcolm, and J. Sikana. 1958. *English and Zulu Dictionary.* Johannesburg: Witwatersrand University Press.

Duany, J. 1985. "Ethnicity in the Spanish Caribbean: Notes on the Consolidation of Creole Identity in Cuba and Puerto Rico, 1762–1868". In *Caribbean Ethnicity Revisited,* edited by S. Glazier, 15–39. New York: Gordon and Breach Science Publishers.

Edwards, B. 1794. *The History, Civil and Commercial of the British Colonies in the West Indies.* London: Stockdale.

Eguchi, Nobukiyo. 1997. "Ethnic Tourism and Reconstruction of the Carib's Ethnic Identity". In *Ethnicity, Race and Nationality in the Caribbean,* edited by J.M. Carrion, 364–80. Puerto Rico: Institute of Caribbean Studies.

Eisner, G. 1961. *Jamaica 1830–1930: A Study in Economic Growth.* Westport, Conn.: Greenwood Press.

Erlich, A. 1976. "Race and Ethnic Identity in Rural Jamaica: The East Indian Case". *Caribbean Quarterly* 22, no. 1:19–27.

Ernout, A. 1951. *Dictionnaire étymolgique de la langue latine.* Paris: Klincksieck.

Fanon, F. 1950. *Peau noire, masques blancs.* Paris: Seuil.

Ferguson, A. 1966. *An Essay on the History of Civil Society,* 8th edition. Edinburgh: Edinburgh University Press.

Ferguson, G. 1954. *Signs and Symbols in Christian Art.* New York: Oxford University Press.

Figueroa Mercado, L. 1974. *History of Puerto Rico.* New York: Anaya.

Fox, D.J., and V.B. Jordan. 1973. "Racial Preference and Identification of Black, American Chinese and White Children". *Genetic Psychology Monographs* 88:229–86.

Franklin, J.H., ed. 1968. *Color and Race.* Boston: Houghton Mifflin.

Frederickson, G. 1971. "Towards a Social Interpretation of the Development of American Racism". In *Key Issues in the AfroAmerican Experience,* edited by N. Huggins, M. Kilson, and D. Fox, 240–56. New York: Harcourt Brace Jovanovich.

Fried, M.H. 1971. "A Four-Letter Word That Hurts". In *Black Society in the New World,* edited by R. Frucht, 151–58. New York: Random House.

Friedman, J.B. 1981. *The Monstrous Races in Medieval Art and Thought.* Cambridge, Mass.: Harvard University Press.

Gardner, W. 1873. *A History of Jamaica.* London: Cass.

Gergen, K. 1968. "The Significance of Color in Human Relations". In *Colour and Race,* edited by J.H. Franklin, 112–28. Boston: Houghton Mifflin.

Glare, P.G.W., ed. 1982. *Oxford Latin Dictionary.* Oxford: Clarendon.

Glissant, E. 1981. *Le discours antillais.* Paris: Seuil.

Grégoire, Abbé. 1826. *De la noblesse de la peau.* Grenoble: Millon. [Reissued 1996.]

Gregory, S., and R. Sanjek, eds. 1994. *Race.* New Brunswick, N.J.: Rutgers University Press.

Hall, D. 1989. *In Miserable Slavery: Thomas Thistlewood in Jamaica, 1750–1786.* London: Macmillan.

Hall, J.C. 1966. *A Concise Anglo-Saxon Dictionary.* Cambridge: Cambridge University Press.

Herskovits, M. 1941. *The Myth of the Negro Past.* New York: Harper and Bros.

Hertz, F. 1970. *Race and Civilisation.* Translated by A. Levetus and W. Entz. New York: Ktav Publishing House.

Heuman, G. 1981. *Between Black and White: Race, Politics and the Free Colored in Jamaica, 1792–1865.* Westport, Conn.: Greenwood Press.

Hiernaux, J. 1975. *The People of Africa.* New York: Scribners.

Hoetink, H. 1967. *The Two Variants in Carib Race Relations: A Contribution to the Sociology of Segmented Societies.* Translated by E.M. Hookykaas. New York: Oxford University Press.

———. 1973. *Slavery and Race Relations in the Americas.* New York: Harper and Row.

———. 1985. " 'Race' and Color in the Caribbean". In *Caribbean Contours,* edited by S. Mintz and S. Price, 55–84. Baltimore: Johns Hopkins University Press.

Horowitz, M. 1960. "Metropolitan Influences in the Caribbean: The French Antilles". In *Social and Cultural Pluralism in the Caribbean,* edited by Vera Rubin. *Annals of the New York Academy of Sciences* 83:802–8.

———. 1967. *Morne Paysan: Peasant Village in Martinique.* New York: Holt, Rhinehart and Winston.

Hraba, J., and C. Grant. 1970. "Black Is Beautiful". *Journal of Personality and Social Psychology* 16:398–402.

Hutton, C. 1996. " 'Roast Breadfruit': The Philosophy and Psychology of Freedom by Submission and Subjection". Typescript.

Isaacs, H. 1968. "Group Identity and Politial Change: The Role of Color and Physical Characteristics". In *Color and Race*, edited by J.H. Franklin, 75–97. Boston: Houghton Mifflin.

Jahn, J. 1961. *Muntu: An Outline of the New African Culture*. New York: Grove Press.

Jensen, A. 1969. "How Much Can We Boost IQ and Scholastic Achievement?" *Harvard Educational Review* 39:1–123.

Jimenez Roman, M. 1996. "Un hombre (negro) del pueblo: Jose Celso Barbosa and the Puerto Rican 'Race' toward Whiteness". *Centro* 8:8–29.

Johnson, H., and K. Watson, eds. 1997. *The White Minority in the Caribbean*. Kingston, Jamaica: Ian Randle Publishers.

Jordan, W. 1969. *White Over Black: American Attitudes Toward the Negro: 1550–1812*. Baltimore: Penguin.

———. 1974. *The White Man's Burden: Historical Origins of Racism in the United States*. New York: Oxford University Press.

Katz, P.A. 1983. "Developmental Foundations of Gender and Racial Attitudes". In *The Child's Construction of Social Inequality,* edited by R.L. Leahy, 41–78. New York: Academic Press.

———. 1987. "Developmental and Social Processes in Ethnic Attitudes and Self-identification". In *Children's Ethnic Socialization: Pluralism and Development*, edited by J.S. Phinney and M.J. Rotheram, 92–100. Newbury Park: Sage.

Kinsbruner, J. 1990. "Caste and Capitalism in the Caribbean: Residential Patterns and House Ownership Among the Free People of Color of San Juan, Puerto Rico, 1823–46". *Hispanic American Historical Review* 70, no. 3:433–61.

Kovats-Beaudoux, E. 1983. "Les blancs créoles: Continuité ou changement?" *Les Temps Modernes, Antilles* (April–May): 1907–23.

Kristeller, P. 1955. *Renaissance Thought*. New York: Harper and Row.

Kurath, H., and S. Kuhn. 1958. *Middle English Dictionary*. Ann Arbor: University of Michigan Press.

Ladero Quesada, M. 1967. "La esclavitud por guerra a fines del siglo XV: El caso de Málaga". *Hispania* 27:64–85.

Leiris, M. 1955. *Contacts de civilisation en Martinique et en Guadeloupe*. Paris: UNESCO.

Leverett, F., ed. 1843. *Lexicon of the Latin Language*. Boston: Wilkins and Carter.

Levy, J. 1986. "The Economic Role of the Chinese in Jamaica: The Grocery Retail Trade". *Jamaican Historical Review* 15:31–49.

Lewis, B. 1979. *Race and Color in Islam*. New York: Octagon Books.

Lewis, G. 1963. *Freedom and Power in the Caribbean*. New York: Monthly Review Press.

———. 1971. "Color and Society in Puerto Rico". In *Black Society in the New World*, edited by R. Frucht, 177–84. New York: Random House.

———. 1972. *The Virgin Islands: A Caribbean Lilliput*. Evanston, Ill.: Northwestern University Press.

Lewontin, R. 1996. "Of Genes and Genitals". *Transition* 69:178–93.

Lind, A. 1958. "Adjustment Patterns Among the Jamaican Chinese". *Social and Economic Studies* 7:144–64.

Little, K. 1971. "The Social Foundations of Racism". In *Black Society in the New World*, edited by R. Frucht, 159–67. New York: Random House.

Long, E. 1774. *The History of Jamaica*, 3 vols. London: Lowndes.

Lowenthal, D. 1972. *West Indian Societies*. London: Oxford University Press.

Mansingh, A., et al. 1976. "Indian Heritage in Jamaica". *Jamaica Journal* 10: 10–19.

Maquet, J. 1961. *The Premise of Inequality in Ruanda: A Study of Political Relations in Central Africa Kingdom*. London: Oxford University Press.

Marouzeau, J. 1949. *Quelques aspects de la formation du latin littéraire*. Paris: Klincksieck.

Martin, G. 1948. *Histoire de L'esclavage dans les colonies françaises*. Paris: Presses Universitaires de France.

McDonald, I. 1997. "Katha; or A Culture for the World". *Vista* 4, no. 2:1–4. [National Commercial Bank Group in association with the Faculty of Arts, University of the West Indies, Jamaica.]

Miles, W. 1986. *Elections and Ethnicity in French Martinique: A Paradox in Paradise*. New York: Praeger.

Millar, J. 1902. *The Origin of the Distinction of Ranks*. London: Blackwork.

Miller, E. 1969. "Body Image, Physical Beauty and Colour Among Jamaican Adolescents". *Social and Economic Studies* 18:72–79.

———. 1973. "Self-Evaluation Among Jamaican High School Girls". *Social and Economic Studies* 22:407–26.

Mintz, S. 1974. *Caribbean Transformations*. Chicago: Aldine.

———. 1996. "Ethnic Difference, Plantation Sameness". In *Ethnicity, Social Structure, and National Identities in the Caribbean: Essays in Honor of Harry Hoetink*, edited by G. Oostindie, 39–52. London: Macmillan.

———, ed. 1989. *Caribbean Transformations*. New York: Columbia University Press.

Moreau de St Méry, M.L.E. 1958 [1797]. *Description de la Partie Française de l'Ile de St Domingue*, 3 vols. Paris: Société de l'Histoire des Colonies Françaises et Librarie Larosse.

Morey, C. 1942. *Early Christian Art*. Princeton: Princeton University Press.

Murphy, J. 1972. *Luganda–English Dictionary*. Washington, D.C.: Consortium Press.

Newman, R.M. 1990. *An English–Hausa Dictionary*. New Haven: Yale University Press.

Ortiz, Fernando. 1954. Prologue. *La Fiesta de Santiago Apostal en Loiza Aldea*, by Ricardo Alegria. San Juan, Puerto Rico: Colección de Estudios.

Owen, N. 1975. "Land, Politics, and Ethnicity in a Carib Indian Community". *Ethnology* 14, no. 4:385–93.

Palmer, L. 1954. *The Latin Language.* London: Faber and Faber.

Patterson, H.O. 1967. *The Sociology of Slavery.* London: MacGibbon and Kee.

Pedreira, A.S. 1969. *Insularismo.* Rio Piedras: Editorial Edil.

Pelleprat, Le père P. 1655. *Relation des Missions des Pères de la Compagnie de Jésus dans les Iles et dans la terre Ferme de l'Amérique Méridionale.* Paris.

Pitt-Rivers, J. 1968. "Race, Color, and Class in Central America and the Andes". In *Color and Race,* edited by J.H. Franklin, 264–81. Boston: Houghton Mifflin.

Pluchon, P. 1984. *Nègres et Juifs au XVIIIe siècle.* Paris: Tallandier.

Pollard, V. 1994. *Dread Talk.* Kingston, Jamaica: Canoe Press.

Proyart, Father. 1776. *Histoire de Loango, Kakongo et autres royaummes.* Paris.

Ramsey, P. 1987. "Young Children's Thinking About Ethnic Differences". In *Children's Ethnic Socialization: Pluralism and Development,* edited by J.S. Phinney and M.J. Rotheram, 56–72. Newbury Park: Sage.

Raveau, F. 1968. "An Outline of the Role of Color in Adaptation Phenomena". In *Color and Race,* edited by J.H. Franklin, 98–117. Boston: Houghton Mifflin.

Roberts, G. 1954. "Immigration of Africans into the British Caribbean". *Population Studies* 7:235–61.

Revert, E. 1949. *La Martinique.* Paris: Nouvelles Editions Latines.

Rodney, W. 1969. *Groundings with My Brothers.* London: Bogle-L'Ouverture.

Russell, J.B. 1977. *The Devil: Perceptions of Evil from Antiquity to Primitive Christianity.* Ithaca: Cornell University Press.

Safa, H. 1998. Introduction. *Latin American Perspectives* 25, no. 3:3–20.

Sanjek, R. 1971. "Brazilian Racial Terms: Some Aspects of Meaning and Learning". *American Anthropologist* 73:1126–43.

———. 1994a. "The Unending Inequalities of Race". In *Race,* edited by S. Gregory and R. Sanjek, 1–17. New Brunswick, N.J.: Rutgers University Press.

———. 1994b. "Intermarriage and the Future of Races in the US". In *Race,* edited by S. Gregory and R. Sanjek, 103–30. New Brunswick, N.J.: Rutgers University Press.

Schafer, D. 1974. *The Maroons of Jamaica: African Slave Rebels in the Caribbean.* Ann Arbor: University Microfilms.

Schoelcher, V. 1976 [1842]. *Des colonies françaises: Abolition immédiate de l'esclavage.* Reprint, Basse-Terre: Sociétés d'Histoire Guadeloupe/Martinique.

Schuler, M. 1980. *Alas, Alas, Kongo: A Social History of Indentured African Immigration into Jamaica, 1841–1865.* Baltimore: Johns Hopkins University Press.

Seda Bonilla, E. 1961. "Social Structure and Race Relations". *Social Forces* 40, no. 2:141–48.

———. 1976. *La cultura política de Puerto Rico.* Rio Piedras, Puerto Rico: Ediciones Amauta, 1976.

————. 1980. *Requiem para una cultura: Ensayos sobre la socialización del puertorriqueño en su cultura y ambito de poder.* Rio Piedras, Puerto Rico: Ediciones Bayoán.

Semaj, L. 1980a. "Race and Identity and Children of the African Diaspora: Contributions of Rastafari". *Caribe* (December): 14–18.

————. 1980b. "The Development of Racial Evaluation and Preference: A Cognitive Approach". *Journal of Black Psychology* 6:59–79.

————. 1981. "The Development of Racial-Classification Abilities". *Journal of Negro Education* 50:41–47.

Senghor, L. 1964. *Négritude et Humanisme.* Paris: Seuil.

Senior, C. N.d. "Bountied European Immigration into Jamaica, with Special Reference to the German Settlement at Seaford Town up to 1650". Manuscript, West India Collection, Main Library, University of the West Indies, Jamaica.

Shepherd, V. 1994. *Transients to Settlers: The Experience of Indian Settlers in Jamaica 1845–1950.* Leeds: Centre for Research in Asian Migration, University of Warwick/Peepal Tree Books.

————. 1988. "Indian and Blacks in Jamaica in the Nineteenth and Early Twentieth Centuries: A Micro-Study of the Foundations of Race Antagonisms". *Immigrants and Minorities* 7, no. 1:95–112.

Société d'Histoire de la Guadaloupe (SHG). 1996. *Cahier de Marronnage du Moule.* Edited by J. Adelaide-Merlande for the Société d'Histoire de la Guadeloupe. Basse-Terre: SHG.

Shills, E. 1968. "Color, the Universal Intellectual Community, and the Afro-Asian Intellectual". In *Color and Race,* edited by J.H. Franklin, 1–17. Boston: Houghton Mifflin.

Simons, R.D. 1961. *The Colour of the Skin in Human Relations.* Amsterdam: Elsevier.

Sio, A. 1976. "Race, Colour and Miscegenation: The Free Coloured of Jamaica and Barbados". *Caribbean Studies* 16:5–21.

Sméralda-Amon, J. 1994. "Quelques éléments de réflexion sur l'auto-représentation et la représentation des Indo-Martiniquais". In *Présence de L'Inde dans le monde,* edited by G. L'Etang, 182–202. Paris: Harmattan.

Smith, M.G. 1965. *The Plural Society in the British West Indies.* Berkeley: University of California Press.

Snowden, F.M. Jr. 1983. *Before Color Prejudice: The Ancient View of Blacks.* Cambridge, Mass.: Harvard University Press.

Speke, J.H. 1906. *Journal of the Discovery of the Nile.* London: Ernest Rhys [edition Everyman's Library].

Steward, J. 1965. *The People of Puerto Rico.* Urbana: University of Illinois Press.

Sued Badillo, J., and A. Lopez Cantos. 1986. *Puerto Rico Negro.* Rio Piedras, Puerto Rico: Editorial Cultural.

Suvélor, R. 1983. "Eléments historiques pour une approche socio-culturelle". *Les Temps Modernes, Antilles* (April–May): 2179–93.

Sylvain, S. 1936. *Le créole haitien: Morphologie et syntaxe.* Wetteren: de Meester.

Taylor, Douglas. 1951. *The Black Caribs of British Honduras.* Viking Fund Publications in Anthropology, no. 17. New York: Viking Fund.

Toller, T.N., ed. 1898. *An Anglo-Saxon Dictionary.* Oxford: Oxford University Press.

Trouillot, M-R. 1994. "Culture, Color and Politics in Haiti". In *Race,* edited by S. Gregory and R. Sanjek, 146–74. New Brunswick, N.J.: Rutgers University Press.

Tucker, T. 1931. *A Concise Etymological Dictionary of Latin.* Halle (Saale): Niemeyer.

Vaccari, O. 1967. *The English–Japanese Dictionary.* Tokyo: Vaccari Language Institute.

van den Berghe, P. 1967. *Race and Racism: Comparative Perspective.* New York: Wiley and Sons.

Vaughan, G.M. 1987. "A Social Psychological Model of Ethnic Identity Development". In *Children's Ethnic Socialization: Pluralism and Development,* edited by J.S. Phinney and M.J. Rotheram, 74–91. Newbury Park: Sage.

Verlinden, C. 1955. *L'Esclavage dans l'Europe Médiévale,* vol. 1. Bruges: University of Ghent.

Voltaire. 1963. *Essai sur les Moeurs,* 2 vols. Paris: Garnier Frères, new edition.

Wagatsuma, H. 1968. "The Social Perception of Skin Colour in Japan". In *Color and Race,* edited by J.H. Franklin, 129–65. Boston: Houghton Mifflin.

Walcott, Derek. 1962. *In a Green Night.* London: Jonathan Cape.

Whitehead, J. 1964 [1899]. *Grammar and Dictionary of the Bobangi Language.* London: Gregg Press.

Williams, E. 1966. *Capitalism and Slavery.* New York: Putnam.

———. 1971. "The Origin of Negro Slavery". In *Black Society in the New World,* edited by R. Frucht, 3–25. New York: Random House.

Williams, J.E. 1979. "Comment on Bank's 'White Preference in Blacks: A Paradigm in Search of a Phenomenon' ". *Psychological Bulletin* 86:28–32.

Williams, J.E., and J.K. Morland. 1976. *Race, Color and the Young Child.* Chappel Hill: University of North Carolina Press.

Williamson, J. 1817. *Medical and Miscellaneous Observations Relative to the West India Islands.* Edinburgh: Smellie.

Wintz, Revd R.P. 1909. *Dictionnaire Français-Dyola et Dyola-Français.* Elkine (Cassamance): Mission Catholique.

Yelvington, K.A. 1993. *Trinidad Ethnicity.* Knoxville: University of Tennessee Press.

Zenon Cruz, I. 1974. *Narciso Descubre su Trasero.* Humacao, Puerto Rico: Editorial Furidi.

Index